BARCELONA
& CATALONIA
World Travel Guide

Author: **Xavier Barral i Altet** and **Clotilde de Bellegarde-Barral**
Translation: **Penelope Poulton**
Editor: **Lisa Davidson-Petty**
Photo credits: **Diaf:** Belly, p. 103; J. Gabanou, pp. 50, 156;
D. Lerault, pp. 58, 63, 64, 161, 169; Pratt-Pries, pp. 39, 77, 81, 111,
115. — **Explorer:** Lenars, p. 55; R. Nowitz, p. 127; P. Tétrel, p. 136.
— **N. Lejeune:** pp. 23, 27, 31, 72, 93, 107, 119, 139, 143, 151,
177, 181. — **Rapho:** H. Donnezan, p. 34; B. Wassman, p. 14. —
Stock-Image: J. Boorman, p. 155.

This edition published in Great Britain by **Bartholomew,** 12 Duncan
Street, Edinburgh, EH9 1TA.
Bartholomew is a Division of HarperCollins*Publishers.*
This guide is adapted from *à Barcelone et en Catalogne,* published by
Hachette Guides de voyage, 1990.

British Library Cataloguing in Publication Data
Barral i Altet, Xavier
Barcelona & Catalonia. — (Bartholomew world travel guide).
1. Spain. Catalonia — Visitors' guides
I. Title II. Bellegarde-Barral, Clotilde de III. [A Barcelone et en
Catalogne. *English*]
914.670483

ISBN 0-7028-1286-2

Printed in France by Aubin-Imprimeur, Poitiers

· Bartholomew ·

BARCELONA & CATALONIA
World Travel Guide

Bartholomew
A Division of HarperCollinsPublishers

HOW TO USE YOUR GUIDE

● Before you leave home, read the sections 'Planning Your Trip' p. 17, 'Catalonia in the Past' p. 35, 'Catalonia Today' p. 49, and 'Practical Information' p. 21, which includes advice on accommodation, local transport, safety precautions, and so on to help you organize your trip.

● The rest of the guide is for use once you arrive. It includes background information and addresses (hotels, restaurants, nightlife, shopping, entertainment, etc.) for each itinerary. See 'Contents' on the page opposite.

● To locate a site quickly, or find out about a famous person or event, use the 'Index' p. 191.

● To locate recommended sites, hotels and restaurants easily on the maps, refer to the map coordinates printed in blue in the text. Example: Cathedral, I, C2.

SYMBOLS USED

Sites, monuments, museums, points of interest

*** Exceptional
** Very interesting
* Interesting

Hotels

▲▲▲▲▲ Deluxe hotel
▲▲▲▲ Luxury hotel
▲▲▲ First-class hotel
▲▲ Comfortable hotel
▲ Modest hotel

Restaurants

◆◆◆ Excellent cuisine; expensive.
◆◆ Good food; moderate to expensive.
◆ Inexpensive.

MAPS

CONTENTS

BARCELONA I, CENTRE

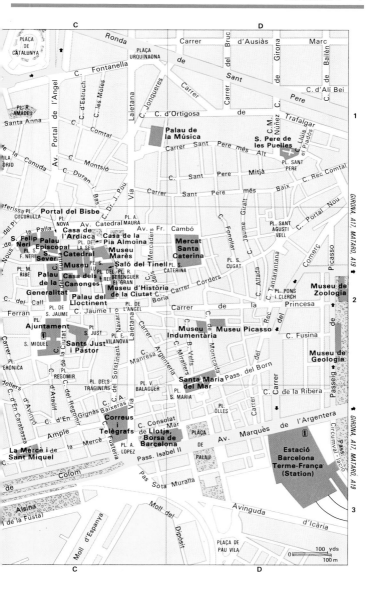

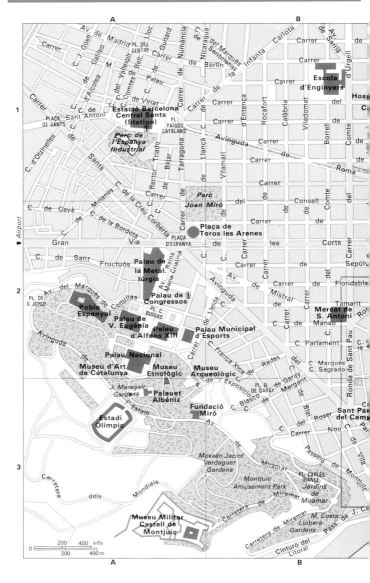

BARCELONA II, GENERAL MAP

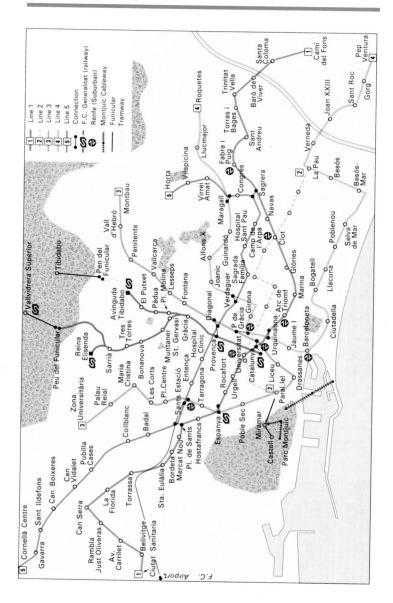

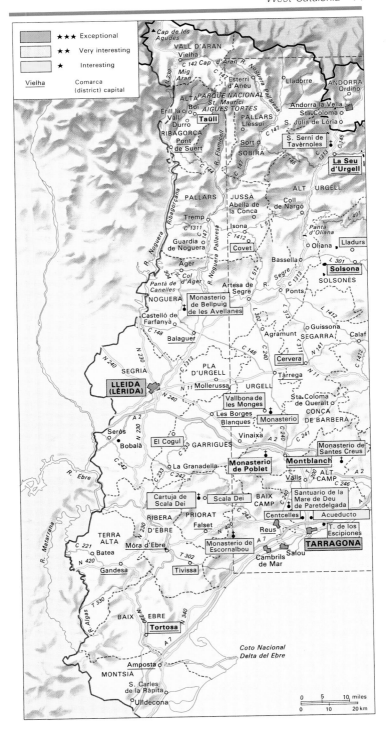

Legend

★★★ Exceptional
★★ Very interesting
★ Interesting

Vielha — Comarca (district) capital

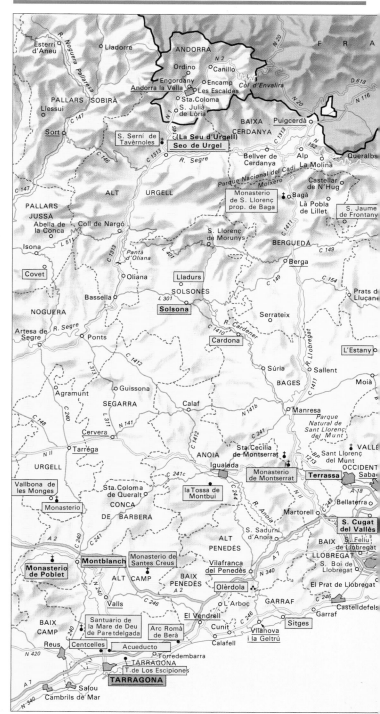

EAST CATALONIA

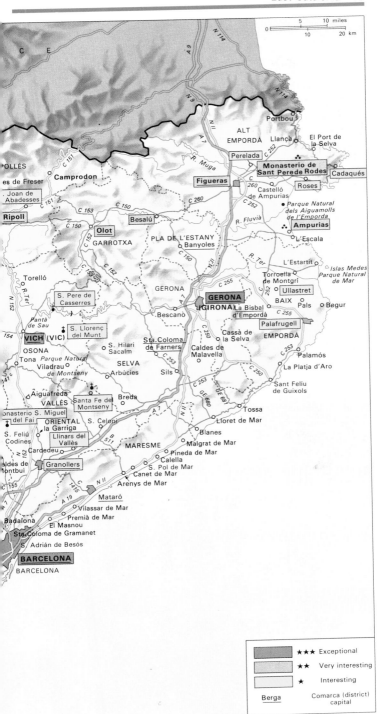

★★★ Exceptional

★★ Very interesting

★ Interesting

Berga Comarca (district) capital

INTRODUCTION TO BARCELONA AND CATALONIA

Catalonia is protected by the wild escarpments of the Pyrenees and lined with the creeks and beaches of the Mediterranean. At its heart lies the cosmopolitan capital of Barcelona, seat of congresses and manifold international events, host to the Summer Olympic Games of 1992.

Life in Catalonia is characterized by a radiant, golden light, a perpetually blue sea, abundant flowers, lively nights, the warm sounds of *sardana* and *habanera* music, and the pleasures of Spanish cuisine enhanced by many a light, fruity wine.

The Catalan people have a history, language and culture more than a thousand years old; they like visitors to respect this and to be able to distinguish their area of the country from the rest of Spain. Don't let the quest for sun, sea and relaxation make you forget Catalonia's artistic wealth, built up since Antiquity; the ancient Greek towns of Empuries (Ampurias) and Tarragona are just two examples.

Moving inland from the coast you reach the Pyrenees, today a popular spot for winter sports and summer hiking. During the Middle Ages these mountains, located in the heart of what was known as Old Catalonia, were the primary cultural centre. It was from them that the reconquest of the south began, towards New Catalonia, which rubbed shoulders with Islam, and towards the Balearic Islands and Valencia. Roman monasteries, Gothic cathedrals and Cistercian austerity are all reminders of this past. Moreover, because of its harbour, Catalonia was a natural centre for cultural and commercial exchange, forming a link between the Iberian peninsula and the rest of Europe.

Catalonia has an impressive list of illustrious names to its credit: the architect Gaudí, whose work was declared by UNESCO to be part of the world's cultural heritage, the painters Picasso, Miró, Dalí and Tàpies; the cellist Pau Casals; and the opera divas Montserrat Caballé and Josep Carreras.

Catalonia offers visitors the happy choice between sunny beaches and a region rich in history and art. In fact, there's no need to choose, it's easy to combine both!

The Plaça Reial is right in the heart of the old quarter of Barcelona, itself the centre of a region with a rich past and a promising future.

Catalonia in brief

Location: in the north-eastern part of the Iberian Peninsula. Catalonia's northern boundary is formed by the Pyrenees, its eastern by the Mediterranean.

Borders: northern, France, across the Pyrenees; southern, Valencia; western, Aragón.

Surface area: 12,328 sq mi/31,930 sq km.

Population: 6,077,096 inhabitants.

Capital: Barcelona.

Main towns: Girona (Gerona), Lleida (Lerida), Tarragona.

Administration: Catalonia is one of Spain's 17 *Comunidades Autónomas* (Autonomous Communities) and is comprised of 41 *comargues* (districts), each with its respective capital.

Language: Catalan (predominant) and Spanish (Castilian).

Religion: Catholicism.

Government: autonomous government, the *Generalitat de Catalunya*. The president of the *Generalitat* is Jordi Pujol.

PLANNING YOUR TRIP

▬ WHEN TO GO

Catalonia is a delightful region to visit all year round. The geographical variety is ideal for sports activities in any season.

Catalonia has a mild and temperate climate, comparable to that of towns like Nice and Genoa. Two factors are responsible: the sea, which mitigates extreme temperatures, and the crown of hills that surrounds the city, protecting it from cold northern and westerly winds.

Summers are hot and humid, winters short and moderately cold with rare snow. Spring and autumn are warm and pleasant with some light rain (14 in/365 mm).

Average temperatures

January	48° F/ 9° C	July	77° F/25° C
February	52° F/11° C	August	73° F/23° C
March	54° F/12° C	September	72° F/22° C
April	55° F/13° C	October	63° F/17° C
May	66° F/19° C	November	55° F/13° C
June	72° F/22° C	December	48° F/ 9° C

▬ GETTING THERE

Plane

Barcelona's airport, El Prat, is 9 mi/14 km south-west of the town and services more than 220 flights a day. There are hourly flights between Madrid and Barcelona. Train and bus services shuttle passengers into the city centre.

Train

From London, trains leave Victoria station around 9am for Paris. Once there, you'll have to cross town from the Gare du Nord to the Gare d'Austerlitz.

Euro City or *Talgo*, leaves Paris every night at 9pm and arrives in Barcelona the following morning at 8:30am. The stops are Limoges (12:15pm), Figueres (6:55am) and Girona (7:15am). An alternative from Paris is to take the daily TGV (highspeed train) from the Gare de Lyon at 11:45am and then to change in Avignon at about 3:45pm (or in Montpellier) for the *Talgo* from Geneva, which reaches Barcelona at 9:15pm.

The daily *Talgo* from Geneva to Barcelona leaves in the morning and stops at Aix-les-Bains, Chambéry, Grenoble, Valence, Avignon, Montpellier, Figueres and Girona.

Car

If you are driving into Catalonia from France you can cross the border south of Perpignan or at various passes in the Pyrenees. You can drive the trip from London to Barcelona on highways (with tolls), passing through Paris to take the Autoroute du Sud via Lyon, Montpellier, Perpignan and La Jonquera which then becomes the A7 to Barcelona (92 mi/149 km) via Figueres and Girona. You turn off it to reach the towns along the Costa Brava. The highway continues south of Barcelona to Tarragona and the Costa Dorada.

From Andorra you cross into Catalonia at La Seu d'Urgell. Other routes from the Pyrenees cross through Vall d'Aran, Puigcerdá and Camprodón, while the coast road on the Mediterranean passes through Portbou.

There are good roads connecting Barcelona and Catalonia to the rest of Spain, especially the A2 highway, which links Barcelona and Lleida to Zaragoza and Madrid, and the Mediterranean A7, which links Barcelona and Tarragona to the south and Valencia.

ENTRY FORMALITIES

Passports

At the time this book went to press, visitors from Great Britain, like other members of the EEC, needed a valid passport or national identity card to enter Spain. Americans, Australians, Canadians and New Zealanders need a valid passport and sometimes a visa. It is best to check with your consulate before leaving.

Driving

Drivers need a valid driver's license (not necessarily international but you should check with the consulate), car registration papers and a Green Card for international insurance, with Spain mentioned on it.

Boats

A valid sailing license is all that is required if you wish to bring a boat into Catalonian waters.

Animals

If you wish to enter with a dog or cat you should have a rabies vaccination certificate and a document (stamped by a veterinarian less than three months before departure) indicating that the animal is in good health.

MONEY

The local currency is the peseta. Banknotes are issued in denominations of 500, 1000, 2000, 5000 and 10,000 pesetas; coins in 1, 5, 25, 50, 100, 200 and 500 pesetas.

Credit cards, especially Visa, American Express and Diner's Club, are widely accepted in Barcelona and in Catalonia's main towns.

A typical daily budget

The average price for a double room in a ▲▲▲ hotel is 8000 to 12,000 pesetas.

Breakfast can be from 150 pesetas (white coffee and a croissant) to 500 pesetas (full Catalan breakfast).

Lunch with a set menu usually begins at 700 pesetas. Count on an average of 1000 to 1500 pesetas.

Dinner prices can vary greatly, with a simple meal starting at about 800 pesetas. For a typical fish meal, count on an average of 2500 pesetas.

An average taxi fare in Barcelona is about 500 pesetas, a visit to a museum 200, and a show between 500 and 1000 pesetas.

WHAT TO PACK

The clothes you should take will depend on the season: a bathing suit and lightweight clothing for summer, a light sweater or jacket for the evening in spring and autumn and warm clothes (although you can safely leave your overcoat behind!) in winter.

BEFORE YOU LEAVE: SOME USEFUL ADDRESSES

Australia

Embassy
15 Arkana St., Yarralumla, ACT 2600, Canberra, ☎ (44) 73 3555 and 73 3845.

Consulates
50 Park St., 7th floor, NSW 2000, Sydney, ☎ (2) 261 2433 and 261 2443; 766 Elisabeth St., WIC 3000, Melbourne, ☎ (03) 347 1966.

Tourist office
203 Castlereagh St., suite 21a, 2000 Sydney, ☎ (612) 264 7966.

Canada

Embassy
350 Sparks St., suite 802, Ottawa, Ontario K1R 7S8, ☎ (613) 237 2193/94 and 237 2183.

Consulates
1 Westmount Sq., suite 1456, Montreal, Quebec H3Z 2P9, ☎ (514) 935 5235/36; 1200 Bay St., suite 400, Toronto, Ontario M5R 2A5, ☎ (416) 967 4949 and 967 4960; 700 Gerogia St. W., suite 1100, Pacific Centre, Vancouver, British Columbia V71 1A1, ☎ (604) 688 9471.

Tourist office
102 Bloor St. W., suite 1400, Toronto, Ontario M5S 1M8, ☎ (416) 961 3131.

Great Britain

Embassy
24 Belgrave Sq., London SW1X 8QA, ☎ (071) 235 5555.

Consulates
20 Draycott Pl., London SW3 2RZ, ☎ (071) 581 5921/22/23; suite 1a Brookhouse, 70 Spring Gardens, Manchester M2 2BQ, ☎ (61) 236 1233 and 236 1261; 63 N. Castle St., Edinburgh EH2 3LJ, ☎ (31) 220 1843.

Tourist office
57-58 St James's St., London SW1A 1LD, ☎ (1) 499 1169 and 499 0901.

Ireland

Embassy
17A Merlyn Park, Ballsbridge, Dublin 4, ☎ (353) 69 16 40 and 69 25 97.

United States

Embassy
2700 15th St. NW, Washington DC 20009, ☎ (202) 265 0190/91.

Consulates
545 Boylston St., suite 803, Boston, Massachusetts 02116, ☎ (617) 536 2506 and 536 2527; 180 N. Michigan Ave., suite 1500, Chicago, Illinois 60601, ☎ (312) 782 4588; 2411 Fountain View, suite 130, Houston, Texas 77057, ☎ (713) 783 6200; 6300 Wilshire Blvd., suite 1530, Los Angeles, California 90048, ☎ (213) 658 6050;

151 Sevilla Ave., Coral Gable, Miami, Florida 33134, ☎ (305) 446 5511/12/13; 2102 World Trade Center, 2 Canal St., New Orleans, Louisiana 70130, ☎ (504) 525 4951 and 525 7920; 150 E. 58th St., floor 16, New York, New York 10155, ☎ (212) 355 4080/81/82.

Tourist offices

Water Tower Pl., suite 915 E., 845 N. Michigan Ave., Chicago, Illinois 60611, ☎ (312) 642 1992; 8383 Wilshire Blvd., suite 960, Beverly Hills, California, ☎ (213) 658 7192; 1221 Brickell Ave., Miami, Florida 33131, ☎ (305) 1992; 665 Fifth Ave., New York, New York 10022, ☎ (212) 759 8822.

PRACTICAL INFORMATION

ACCESS

If you fly to Barcelona, there are train and bus services into the city centre from El Prat airport (7 mi/12 km south-west of town).

The train journey takes 15 minutes, with a service to Estació de Sants, Barcelona's main station (plaça Països Catalans, II, A1, ☎ 322 4142), every half hour from 6:30am to 11pm. Trains from the city to the airport run from 6am to 10:30pm.

The bus takes half an hour, with an EA line bus every 40 minutes from the airport to plaça d'Espanya; buses in the opposite direction run from 7:15am to 9:15pm. There's a night service from the airport, with an EN line bus every 80 minutes, from 10:30pm to 2:30am. Buses run from plaça d'Espanya to the airport from 11:10pm to 3:10am.

The international express *Talgo* trains from Paris and Geneva also arrive at Sants station, stopping first at Passeig de Gràcia station in the heart of town.

If you arrive in Barcelona by car from France, you have 92 mi/149 km of continuous highway (with tolls) from the border, the A7. The speed limit is 74 mph/120 kph and there are five service stations: La Jonquera-Empordá (18 mi/29 km), Girona (22 mi/35 km farther), La Selva (10 mi/16 km farther), Montseny (19 mi/31 km) and Montcada (17 mi/27 km). The highway leads into Barcelona on avinguda de Meridiana. You can, however, bypass the town on the ring-road (beltway) if you are heading towards Tarragona or Lleida (Lerida).

ACCOMMODATION

Hotels

Every year the *Generalitat de Catalunya* publishes a guide, *Catalunya Hotels*, that includes everything from luxury hotel complexes to the smallest family-run establishment, with the exception of inns *(fondes)* and guest houses *(cases d'hostes)*.

Not every hotel has a restaurant and when there is one, half-board is more common than full board.

Cheaper than hotels, boarding houses are recognizable by the letters Hs, HsR or P. Families do not often take in paying guests, even in small villages.

Hotel symbols:
H: hotel
HR: *hotel residència*
HA: *hotel apartaments*
RA: *residència apartaments*
M: motel
Hs: *hostal*
HsR: *hostal residència*
P: *pensió.*

The letter R (residència) means that there is no restaurant although the hotel may serve breakfast and there may be a bar.

H and HR establishments are graded from one to five stars, HA and RA from one to four stars, and M, Hs, HsR and P from one to three stars.

The state-run *Paradors* are unique to Spain and are in a category of their own. These are converted castles, palaces, monasteries and convents located in beautiful settings. Considered to be luxury establishments, they are not excessively expensive for what they offer.

Hotels are fullest in summer, over Christmas and Holy Week, and during local festivals (see p. 24).

Prices are normally checked by the Catalan tourist board. They are always shown without the tax included and vary according to the season. You should find an official list at the hotel reception and in your room. The price for a single room should be between 60% and 80% that of a double. An extra bed should not cost more than 60% the price of a single or 35% the price of a double.

For Barcelona hotels, see p. 79

Campgrounds

Catalonia has 70% of Spain's total camping capacity with over 300 campgrounds. A guide to facilities in Catalonia is published each year by the *Generalitat* and can be obtained free of charge from tourist offices.

Most campgrounds give special rates outside the tourist season (June, July and August) and there is a reduction for children under 10.

You should reserve in advance. For further information, contact the **Barcelona Camping Organization, ☎** (93) 317 44 16.

▬ *BEACHES*

Catalonia's eastern boundary, the Mediterranean, has 301 mi/485 km of beaches. The Costa Brava in the north is characterized by a steep coastline and a succession of creeks, while the Maresme coast just north of Barcelona is a series of long beaches. South of the city, on the Garraf coast and especially on the Costa Dorada, there are beaches of fine sand as far as the eye can see.

Most beaches in Catalonia are accessible by car. They are popular in summer and generally offer good facilities, including restaurants and bars. There is also a wide choice of water sports: sailing, windsurfing, water-skiing, etc. Special care is taken today to preserve their natural beauty and they are quite clean and unspoiled — in spite of the intense development that took place from 1950-1970. Depending on local weather, the beach season lasts from Easter to October with an average of 204 sunny days a year.

Sun. Sand. Bullfighting. Paella. These are the images conjured up in the mind of many visitors who too often forget that while Catalonia offers opportunities for rest and relaxation, it is also a land of great cultural interest. Enjoy the beaches, yes — but don't limit your horizons to the burning sand.

▬ *BUSINESS HOURS*

As in other Mediterranean countries, there is a lot of flexibility where time is concerned. Punctuality does not always seem to be a priority in Catalonia; this said, however, don't assume it to be the rule in all cases.

In large towns, of course, public establishments are scrupulous about keeping to official working hours, but don't be surprised if you are given an appointment for 'between 9 and 10'. This is part of the relaxed way of life from which you can profit while on holiday. Allowances are sometimes made in small towns where, for example, public ceremonies may be announced for half an hour earlier than the time they have actually been planned to begin.

The lovely sand beaches of Costa Daurada are a perfect place to stop for a rest between two visits to the monasteries near Tarragona.

As a general rule, shops close between 2 and 4pm for lunch. After 8pm, once the shops have shut, the evening strolls and nightlife begin.

Banks
Banks are open Monday to Friday 8:30am-2pm; Saturday 9am-12:30pm.

Post offices
Post offices are usually open Monday to Friday 9am-2pm; some open in the afternoons 5-8pm.

Restaurants
Restaurants normally open 1-4pm for lunch and again in the evening 9-11pm.

Shops
Shops are open 9 or 10am-1:30 or 2pm; 4 or 4:30-7:30 or 8pm.

Tourist information
Tourist Information Offices keep the same hours as banks and shops.

▬ COURTESY

Courtesy is the rule in Catalonia. For greetings, handshakes are frequent though not automatic; only good friends kiss when they meet. If you speak Catalan, the polite form of 'you' is a must, especially with the older generation, although the informal 'you' has become common with the young over the past few years. Don't be surprised if a stranger uses this with you — it is merely a sign that times are changing. If you don't speak Catalan, Spanish will always be understood, of course, and failing that, English or French. Although it is not considered impolite to address a Catalan in another tongue, the local people like foreigners to be aware that Catalan is the regional language (see p. 29).

CURRENCY EXCHANGE

Although you can change money in Catalonia in a great many banks, your best bet is to go to the main ones. Some big hotels and travel agencies have exchange facilities, as do Barcelona's stations and El Prat airport *(open daily 7:30am-11pm)*.

ELECTRICITY

The electric current is 220-230 volts AC although some hotels have 110-125 volt plugs in bathrooms. The plugs are generally of the universal round variety with two prongs. It would be a good idea to bring an adaptor for such small appliances as razors, hairdryers and so on.

EMERGENCIES

Each town has a hospital and an emergency service in case of accident or illness. Apart from these, there are a lot of private doctors who post their surgery hours. As in other continental European countries, the price of a consultation depends on the doctor's specialization. Your travel agent can advise you on appropriate health insurance.

Pharmacies *(farmacias)*, easily recognizable by a blue or green cross, keep the same business hours as shops. If closed, they post on their doors the addresses of the nearest open pharmacy, so that, in the event of an emergency, you will always be able to find what you need, even on a Sunday or holiday. You can also check the list of *Farmaciàs de Guerdia'* (pharmacies open) in one of the local newspapers.

FESTIVALS

Religious holidays
See also 'Festivals', p. 82 in Barcelona section.

March or April: Holy Week

Many Catalan villages commemorate Holy Week and Easter with music and theatrical events. Religious festivals are extremely popular and are mainly composed of representations of the *Via Crucis* (Way of the Cross), processions, plays and performances of the Passion of Christ, *caramelles* (chorals) and *cururulles* (parades of hooded penitents). Mention should also be made of the processions in Girona, Tarragona, Badalona and Tortosa, and the *Via Crucis* in Sant Hilari Sacalm in which actors perform various scenes. The most popular procession of all, which takes place in the village of Verges, is accompanied by 'the dance of Death' and dates from the 15th century.

The afternoon procession in Barcelona on Good Friday is preceded by the Adoration of Christ of Lepanto. The most renowned Passion plays, including the death and resurrection of Christ, are performed in Olesa and Esparraguera near Barcelona. On Easter Sunday (and sometimes also on one or two following Sundays), groups of young people in Catalan costume sing *caramelles* in the streets and squares. These humorous popular songs, part of a strong village tradition, are sung to wish for happiness and well-being. The singers often carry large ribboned baskets into which people put gifts of food. Easter is celebrated with *mones* — various types of cakes and chocolates shaped into figurines, often accompanied by eggs that are either decorated or made of chocolate. It is customary in Catalonia for a godmother to give her godchild *palma* on Palm Sunday and a godfather to give *mona* on Easter Monday.

April 23: Feast of St George (Sant Jordi), or the Festival of Catalonia, roses and books

Ever since the Middle Ages, the Catalan nobility has considered St George to be its patron saint. In the 15th century the *Generalitat* placed itself under the saint's protection by adopting St George's cross as its emblem. In 1456 the Parliament *(Cortes)* decided that his feast day should be celebrated throughout Catalonia and in 1660 the Church recognized him as patron saint of Catalonia. Long after the Middle Ages the holiday was known for its flower market in del Bisbe street, which was moved in the 19th century to the courtyard of the *Generalitat* palace. The inhabitants of Barcelona would go to the palace chapel to worship the relics of St George.

The feast of St George remains the *Generalitat's* most important holiday — characterized by abundant displays of brightly coloured roses, a book fair and the chiming of church bells. Moreover, because it coincides with the arrival of Spring, it also serves as the Festival of Love, during which joyful crowds throng the streets. The cultural aspect of the holiday is provided by the *Dia desl llibre* ('Day of the book'), a book fair in which newly published works are displayed. The triple function of the festival has given rise to its triple motto: 'Homeland, Love, Culture'.

FOOD AND DRINK

Catalan cuisine is distinctive for its variety, its contrasting flavours and unusual mixtures of ingredients, made possible by a multitude of natural produce. Without attempting to be refined, traditional dishes are made from whatever the land and sea have to offer on a daily basis.

Typical dishes

At the base of Catalan cooking are sauces like *samfaina* (made of peppers, tomatoes and aubergines) and *picada* (pine nuts, almonds, hazelnuts, garlic and toasted breadcrumbs ground up in a mortar). The varied mixtures stem from the necessity to use everything available — especially where the cuisine of poorer people is concerned; the results of such necessity are delightful.

The queen of soups is the *escudella*, a version of the universal *carn d'olla* (stew) enriched with *pilota* (minced meat, breadcrumbs, egg and spices). One of its variations is *escudella de pagès* or *escudella barrejada* — a hotpot with beans, rice, noodles, spicy sausages and vegetables.

The Mediterranean naturally supplies a rich variety of fish for the dishes that are so popular now in Catalonia. Surprisingly, the art of seafood cooking came into its own here less than a century ago. Fish in a sauce, *sarsuela (zarzuela)*, is popular in Barcelona and, like *graellades (parrilladas)* or platters of grilled seafood, uses a large variety of seafood including lobster, grouper, mussels, cuttlefish. There is also a wide range of rice *a la marinera*, which is similar to Valencian paella. Cod is popular, often accompanied by *samfaina*, potatoes and *alioli* (crushed garlic and olive oil sauce); be sure to try cod fritters or the cod served during Lent.

In the Pyrenees you will find game dishes (wild boar, mountain goat), hearty *estofats* (stews) and freshwater fish (trout). Snails (*cargols*) are cooked to perfection in the Lleida (Lerida) region. In agricultural areas where there is a wide variety of vegetables, you will come across typically

---

Bon profit!

A Catalan meal can be a unique experience, mainly because of the great variety of products used in the dishes.

A meal on the Mediterranean coast includes a wide choice of fish and seafood, of course, which you can have grilled (*parrillada*), with a sauce (*zarsuela*), or in a kind of soup (*suguet*, fishermen's fish stew).

On the other hand, a mountain meal normally consists of delicious rice-based dishes to accompany rabbit, with broad beans, sausages, green beans or mushrooms (*rovellons*).

Desserts include *crema cremada*, a typical Catalan cream mixture, a kind of biscuit roll known as gypsy's arm', and *coques* (cakes with pine kernels).

Bon profit! (Hearty appetite!).

Pastry Calendar

Special Catalan pastries and desserts are prepared for each religious festival. *Torrons* (a kind of nougat) are eaten at Christmas, *tortells* (pastries) and *roscons* (fondants) at Epiphany and the feast of St Anthony, and *bunyols* (doughnuts) during Lent. *Mones* (cakes and chocolates shaped into figurines) accompany hard-boiled eggs at Easter, *coques* (cakes with pine kernels) are eaten on Christmas or New Year's Eve and *panellets* (almond paste) on All Saints' Day. *Crema cremada* (crème brûlée) and *mel i mató* (curd cheese with honey) can be savoured whatever the season.

Catalan broad beans, sometimes mixed with peas, or green beans (*montgetes*) accompanying pork dishes.

Many types of sausages can be found on Catalan tables throughout the year. Among these are the large *botifarres* (including raw, cured, dry sausages, sweet sausages from Girona, *negra* or *de sang*, black pudding); *Botifarra de perol* (with tripe); and other varieties, including *llonganissa*, *fuet* and *espatec*. *Xoric*, a sausage from Pallars made of pork or wild boar, and *girella*, liver and rice sausage, are typical Pyrenean dishes. Equally popular are copious mixed salads dressed with olive oil and served at the beginning of a meal.

Most meals are accompanied by *pà amb tomàquet*: fresh country bread (sometimes toasted) rubbed with a cut tomato and occasionally garlic and sprinkled with olive oil. It is often very salty and usually served with pork and traditional Catalan dishes.

Breakfast and snacks

Continental breakfasts are rare outside large hotels but a visitor to Barcelona will have no trouble finding a bar or café (there's one about every two blocks!) in which to have a quick breakfast. This usually consists of coffee with a little milk or a *tallat* (*cortado* in Castilian: a small amount of coffee generally served in a glass with a drop of milk), accompanied by a croissant, a *xuixo* (cream doughnut), an *ensaïmada* (typically Majorcan roll) or other cakes. For a more substantial breakfast you can ask for a 'sandwich' — a kind of hot snack of toasted cheese with ham. For a cold loaf sandwich, ask for an *entrepà* (Catalan) or *bocadillo* (Castilian) with ham, cheese or chorizo, which will be prepared for you on the spot with tomato bread (*pà amb tomàquet*). Another option is to go to a more modern establishment, the croissant shop, where you have a wide choice of croissants and sandwiches.

Because of the long working hours in the morning (9am-2pm), Catalans usually have two breakfasts; coffee early on and then a larger snack with sandwiches around 11 am.

A *granja*, a kind of milk bar, is the place to go for a copious breakfast or afternoon tea. As you walk by, you will be greeted by the irresistible smell of hot chocolate or caramel. A quiet family atmosphere usually reigns in a *granja*, making it a pleasant place to take a break in a busy day. Here you will find a variety of specialities including thick, hot, full-flavoured chocolate, *nata* (thick sweet Chantilly cream) or *crema catalana* (crème brûlée with eggs and cinnamon). A good *granja* will also serve *mel i mató* (curd cheese with honey), *mató* from Pedralbes (another kind of thick cream with eggs) served in earthenware dishes, and hot *ensaïmadas*.

While bars are generally open from 8am-11pm, *granjas* tend to close for lunch and at 8pm.

Wine

The tremendous variety of different landscapes in Catalonia is reflected in its wine production. The 247,110 ac/100,000 ha of vineyards, the 66 million gallons/3 million hectolitres of wine they produce and the 30,000 families working in the wine business give an idea of the size of this industry in Catalonia.

The entrance to Mercat de Sant Josep is marked by a giant red pepper — one of the main ingredients in many Catalan dishes.

The main wine-growing areas in Catalonia

Penedès: white wines and young, light, fruity *caves* (champagnes). Best vintages 1963, 64, 65, 69, 70, 72, 73, 75, 76, 78, 80, 82, 83, 85 and 87.

Alella: smooth, mellow whites; *marfil* (ivory) type. Best vintages: 1964, 67, 68, 70, 72, 75, 78, 79, 81, 82, 83, 85 and 87.

Priorat: potent, velvety, full-bodied reds. Best vintages: 1977, 79, 80 and 85.

Tarragona: firm, aged, generous reds. Also whites and rosés. Best vintages: 1967, 78, 79, 80, 81 and 84.

Empordà-Costa Brava: fresh fruity rosés and *garnatxes* (dessert wines). Best vintages: 1966, 67, 73, 78, 79, 81, 83 and 85.

Conca de Barberà: light whites and bright rosés. Best vintages: 1971, 75, 78, 79, 80, 81, 82, 83, 84, 85 and 87.

Terra Alta: strong, dry white wines; rosés. Best vintages: 1966, 71, 73, 79, 82 and 87.

Costers del Segre: reds from different vineyards, whites. Best vintages: 1966, 71, 73, 80, 81 and 85.

The rosés from the Empordà and Costa Brava regions, which are a deep cherry colour, well-structured and fruity, are delicious. The reds are good too, especially the young, highly aromatic ones. Also try *garnatxa*, a smooth, powerful natural dessert wine.

The range of traditional Alella whites, soft elegant wines with a distinctive flavour, is now widening to include new varieties.

Penedès is without doubt the most prosperous wine-growing region in Catalonia. The whites figure among the great names — *macatau*, *xarel-lo* and *pavellada*; these are dry, fresh, slightly acidic, aromatic wines.

A favourite among Catalans is *cava*, local champagne, a sparkling wine that is slightly sweeter than the French equivalent. Traditionally associated with the town of San Sadurni d'Anoia, *cava* is produced in different parts of Penedès and in the Tarragona region. The one from Perelada in the Empordà region is also greatly appreciated.

The widest variety of wines comes from the Tarragona region. They range from the light wines of Conca de Barberà, to the legendary nectar of Priorat and the Tarragona classics — not forgetting the honest little wines typical of Camp and Ribera. Of the less well-known family-produced wines, the *moscatells* and *rancis*, which are intended to accompany desserts and pastries, are well worth trying.

Summer drinks

Morxata de xufla (*horchata de chufa* in Castilian) is a refreshing milky drink which originated in Valencia and is made from a *xufla* base (edible rhizomes known as tiger-nuts) with sugar and water. Most bars serve it during the summer but it is best to order it in places that make their own.

Other summer drinks include vegetable milk and *granissats* (drinks with a crushed ice base). The most popular flavours are coffee and lemon although you will also find other fruit and chocolate.

Finally, as in most Mediterranean countries, there is a wide choice of ice cream which can be made into *batuts* (milk shakes).

The aperitif

An aperitif at midday or in the evening is a veritable ritual, whether savoured alone or in a group. As meal times are quite late in Catalonia (between 2 and 4pm for lunch and from 9:30 or 10pm onward for dinner), it is customary after work to drop into one of the many bars or taverns to have a drink (alcoholic or otherwise) accompanied by *tapas*: these snacks, originating in other parts of Spain, were brought to Catalonia by immigrants from those provinces. *Tapas* consist of small portions of meat, fish, seafood, sausages, croquettes, olives and so on, and sometimes serve as a meal in themselves. The idea is to vary your choice, hopping from bar to bar trying out different specialities.

▬ GETTING AROUND

By car

Traveling by car is the most practical way of getting around Catalonia. The main towns in Catalonia — Girona, Barcelona, Tarragona and Lleida — as well as the Costa Brava and the Costa Dorada, are all linked by highways (with tolls) where the speed limit is 75 mph/120 kph. You can easily reach Girona or Tarragona from Barcelona in less than an hour and a half, a little longer for Lleida.

Four-lane roads (dual carriageways) are on the increase in Catalonia; the speed limit on them is 60 mph/100 kph. The limit on other roads is 55 mph/90 kph; in towns it is 35 mph/60 kph. Finally, if you have a caravan (trailer), you should never exceed 50 mph/80 kph. It is unwise to try visiting the centres of large towns by car, especially Barcelona.

Filling stations sell super, regular and diesel. As in other continental countries, the highway code requires drivers to give way to traffic coming from the right. The local automobile club, the *Reial Automòbil Club de*

Catalunya (RACC), offers services similar to those of clubs in other European countries.

By train

You can reach all rail destinations in Catalonia from Sants and Passeig de Gràcia, Barcelona's main rail stations. The Spanish railway network operating throughout the country is known as RENFE *(Red Nacional de los Ferrocarriles Españoles)*. You can buy RENFE tickets in travel agencies. There are special passes entitling you to unlimited rail travel over a period of 8, 15, or 22 days. A *Tarjeta Dorada* pass gives a reduction of 50% and, if you are under 26, an InterRail or Eurail Youthpass also entitles you to reduced fares.

The *Generalitat* of Catalonia runs a network of trains from Barcelona to various towns in Catalonia. Trains from plaça d'Espanya station run to Igualada, Montserrat and Manresa, while others from plaça de Catalunya go to Sabadell, Terrassa and Sant Cugat.

▬ *LANGUAGE*

The two official languages of Catalonia are Castilian Spanish and Catalan. However, in recent years Catalan has become the predominant language. This guide uses the Catalan spelling because this is what a visitor is most likely to encounter (street signs, directions). English is often understood in the main tourist centres. See 'Useful Vocabulary' p. 185 for a list of useful terms, with the Catalan and Castilian equivalents.

The people of Catalonia have fought hard to keep the Catalan language alive. It was initially outlawed in 1923 by the Madrid government, and Franco later hardened the position against the Catalan culture. Schools were forbidden to teach in Catalan and no books could be published in the language. Nevertheless, it thrived underground and is now replacing Castilian Spanish throughout the region. You will hear it everywhere: it is taught in schools and used in newspapers, on the radio and on television. It is also used in the fields of literature and science and the region possesses a dynamic publishing system that produces an impressive amount of books.

The first words of Catalan, originally a Romance language, appeared in Latin texts in the 9th century. It is a language in its own right and, logically enough, local people will not appreciate suggestions that their language is merely a dialect.

▬ *MEDIA*

Press

Catalonia's daily newspapers appear in either Catalan or Castilian. For a long time the *La Vanguardia* daily had the biggest circulation in Spain despite the fact that it was produced in Barcelona. In the 1970s it stabilized at about 200,000 copies and since 1987 it has been overtaken by *El País*. *La Vanguardia* continues to be Catalonia's main newspaper followed by *El Periódico*, *El País* (thanks to its Barcelona edition) and *Avui*. This last has a circulation of about 40,000 and was the only exclusively Catalan daily until the reappearance of *Diari de Barcelona*.

You can easily find international newspapers in all the larger towns.

Radio and television

Catalonia's radio stations broadcast either in Catalan and Castilian or in Catalan exclusively. The two national Spanish television channels TVE1 and TVE2, broadcast programs for Catalonia in Catalan. Furthermore, the second channel is now established regionwide. Catalonia also has its own autonomous, high-quality channel, TV3, which is widely broadcast within Catalan borders. A new channel, Canal 33, broadcasts over a smaller area, basically sports, culture and local news programs. Regional channels are making a big effort to create new programs and dub all foreign films into Catalan.

NIGHTLIFE

Catalonia is renowned for the quality and diversity of its nightlife, especially Barcelona which is considered a kind of nocturnal paradise where life never slows down. (See 'Barcelona', p. 89.)

ORGANIZING YOUR TIME

The time you spend visiting Catalonia will depend on the kind of holiday you are looking for. In the section on Barcelona you will find several itinerary suggestions ranging from a one- or two-day visit, up to a whole week. There are also suggestions for visiting the rest of Catalonia.

If you plan to spend a week on the Costa Brava, you will need a day to see Girona, half a day for Figueres and another half day for the ruins of Empuries or for Cadaqués and Sant-Pere-de-Rodes.

If you have a week on the Costa Dorada, you will need a day for Tarragona and another for the monasteries of Poblet and Santes Creus, with a visit to Montblanc on the way.

Include at least a day in the itinerary suggestions above for Barcelona; you must not leave Catalonia without seeing it.

If you plan to stay for two weeks, you could spend three days in Barcelona and then follow one of our itineraries to Lleida, Tarragona, the Pyrenees or Andorra.

POST OFFICE

Post offices are generally open Monday to Friday 9am-2pm (some re-open in the afternoon). To collect your 'poste restante' (General Delivery) mail you will need a means of identification. The main post office, plaça Antoni Lòpez, I, C3, is open Monday to Saturday 8:30am-10pm, Sundays 10am-noon.

Stamps are on sale in post offices and tobacconists.

PUBLIC HOLIDAYS

January 1: New Year's Day *(Cap d'any)*.
January 6: Epiphany *(Reis)*.
March-April: Good Friday *(Divendres sant)*.
March-April: Pentecost *(Pasqua)*.
May 1: Labour Day *(Festa de Treball)*.
June 24: Feast of St John *(Sant Joan)*.
August 15: Assumption *(Mare de Déu d'Agost)*.
September 11: National Day *(Onze de Setembre)*.
September 24: Feast of Our Lady of Mercy *(Mare de Déu de la Mercè)*, in Barcelona only.
October 12: Festival of the Hispanic world, Feast of the Virgin of Pilar *(Hispanitat, Mare de Déu del Pilar)*.
November 1: All Saints' Day *(Tots Sants)*.
December 8: Feast of the Immaculate Conception *(Puríssima Concepció)*.
December 25: Christmas Day *(Nadal)*.
December 26: Feast of St Stephen *(Sant Esteve)*.

SAFETY PRECAUTIONS

Keep an eye on your belongings in large towns and on beaches. When you arrive, pay attention to your luggage and don't change more money than is necessary to get you to wherever you are staying. Never leave your car unguarded if it contains luggage and don't leave personal documents, radios, cameras or videos in sight.

Two policemen from the mounted squad of Barcelona.

When out walking, be circumspect about street hawkers and don't carry large sums of cash. Handbags, photo or video cameras should be carried bandoleer fashion with the straps slung diagonally across your chest.

Although Catalonia is not regarded as a dangerous region, petty crime in certain quarters of Barcelona is common. Simply be careful at all times. As for going out at night, don't venture out alone without enquiring beforehand whether the area you're visiting is safe or not.

▬ SHOPPING

Most shops are open from 9am-1 or 1:30pm and again from 4pm or 4:30-8pm. Department stores, some boutiques and shopping arcades do not shut for lunch, especially in town centres. Many of the shops have sales from the second week in January to the end of February and (mainly in large towns) in July and August.

Catalonia offers a rich variety of places to shop, ranging from department stores to the tiniest boutiques, and including a large number of outdoor markets. Among cottage industry products to bring back home, you will find pottery, glassware, wrought ironwork, enamels, lace, leather and secondhand goods.

Lace

Making bobbin-lace is still a popular craft in Catalonia and in spite of industrial competition, you can sometimes see village women at work on it. A pattern is fixed to a small cushion with little wooden pieces called *boixets* ('bobbins'). The thread they use is of the highest quality. Among the specialities of the trade are the black lace of Arboç del Penedès and the white lace of Arenys de Mar.

Ceramics

The ceramics tradition dates back to the Middle Ages and is still a widely established cottage industry in Catalonia. There are many regional varieties ranging from the production of Verdú (Urgell) to that of La Bisbal (Baix Empordà). Some Catalan potters are internationally renowned; among the best-known are Josep Llorenç Artigas and Antoni Cumella.

▬▬ SPORTS

For information on sporting activities contact the **Direcció General d'Esports,** Generalitat de Catalunya, Barcelona, av. Països Catalans, 12 Esplugues de Llobregat, ☎ (93) 371 9011.

Ballon (soccer) and basketball

Soccer is the most popular sport in Catalonia and the rivalry between Barcelona's two teams, the 'Barça' or Football Club of Barcelona and the 'Espanyol' or RCD Español, constantly makes the news (see 'Sports' p. 93 in Barcelona section).

Basketball is Catalonia's second most popular sport. The 'FC' of Barcelona and the 'Jovenut de Badalona' feature among leading international clubs.

Golf

Golf enthusiasts know that the region possesses a number of pleasant modern courses. The success of Severiano ('Seve') Ballesteros has certainly contributed to the increasing popularity of the sport here.

Catalonia has nine clubs scattered throughout the region — near Barcelona, on the Costa Brava, on the Costa Dorada and at the foot of the mountains.

Reial Club de Golf de Cerdanya (18 holes): this is located in Cerdaña, 0.6 mi/1 km from Puigcerdà in the middle of the Pyrenees; 1.8 mi/3 km from the French border (frontier post: Bourg Madame) and 87 mi/140 km north of Barcelona. Apartat de Correus, 63-17520 Puigcerdà, ☎ (972) 88 1338/(972) 88 0950. International competitions are held twice during Holy Week and in August and September.

Club de Golf Costa Brava (18 holes): on the Costa Brava; 62 mi/100 km north-east of Barcelona and 68 mi/110 km south of Perpignan (exit 9 on highway A7 towards Sant Feliu de Guíxols). La Masia, 17246 Santa Cristina d'Aro, ☎ (972) 83 7150/(972) 83 7152.

Club de Golf Costa Dorada (9 holes): 3.1 mi/5 km from Tarragona, (access N340 and highway N7). Apartat de Correus, 600-43080 Tarragona, ☎ (977) 65 541.

Reial Club de Golf El Prat (27 holes): 9 mi/15 km south-west of Barcelona between the airport and the beach. Apartat de Correus, 10-08820 El Prat de Llobregat, ☎ (93) 379 0278. One of the best-known clubs in Catalonia with three different courses, it was designed by Xavier Arana and holds many international competitions.

Club de Golf Llavaneres (9 holes): in Sant Andreu de Llavaneres, 21 mi/34 km north-east of Barcelona, overlooking the Maresme coast (6.2 mi/10 km beyond the end of the A19, the Barcelona-Mataró highway). 08392 Sant Andreu de Llavaneres, ☎ (93) 792 6050. The smallest course in Spain with very steep slopes.

Club de Golf Sant Cugat (18 holes): 0.6 mi/1 km from the centre of Sant Cugat del Vallès, 12 mi/20 km north of Barcelona (access: highway A7 or city trains from the centre of Barcelona). 08190 Sant Cugat del Vallès, ☎ (93) 674 39 58. In addition to the 18 holes there are three extra ones for beginners.

Club de Golf Terramar (18 holes): at the end of the long Passeig Marítim of Sitges, parallel to the beach, 23 mi/37 km south-west of Barcelona. Apartat de Correus 6-08870 Sitges, ☎ (93) 894 0580/(93) 894 2043.

Club de Golf Pals (18 holes): on the Pals beach (Costa Brava), 3.1 mi/5 km from Begur, 25 mi/40 km from Girona and Figueres, 84 mi/135 km north-east of Barcelona. Platja de Pals, 17256 Pals, ☎ (972) 63 6006. One of the most successful in Spain.

Club de Golf Vallromanes (18 holes): on the eastern slope of the mountains that separate Maresme from Montseny, 4.6 mi/7.5 km off the Masnou-Granollers road, 14 mi/23 km north-east of Barcelona. Apartat de Correus, 43-08170 Montornès del Vallès, ☎ (93) 568 0362.

Skiing

There are a great many ski resorts in the Pyrenees. The oldest are La Molina and Núria, while one of the most famous is Baqueira-Beret in the Aran valley, which is frequented by the King of Spain, Juan Carlos, and his family. All the resorts have excellent slopes and are equipped with modern facilities. There are 11 resorts in Catalonia for Alpine skiing (open from December to May) and 11 for cross-country skiing.

Once the snow has melted, these mountains make ideal spots for hunting, hiking or simply enjoying the pure air and delightful landscapes.

▬ TELEPHONE

To telephone you will need a stock of 5, 25 and 100 peseta coins, although some phones accept credit cards.

You cannot call collect (reverse charges) from a telephone booth.

For information dial **003**.

Each province has regional and city codes. To call from one province to another when in Spain you need to dial **9**, the first number in any provincial code. The 9 is not necessary when calling from abroad.

To make an international call from Catalonia: dial **07**, wait for the dialing tone then dial the international code for the country in question (44 for the United Kingdom, 1 for Canada and the United States, 61 for Australia, 64 for New Zealand) and finally the number.

Telephone area codes for towns and cities listed in this guide:
- Barcelona: **93**
- Lleida: **973**
- Ripoll: **972**
- La Seu de Urgel: **973**
- Tarragona: **977**
- Vic: **93**

▬ TIPPING

Service is never included in restaurant or café bills or in taxi fares. It is therefore customary to leave a tip of around 10% of the price.

▬ TOILETS

You will find public toilets in train stations and museums, or near beaches and markets. In Barcelona they are often located at basement level along with other facilities.

In Catalan you ask: *'On es troben els lavabos* (or *'el bany'/'els serveis'*), *si us plau?'*. The equivalent in Castilian is: *'Donde se encuentran los lavabos* (or *'el bano'/'los servicios'/'los aseos'*), *por favor?'*

▬ TOURIST INFORMATION

There are two types of tourist information offices in Catalonia. The first, run by the *Generalitat* of Catalonia, provides geographical and cultural information, regional maps and general advice of all kinds. The second, a municipal tourist bureau (which in some towns is combined with the former) is where you will be given practical details concerning hotel accommodation, guided tours, concerts and so on.

▬ WORSHIPPING

Roman Catholicism is by far the most widespread religion. However, there also exist Orthodox Catholic, Protestant, Catalan, Spanish and foreign denomination churches. Synagogues and mosques are mostly located in Barcelona.

CATALONIA IN THE PAST

The fate of Catalonia was shaped by its position in the Mediterranean; early conquests by the Greeks, Romans and Carthaginians all left their mark on the character of the north-east of Spain. In addition, a remarkable climate and abundance of natural resources meant that Catalonia could turn away from central Spain and enjoy an autonomous destiny.

The oldest known inhabitants in Catalonia were the Iberians who crossed the Straits of Gibraltar from Africa. Around 990 BC Celts from the north moved to the northern and central sections of Spain, gradually mixing with the Iberians to form what is now referred to as the Celto-Iberian people. Rather than adopting the Iberian customs, the Celts were able to impose their own and thus retained a strong identity throughout their migrations.

The high level of skill achieved by the Iberians in the art of metallurgy attracted traders from other regions of the Mediterranean. The neighbouring sea-farers of Greece, for example, attracted by potential trade prospects, founded the coastal colonies of Emporium (present-day Empuries) and Rhode (Roses). The Greek legacy to Spain includes not only their love of the bull, wine and olives, but also a specific artistic sensibility.

In 237 BC, the Carthaginians founded Barcelona, a former Iberian town. They named it Barcino after a Punic family called Barca, of which both Hamilcar and Hannibal were members. In 218 BC, to stem the progress of Carthaginian power in Spain, the Romans founded their first province on the peninsula, north of the Ebro River, with Tarraco (Tarragona) as its capital. The second Punic War (218-202 BC), led by Rome against the Carthaginians, ended with the defeat of Hannibal, the Carthaginian general. After being conquered by the Romans, Barcelona was made a colony.

The first Visigoth monarch, Ataulphus, settled in Barcelona in AD 415 and the Roman province of Tarraconensis came under Visigoth control. The Visigoths (who by this time had been Romanized) were driven out of their settlements to the north by Clovis and the Franks of Aquitaine. After their defeat at Vouillé, they settled mainly in Spain, gathering in Old Castile to found the kingdom of Toledo, which adopted the main elements of

This monument to Christopher Columbus, erected in the 19th century, serves as a reminder that, after his discovery of America, the great explorer sailed into the harbour of Barcelona.

the political and administrative structures of the kingdom of Toulouse.

In AD 587, the Visigoth king, Recared I, renounced allegiance to Arian religious doctrines and espoused orthodox Christian thought. Of course, Christianity had been introduced centuries before, during the rule of Nero (1st century): St Paul is said to have visited Spain between AD 63 and 67 and Christ's disciple, St James, is believed to have preached there. But following the conversion of Recared I, Catholicism spread rapidly, especially among the more Romanized regions, such as Catalonia. The cults of Saints Prosper, Augury and Eulogy took hold in Tarragona while the population of Barcelona was influenced by the strong personality of St Pacian. The Arabs entered the peninsula in 711. By 715 they were in Catalonia, destroying Tarragona and occupying Barcelona. When they defeated Roderic, the last king of Toldeo, Akhila, who reigned in Tarraconensis, sided with them. The Muslim advance toward the north was soon halted by the Franks who, having expelled Islam from Septimania (part of southern France around Carcassonne and Narbonne), continued pressure to the south. Girona was abandoned by the Muslims in 785. To protect himself against the Muslim invasion, Charlemagne established what was known as the Spanish March (a buffer zone between Christian and Muslim Spain) and gave his own son, Louis the Pious, the responsibility of reorganizing the territory. Barcelona capitulated in 801 and became the capital of the Spanish March. New territories conquered by the Carolingians were given to the archbishopric of Narbonne. Lands recovered from the Arabs were divided into counties and became dependent on the Carolingian Empire.

REORGANIZATION OF THE COUNTRY

At the end of the 9th century, Guifre el Pelós (Wilfred the Hairy) undertook to free a great many of the Catalan counties from Frankish suzerainty. As Count of Barcelona, Urgell and Besalú, he founded the Royal House of Barcelona which ruled the region for five centuries. One of the many legends from this period claims that Count Guifre was wounded during a battle against the Arabs; he dipped four fingers into his blood and drew them across his gold shield before he died, leaving four red parallel bars — the insignia of the national Catalan coat of arms. In 985 when Count Borrell II called upon Lothaire, King of the Franks, to help protect Barcelona from the Arabs, the king refused his support. This sparked the Catalans' first stirrings of independence.

Ramon Berenguer I, count from 1035 to 1076, widened the former March by reconquering territories occupied by the Arabs. During his reign he assembled the *Cortes* (parliament) and issued the *Usatges,* the first feudal code in Europe. This was a legislative body composed of four parts: legal and feudal practices, a constitutional charter of the territory, the duties of the Prince, and rules concerning navigation and civil legislation.

Ramon Berenguer thus drew up an early outline for the political independence of Catalonia. In addition, under the impetus of the Abbot-Bishop Oliba, the first *Peace and Truce of God* was written. This contributed to the legislative organization of the region at a local level whereby peace was ensured from Saturday evening to the first hour of Monday, prohibiting attacks on persons (whether ecclesiastic or lay) entering or leaving a church.

Anxious to increase its territory, the House of Barcelona undertook a policy of alliance. Through the marriage of Ramon Berenguer III it inherited Provence which it ruled from 1113 to 1245. On the death of Alfonso, the King of Aragon, the marriage in 1137 of Ramon Berenguer IV to Petronila, Queen of Aragon, sealed the union of the Kingdom of Aragon and the County of Barcelona.

With the unification of the two powers, Ramon Berenguer found himself at the head of a heterogeneous state. He kept the title Count of Barcelona, preferring it to King of Aragon. But the union of the two peoples, so advantageous on the surface, was not achieved without difficulty due to their profound temperamental and linguistic differences. On the death of Ramon Berenguer IV, his widow Petronila changed the title of their son from Ramon Berenguer V to the more traditional Aragonese, Alfonso I. During his reign Catalonia's influence spread over the entire region of Languedoc in France from Nice to the Atlantic. For three centuries the Catalan-Aragonese confederation was one of the greatest Mediterranean powers.

THE CRUSADE AGAINST THE ALBIGENSIANS AND THE REIGN OF JAUME I

Following the excommunication of Raymond VI of Toulouse (1207) by the Pope, the Count of Barcelona, Pedro II the Catholic, faced a dilemma: as a lord he was expected to defend Raymond VI but as a Christian prince he was obliged to combat Cathar heresy and obey the Pope. Faced with the intransigence of Simon de Montfort, a papal ally, together with his thirst for conquest, King Pedro chose to defend the barons of Languedoc and take part in the battle of Muret in September 1213.

On his death he was succeeded to the throne by his five-year-old son, Jaume I the Conqueror, whose reign lasted 63 years. In his youth Jaume had to deal with the uprisings of Aragonese nobles who, proud and jealous of their privileges, often created problems that threatened the balance of power in the kingdom.

Jaume the Conqueror's rule was an heroic one. On September 5, 1229, he set out from Salou (a small port near Tarragona) to take Majorca. Three months later he annexed it to the Crown. Several years later, in 1235, he landed at Eivissa (Ibiza) and then in 1238, he conquered Valencia. This was settled by people from the Lleida region to whom the king gave special laws that differed from those in the princedom (Aragon had also kept its own laws).

The taking of Majorca, the first Catalan conquest and annexation outside the continent, marked the beginning of the great Mediterranean expansion. The *Llibre del Consolat de Mar* was written, thanks to these conquests and remained the most consulted maritime code for years after. Meanwhile, inland, the *Cortes* began to operate with its three branches of representatives: ecclesiastic, military and the commons. The long reign and achievements of Jaume I were recorded in a chronicle entitled the *Llibre dels Feyts (Book of Deeds)*.

A MEDITERRANEAN POWER

In 1253, Jaume I divided his immense kingdom between his sons, entrusting Aragon, Valencia and a frontier zone near the Ebro to Alfonso III (the Liberal); Catalonia to Pedro III (the Great); and the Balearic Islands and Montpellier (modern-day France) to Jaume II (the Just). When Alfonso died in 1262, the King had to divide the kingdom again, this time definitively: Catalonia, Aragon and Valencia went to Pedro, and the Balearic Islands, Roussillon, Montpellier, Conflent and Cerdana went to Jaume. This decision gave birth to the Kingdom of Majorca.

While Charles d'Anjou was setting himself up as King of Sicily, the Sicilians called upon Pedro the Great, King of Catalonia and Aragon, to lay claim to this island and assert the hereditary rights of his wife. Pedro was fighting in North Africa at the time, and because he lacked the necessary funds to continue his crusade against the Arabs, he welcomed the appeal and sailed to Sicily, conquering the islands of Djerba, Malta and Gozo on the way.

In view of the usurpations of Charles d'Anjou's rights in Sicily, Pope Martin IV gave him permission to launch a crusade against Catalonia and bequeathed him all of the Catalan kingdoms. Thus the troops of King Philippe III of France prepared to invade Catalonia. When the French army arrived at the gates of Girona, however, Catalonia found in Roger of Llúria the military leader it needed and the French fleet suffered heavy losses at Roses in September 1285.

The administrative structure of Catalonia was further developed in the late 13th century, during the reign of Pedro III, with the creation of the *Generalitat*. It had at first a purely economic function limited to the administration of grants allocated by the *Cortes* to the king. Later, however, it became the actual government of Catalonia and its name was applied to the permanent committee of the *Cortes* of Barcelona.

During this time the Catalan economy benefited from a policy of union and annexation. Thus its unification with Aragon gave Catalonia access to Aragonese products and helped to develop its maritime trade, mainly with Italy. Majorca became a major stopover in the Catalan trade route, especially for the organization and distribution of goods, while Sicily supplied Catalonia with wheat and served as a base for trade with the eastern Mediterranean.

The Catalans also exploited trade routes set up in the south of France, Flanders and England. This prosperity was hard hit, however, at the end of the 14th century when the plague broke out, ravaging towns and countryside alike. The first crisis began

A full-size replica of a royal galley, in Gothic style, exhibited in Barcelona's Museu Marítim.

in 1373 after three long years of rain that resulted in famine. The drop in population caused by starvation coupled with the exodus of rural inhabitants who went to the towns to look for work meant that much less land was cultivated. These difficult conditions were accompanied by social unrest in the peasant class, and between the *Biga* (merchant class) and the *Busca* (the poor). The result was a radical decline in trade and in the economic and social prosperity of Catalonia.

A CHANGE OF DYNASTY

Since the 9th century Catalonia had been governed by descendants of the same royal lineage, one of the important factors that contributed to its political growth and stability. In the second half of the 14th century a series of deaths struck the Catalan dynasty of the counts of Barcelona. The last of the line, Martin the Humane, patron of the arts and letters, died on May 31, 1410, without leaving an heir. His death marked the end of the Catalan-Aragonese dynasty. Thus, just as Catalan was enjoying a certain political maturity with the *Cortes* and *Generalitat*, it was faced with the serious problem of finding a successor to the throne.

In Caspe on June 24, 1412, the Castilian candidate, Fernando of Antequera, was proclaimed King of Aragon and Count of Barcelona. He had benefitted from the support of San Vicente Ferrer (an impassioned and popular orator), and the assistance of the Aragonese antipope, Benedict XIII, all anxious to consolidate their positions.

During the reign of his son, Alfonso V the Magnanimous, non-Catalans were given key positions in the government of Catalonia. In 1442 Alfonso conquered the Kingdom of Naples, where he set up residence, and to his title of King of Naples he added those of King of Hungary and of Jerusalem as well as Lord of Dalmatia, Croatia, Serbia and Bulgaria. His costly military campaigns led to monetary devaluation and an increase in internal struggles between lords and peasants.

Catalan discontent broke out during the reign of his successor, Juan II, who was brought up in Castile and wanted to put an end to Catalan independence. The death of his son, rumoured to have been murdered, gave Catalonia a pretext to rebel against royal power and to appoint a Representative Council of the Princedom of Catalonia. Juan II managed to gain the support of Louis XI, King of France, on the condition that he give up Roussillon and Cerdana. Franco-Aragonese troops laid seige to Barcelona in 1472. Ten years prior to the death of Juan II in 1479 his son, Fernando, married Queen Isabella of Castile thus sealing the unification of the two kingdoms. So began a new chapter in the history of Catalonia which was to last until 1714.

THE CENTURIES OF DECLINE

Officially the marriage of Fernando and Isabella represented the union of the King of Catalonia-Aragon and the Queen of Castile. While the Renaissance was changing the cultural face of Europe, Catalonia, hitherto a flourishing state, began its decline. A Royal Council was put in charge of the country, Castilian troops were sent to Catalonia and Castilian abbots took over the monasteries. This was also the period when Columbus discovered America and economic interest increasingly moved from the Mediterranean to the Atlantic.

The situation improved slightly with the death of Isabella of Castile and the beginning of the reign of Carlos I (Charles V). The emperor was as foreign to Castile as he was to Catalonia but he seemed to favour the latter. Nevertheless, Catalonia's economic insufficiency contributed to its decreasing power. The decline of Catalonia continued under Felipe II — the capital, the Court and all the wealth were centred in Castile.

King Felipe III visited Catalonia only once, when a movement of rebellion was gathering impetus. This is echoed in the literature of the time, which idealized bandits (admired by Cervantes' Don Quixote) who attacked the royal treasury to aid the poor. Serrallonga, Tallaferro and Roca Guinarda are among the best-known of these mythical heroes.

A ban on all trade with America further damaged the Catalan economy. Barcelona lived modestly from the cloth industry, handicrafts and shipping.

The Catalan rebellion broke out once again under Felipe IV who for 16 years ruled under the influence of the Count-Duke of Olivares. The wars conducted abroad had their toll in money and men; Olivares decided to send Castilian troops to Catalonia knowing resources could be found there. Thus in 1634, the *quinto* tax was levied once more. On June 7, 1640, the day of Corpus Christi, the famous 'Corpus of blood' broke out in Barcelona: following the death of a reaper, the people set fire to public buildings and killed members of the royal government, including the viceroy. The song *'Els segadors'* (The Reapers), composed for the occasion, tells of the revolt of the Catalan peasants who, armed with scythes, fought against the Castilian troops. It has since become the national anthem.

The president of the *Generalitat,* Pau Claris, died in 1641 and the Catalans rejected King Felipe's proposal of peace. Perpignan fell into the hands of the French and Lleida into the hands of the Castilians. Barcelona, ravaged by the plague, was besieged in August 1651. After 12 years of war the Catalans were allowed to keep their Constitution. But with the Treaty of the Pyrenees in 1659, Felipe handed over Roussillon, Vallespir, Capcir and a part of Conflent and of Cerdana to France. In this way Catalan territory was divided between Spain and France.

Upon the death of Carlos II, the successor to Felipe IV, Philippe, the French duke of Anjou, was named king as Felipe V. He was the grandson of Louis XIV and, as a French prince, was brought up in the spirit of Bourbon absolutism. Catalonia was then allied with England and recognized by King Charles III of Austria, who entered Barcelona in November 1705. Various offers of peace made by Louis XIV to the Catalans were refused by the *Cortes* on several occasions. However, the Franco-Castilian victory of Brihuega and the death of Emperor Joseph I of Austria in 1711 caused Britain (which feared the union of Spain and the Empire) to seek peace with France.

By the Treaty of Utrecht in 1713, Felipe V was recognized King of Spain and the British troops left Catalonia. As a defender of monarchical centralism, Felipe V did away with Catalan constitutions and imposed the laws of Castile. The *Cortes* of Barcelona met on July 5, 1713, and the people voted their resistance. Barcelona was then besieged by Castilian troops reinforced by a French army commanded by the Duke of Berwick. The defense of the city was led by Rafael de Casanova, advisor-in-chief to the Catalan parliament. Barcelona fell on September 11, 1714. This date is celebrated today as Catalonia's national holiday marking the beginning of Catalan resistance to all invaders.

The *Consell de Cent* (Council of 100), the *Deputation,* the *Generalitat* and other government organizations were dissolved. A period of repression began with the institution of military reform. On January 16, 1716, the *Decreto de Nueva Planta* abolished Catalan autonomy. The King imposed a Captain General as governor of Catalonia; mayors and administrators appointed by the king formed the Royal Audience; Catalan was banned and Castilian declared the official language. A citadel was built at the expense of a whole city quarter, and the University of Barcelona was transferred to the small town of Cervera.

Catalonia ceased to exist as an autonomous entity. More than a century passed before a new separatist movement emerged.

During the period between 1714 and 1833, Catalan culture dropped to the lowest level in its history, though the language continued to be spoken by the people. There was improvement, however, on the economic front; in 1717 internal customs were lifted and Spain became a new outlet for the fast-developing Catalan industry. In 1746 the first cotton factory was built and by 1767 there were 19 more. By 1792 the cotton industry employed 80,000 people in Catalonia and the leather industry was so prosperous that in the last decade of the 18th century Catalonia was exporting 700,000 pairs of shoes to Spain and the Indies.

In 1760, Carlos III permitted the establishment of the *Junta de Comerc de Barcelona,* which dealt with industrial, commercial and agricultural affairs, founded schools and encouraged research. In 1778, he allowed Catalonia to trade with the Americas. Catalan commerce also benefitted from the restoration of peace with Tripoli (1784), Algiers (1786) and Turkey (1793). The population was on the rise in Catalonia (500,000 inhabitants in 1708 and one million by the end of the century). A similar boom took place in Valencia, where flax, silk and ceramic industries were developing and where agriculture was flourishing.

This growth was somewhat slowed by the Carlist Wars and the war against Napoleon, as well as the loss of Spanish colonies in the Americas and the general impoverishment of Spain. However, the rapid development of the metallurgical industry, together with the arrival of the railway and the founding of the first electricity companies and the first banks, raised Catalonia to the rank of a new economic power, created by the Industrial Revolution.

THE FORMATION OF MODERN CATALONIA

The king of Spain, Amadeo de Saboya, abdicated on September 11, 1873, and the First Spanish Republic was declared. The first two presidents were Catalan and under the second, Francesc Pí i Margall, an eminent federalist, a project was put forward to form a group of 16 federate states within the Iberian Peninsula. These ideas were temporarily abandoned when the republic fell and the monarchy was restored.

However, when Queen María Cristina visited Barcelona, members of the *Lliga de Catalunya* (a conservative party formed in 1887) presented her with a project of autonomy. Concurrently, Prat de la Riba, a political theoretician, published his *Compendi de doctrina catalanista,* a kind of national catechism aimed at 'awakening' the masses, that was quickly banned by the police. The nationalist campaign centred on explaining the fundamental differences between state, nation and homeland and also on the change from regionalism to nationalism.

A first attempt to unite the different political trends of Catalanism took place in 1892 with the founding of the Catalanist Union, which drew up the *Bases de Manresa,* expressing the will for political autonomy. In spite of this, the movements were profoundly disunited; one group, led by the young Prat de la Riba, separated from the Catalanist Union and founded the National Catalan Centre. As a result of elections in 1901, another party, the Regionalist Union, joined with the National Catalan centre to form the *Lliga Regionalista* from which emerged such leaders as Cambó and Puig i Cadafalch.

Different divisions of Catalanism grew rapidly and an incident in 1905 accelerated the phenomenon. During the night of November 26, 1905, the offices of the humorous weekly, *Cu-Cut* of Barcelona, which had published a caricature of the army, were burned by a handful of officers. The atmosphere of unrest that followed inspired the burgeoning of increasing numbers of new political groups.

In an attempt to unite the different tendencies, *Solidaritat Catalana* was founded; 41 out of the 44 Catalan deputies elected to the parliament of 1907 came from this group. Francesc Macià was one of the most prominent figures of that period.

A project instituted by the government in Madrid to change the provincial *Deputations* led to the formation of broader bodies, known as *Mancomunitas,* that combined the functions of the four *Deputations* of the provinces. In Valencia, meanwhile, the first Valencian Regionalist Assembly was convened in 1907, following closely behind *Solidaritat.*

At the beginning of this century, Catalonia took part in the industrial development that was sweeping through the rest of Western Europe. Parallel to the Catalan political movement, which sought to gain national autonomy, a proletarian movement began to form, organized mainly by anarchists and revolutionary trade-unionists. It grew in tandem with industrial development and was tightly linked to the European labour movement at the time.

The idea of the *Mancomunitat* was taken up again by Prat de la Riba who, in December 1911, presented a project for the combination of the four Catalan provinces into a single 'Mancommunity'. The *Mancommunitat de Catalunya* was formally constituted on April 6, 1914 with Prat de la Riba as its first president followed by Puig i Cadafalch in 1917. The same year a project for an autonomous Catalonia, presented to the Parliament in Madrid, was firmly rejected. In Valencia, the repeated efforts of the *Lliga* led to the founding of the *Unió Valencianista* in 1917. Five years later Francesc Macià founded the nationalist party *Estat Català.*

The rise of Catalan nationalism was interrupted by General Primo de Rivera's coup d'état. During his military dictatorship, Catalonia lived through a brief period of political repression that included a ban on the use of the Catalan language.

POLITICAL AUTONOMY

The dictatorship began to lose its footing, agitation was on the rise and Primo de Rivera was replaced by another general in January 1930. Secret agreements regarding the proclamation of a Republic were made between Barcelona and Madrid but as Madrid hesitated to take the final step, Francesc Macià, who had founded the coalition party *Esquerra Republicana*, declared the Republic of Catalonia. On the same day the Second Spanish Republic was proclaimed in Madrid. By common accord, the government of the Catalan Republic took the name of the Government of the *Generalitat* of Catalonia.

On June 2, during elections for the first constituencies of the Republic, the *Esquerra Republicana de Catalunya* party won a landslide victory. While some members of the Spanish church opposed the recently proclaimed régime, the Catalan ecclesiastics, under Cardinal Vidal i Barraquer, the Archbishop of Tarragona, accepted the change.

The provisional *Generalitat* government put together a project for the Catalan Statute of Autonomy. The work was done in the winter resort of Núria. Before being presented to the Parliament in Madrid, the project was put before the people of Catalonia on August 2 in a referendum which was won by a large majority.

The Parliament in Madrid, after long debates, accepted an abridged version of the project with limited autonomy for Catalonia that would henceforth have a government, a Parliament and control of all departments concerning administration, justice, culture and the budget.

The first elections of the new Catalan Parliament were won by left-wing parties in November 1932. On December 11, 1933, President Macià died in Barcelona and was succeeded by Lluis Companys.

A conflict soon arose between Barcelona and Madrid concerning the law of *Contractes de conreu* (cultivation contracts), which granted important rights to peasants. It was extremely unpopular with large landowners and the *Lliga;* the latter denounced it and had it declared unconstitutional by the court of Guarantees in Madrid. In this atmosphere of unrest, on October 6, 1934, in Barcelona, Lluis Companys proclaimed the autonomous State of Catalonia within a Federal Spanish Republic. However, due to a lack of military support, the proclamation failed, the Catalan government was imprisoned and a Governor General appointed instead. There was an insurrection the same month.

The Spanish general election of February 1936 was won by the left-wing alliance, the Popular Front. In Catalonia, the *Esquerra* party won, although its leaders were still in prison. When they returned to Barcelona two weeks later, the Spanish Republic, under President Azaña reinstated the Catalan Statute of Autonomy. Furthermore, the agrarian cultivation law was enforced. Four months later, on July 18, 1936, General Franco, together with four other chiefs of staff, launched a military *coup d'état* and civil war ensued.

CIVIL WAR (1936-1939)

The armed uprising led by Generals Sanjurjo, Mola, Franco and Queipo de Llano was rapidly repressed in Catalonia and its leaders were imprisoned. In Barcelona, the Civil Guard supported the government, the population disarmed the army, and the social and proletarian revolt gained impetus, increasing its readiness for defense. This internal revolution affected large sectors of the population intent on combatting fascism. Leading the operations were the two large trade union anarchist groups, the FAI (International Anarchist Federation) and the CNT (Confederation of National Workers). The armed and resolute population prepared for a struggle they knew would be decisive.

The popular anarchist counter-attack in response to the military *coup d'état* was a spontaneous organization of the people into a militia. Several decrees were passed legalizing its power. In 1936 the Catalan economy was totally restructured on a collectivist basis. All companies of more than a hundred workers, together with companies that had been abandoned by their bosses, were collectivized and their management was run by 'Company Committees'.

CATALONIA AND THE FRANCO ERA

General Franco's victory meant the loss of autonomy for Catalonia and the beginning of systematic suppression of the Catalan language and culture. President Companys was executed, the University lost its autonomy, all the chairs of the language, history and law of Catalonia were done away with. There was a total ban on the publication of any newspaper or magazine in Catalan, on using the language in court, in public departments, for any official event or in any official document, even in the choice of Christian names. The names of towns and streets were changed to Castilian Spanish. Catalonia lived through a period of silence and passive resistance.

1959 marked the beginning of a new step towards general recovery. Beside the official single-party bodies there was a strong current of opposition created by the Unified Socialist Party of Catalonia or PSUC (communist), the Socialist Movement of Catalonia or MSC (socialist), the Democratic Union of Catalonia or UDC (Christian-Democrat) and the National Front of Catalonia or FNC (nationalist). Furthermore, worker commissions coordinated the main activities in companies.

The church played an important part in forming Catalonia into what it is today. In 1939 in an attempt to stem the influence of the Catalan church, Cardinal Vidal i Barraquer was exiled for having refused to sign the collective document of the Spanish episcopate in 1937. State Catholicism was instituted in Catalonia with an entire hierarchy imposed by Madrid. Nevertheless, the Catalan language slowly crept back into some church services. On the other hand, the agreement of 1941 between the Spanish government and the Vatican, which was renewed by the 1953 concordat, allowed the government a say in the appointment of bishops which meant that it could enthrone non-Catalan bishops with the aim of 'Castilanizing' the country. In 1963, the Abbot of

CHRONOLOGY

700-500 BC	Trade with the Greek world. Foundation of Empuries.
210 BC	Hannibal crosses Catalonia. The Romans land at Empuries.
AD 415	Ataulphus establishes the capital of the Visigoth kingdom in Barcelona. It later moves to Toulouse and then to Toledo (510).
720	The Arabs cross the Pyrenees after having conquered the Iberian Peninsula.
801	Barcelona is freed from the Arabs by the Carolingians. The Spanish March is established.
985	Destruction of Barcelona during an Arab incursion. Borrell II, Count of Barcelona.
1035-1076	Ramon Berenguer I, Count of Barcelona. Declaration of the *Usatges* of Catalonia.
1137	Unification of Catalonia and Aragon on the death of Alfonso, the last king of Aragon.
1237	Battle of Muret. End of the crusade against the Albigensians. Death of Pedro the Catholic, Count of Barcelona.
1229	Jaume I the Conqueror, Count of Barcelona, sets out from Salou to conquer Majorca.
1238	Jaume I takes Valencia.
1282	Pedro III enters Sicily.
1327	Jaume II conquers Sardinia.
1336-1387	Pedro IV the Ceremonious, King of Catalonia-Aragon.
1410	Death of Martin I the Humane. As he leaves no heir he is the last king of the Catalan dynasty.
1412	The Caspe decision. Fernando of Antequera is crowned King of Catalonia-Aragon.
1442	Alfonso V conquers the Kingdom of Naples.
1469	Marriage of Fernando of Catalonia-Aragon to Isabella of Castile.
1479	Death of Juan II. Unification of the kingdoms of Catalonia-Aragon and Castile.
1640	Corpus of blood. Revolt in Barcelona marking the beginning of the Catalan war against King Felipe IV.
1659	Treaty of the Pyrenees. Felipe IV hands over Roussillon, Vallespir, Capcir and a part of Conflent and of Cerdaña to France.
1716	Nueva Planta Decree. Catalonia is integrated into Spain.
1778	Free trade begins between Catalonia and the Americas.
1873	Declaration of the First Spanish Republic.

Montserrat, dom Aureli Escarré, openly opposed the régime of General Franco in an interview to the French newspaper, *Le Monde.* Following other dissident leaders into exile, his departure was to become a symbol of political change.

CATALONIA AFTER FRANCO

Two very different events mark the evolution of Catalonia in the early 1970 s. The first was the formation of the Assembly of

OF HISTORICAL EVENTS

1874	Restoration of the monarchy. Reign of Alfonso XII (1874-1885).
1914	Formation of the *Mancomunitat de Catalunya*.
1923-1930	Dictatorship of General Primo de Rivera.
1931	Declaration of the Republic of Catalonia in Barcelona and of the Second Spanish Republic in Madrid. The Catalan government becomes the *Generalitat* of Catalonia. Departure of King Alfonso XIII. Alcalá Zamora is the first president of the Spanish Republic.
1932	Catalonia is granted the statute of autonomy and Macià becomes the first president of the *Generalitat* of Catalonia.
1933	Death of President Macià. Lluis Companys is declared President of the *Generalitat* of Catalonia.
1934	Revolution in October. The Catalan government is imprisoned.
1936	General election won by the Popular Front. The Catalan statute of autonomy is reinstated. Civil war breaks out. Decree of collectivization in Catalonia.
1939	Tarragona, Barcelona and Valencia are taken by the pro-Franco army; Franco is in control of the country and is named chief of state.
1945	The *Cortes de Madrid* approve the *Fueros de los espanoles,* the rights and duties of Spanish citizens.
1953	Concordat between Spain and the Vatican.
1970	Meeting of Catalan artists and intellectuals in Montserrat to protest the Burgos trials. Formation of a Commission in Barcelona to coordinate Catalonia's different political forces.
1971	Elections for *Procuradores en Cortes* (members of Parliament). The Catalans propose a conservative team. The first Assembly of Catalonia, a meeting of democratic parties, is secretly held in Barcelona.
1975	Death of General Franco.
1977	First democratic elections for the Spanish Parliament. Formation of a parliamentary assembly in Barcelona. Return of Josep Tarradellas, president of the *Generalitat* in exile.
1978	Drawing up of the Statute of Autonomy for Catalonia.
1979	Approval of the Statute of Autonomy for Catalonia by the Spanish Parliament.
1980	First elections for the Catalan Parliament, renewed in 1984 and again in 1988.

Catalonia in 1971, which, by more or less secretly gathering together members of most of the political forces, began a determined struggle for Catalan recognition. Its slogan was 'Liberty, Amnesty, Statute of Autonomy'. The second event, now considered in contemporary Spanish history to mark the end of an era, was the death of General Franco in November 1975.

On September 11, 1976, an immense demonstration was held in Barcelona which was to have spectacular repercussions. It was a determining factor in the formation (the following

September) of an assembly of members of parliament, and the provisional re-establishment of the *Generalitat* of Catalonia, headed by the president of the former government in exile, Josep Tarradellas.

The role of the new King, Juan Carlos I, was fundamental to the democratic process which led to the elections of the Spanish Parliament, the *Cortes,* in June 1977.

In Catalonia, unlike the rest of Spain, the Union of the Democratic Centre (UCD) did not win; victory went to the socialists (PSC-PSOE) who were followed by the Democratic Union and the communists (PSUC). The demonstration on September 11, 1977, when more than one and a half million people filled the streets of Barcelona, was a powerful confirmation of the people's determination to have their own political legislature. A statute of autonomy *(Estatut de Sau)* was drafted in 1978. It was approved by the Spanish Parliament in 1979 and won massive support in the referendum held in December that same year.

CATALONIA TODAY

A LAND BETWEEN SEA AND MOUNTAIN

Catalonia's landscapes are extremely varied. The Pyrenees are a succession of alpine meadows, fir and pine forests, valleys, lakes and high peaks (Estats: 10,305 ft/3141 m; Puigmal: 9557 ft/2913 m). The Catalan Pyrenees, a continuation of the Aragonese Pyrenees, cover an area from the Maladeta massif to the Mediterranean. They form a vast barrier that stretches over the Alberes mountains to Cape Creus before plunging into the sea. The range is punctuated by the deep cuts of the Segre and Nogueras valleys and the Vallespir, Cerdana and Vall d'Aran basins.

The Aigües Tortes Y Lago de San Mauricio National Park spreads between the valleys of Noguera de Tor and Noguera Pallaresa, both marked by glacial erosion. There are chamois and ibex in the higher regions of the park while the woods shelter wild boar and capercaillie (large woodgrouse).

The mountain landscape changes farther south to lower massifs: the Cadi and Montserrat ranges. The Montserrat Sierra is a most unusual natural formation, consisting of Eocene strata carved by erosion into steep serrated cliffs above which rise strangely shaped rocks and crags.

The Olot region of Catalonia is a volcanic area that dates back to the Tertiary period when the Pyrenees were formed. This action disfigured the ancient geological platform and freed lava flows. Today the extinct volcano cones are covered with a clay soil. The fertility of the soil combined with a rainy climate favour the growth of grasslands and woods that hide the craters.

The Sierra of Montseny in the heart of Catalonia consists of a granite base covered with holm oak, cork, pine and beech forests where crop cultivation alternates with natural vegetation.

In southern Catalonia near the Costa Dorada, the mountain landscapes become harsh and rocky, with dwarf palm trees growing in the red earth.

The Costa Dorada is an immense sandy strip that stretches along the coasts of the provinces of Barcelona and Tarragona. The coastal plain of Maresme, covering the area from the Tordera river to Barcelona, spreads over fertile land suitable in the lower reaches for market gardening and higher up for the

growing of cereals, vines and olives. The Tarragonese coastline from Barcelona to the Ebro river is characterized by hills covered in pine plantations, below which runs a strip of fine sand.

The lower valley of the Ebro and its delta, vast stretches of farmland bordered by green hills, form a natural reserve where many different species of migratory bird shelter among the reeds.

The rugged Costa Brava coastline rises in steep pine-covered cliffs above the sea and runs the length of the province of Girona from Cape Creus to Blanes. From the last foothills of the Alberes mountains which form vast bays between Portbou and Roses, the coast continues south along the fertile, swampy Empordà plain to Begur before giving way to the beaches that stretch to Blanes. The rich botanical garden in Blanes is full of Mediterranean and exotic plant species.

THE CATALAN ECONOMY

Catalonia is a vibrant, competitive economic entity, a link between northern Europe and the Mediterranean basin. In order to count among the most active champions of the European market, Catalonia is encouraging development in social, cultural and technical domains. Added to this challenge is the organization of the 1992 Olympic Games. These two objectives, are currently boosting the Catalan economy, which is experiencing rapid growth.

Although Catalonia lacks energy and mineral resources, it has some large industries. The economy relies upon industrial companies that attract workers in large numbers from Andalusia. Despite the fact that Catalonia covers only 6.3% of Spain's surface area and has only 15% of the country's population, it is the leading industrial zone of the Iberian Peninsula, supplying 20% of the gross national product and 21% of the exports. Finally, Catalonia's gross domestic product is 20% higher than the national Spanish average.

As Europe's 11th most important industrial region, Catalonia is the most dynamic part of the Iberian Peninsula, followed by Madrid and the Basque Country

Industrial wealth is not, however, evenly spread throughout Catalonia; 85% of the companies are concentrated in Barcelona while the petrochemical industry is centred in Tarragona and the timber and cork trades in Girona.

The percentage of Catalonia's working population follows the same pattern as in most industrial countries, with 7% involved in farming, 49% in industry and 44% in the services sector. This last accounts for more than half Catalonia's gross domestic product, followed by industry and to a lesser degree, building, farming and fishing. The rate of unemployment (12%) is relatively low when compared to the rest of Spain.

The stupendous coastline of the Costa Brava with its steep cliffs plunging into the Mediterranean Sea.

If iron and steel production is the prerogative of the Basque Country and Asturias, the metal-working industry, a thriving sector which benefits from foreign investment, remains that of Catalonia, covering the domain of light engineering and the manufacture of transport equipment. The automobile industry is also important in Catalonia, accounting for 50% of the national production of SEAT (the Spanish car manufacturing company).

Catalonia excels in rubber processing and plastics, overtaking the Basque Country in this field. It is also ahead of Madrid in the chemical industry, in the manufacture of products used in agriculture, industry and pharmaceuticals.

Catalonia also takes part in European science and technology research programs. The computer sector is developing fast and Catalonia runs a close second to Madrid in the manufacture of electronics equipment such as components and integrated circuits.

While the chemical, metallurgical, food, leather and shoe industries are expanding, the textile industry, which dates back to the Middle Ages, is showing a noticeable drop in production. Even so, Catalonia still leads Spain in the textile and clothing industries, employing more workers in the spinning and weaving sectors than any other region.

The present boom in the tertiary sector, mainly in banking, tourism and trade, is in part due to the 1992 Olympic Games. The games should indeed reinforce development in this healthy area of the Catalan economy, a sector which is being further boosted by massive domestic and foreign tourism. Every year millions of visitors (14 million in 1987) invade the Costa Brava and Costa Dorada and in turn ensure the development of the region's roads, hotels, campsites, golf courses, marinas, thermal spas and so on. Some coastal towns appear to have been fully taken over by tourism (mainly German).

With the Olympic Games in mind, foreign banks have set up offices in Barcelona and have thus increased the activity of Catalonia's financial sector, which ranks fifth on the European scale. Catalonia further benefits from the significant industrial investment throughout the region and the new jobs thereby created. Among the large-scale projects in Catalonia today are the reorganization of Barcelona airport, the building of a ring-road (beltway), the completion of a major metro line, and urban, touristic and commercial promotion on a regional scale.

Agriculture, now highly mechanized, accounts for only 3% of Catalonia's income although Catalonia is Spain's leading farming region. While the wetter northern part of Catalonia grows mainly fodder crops and concentrates to a lesser extent on stock raising, the Mediterranean areas are more diversified with vineyards, olives, almonds and market gardening. The abundance of fruit, vegetables and wine compensate for the shortage of meat. The most common type of farm is the *masia*, managed and worked by a landowner who employs few workers because of advanced mechanization (unlike the *latifundia* or great landed estates that still exist in the south of Spain).

AUTONOMOUS CATALONIA

Catalonia is a comunidad autónoma (an autonomous community) of Spain and is divided into four provinces, each with its own capital: Barcelona, Girona, Lleida and Tarragona. Catalonia is further divided into 41 natural divisions called *comarques* with their respective capitals (see maps p. 11 and pp. 12-13).

In the past, Catalonia was comprised of the *Principat* (the collective name given to the four provinces), Andorra, a narrow frontier zone that now belongs to Aragon, and Roussillon, Cerdaña, Conflent, Vallespir and Capcir (regions that today form part of the French *Pyrénées Orientales*, with Cerdaña and Vallespir being cut in two by the modern border).

Apart from the areas mentioned above, the lands beyond the present-day boundaries of Catalonia that form a linguistic and cultural Catalan entity include the autonomous community of Valencia (part of the former kingdom of Catalonia-Aragon) with its three administrative provinces (Valencia, Alacant and Castelló), and the five Balearic Islands. Furthermore, Catalan is still spoken in the town of Alghero in Sardinia (see 'Catalonia in the past' p. 35), while in Andorra, Catalan shares the status of official language with French.

POLITICAL STATUS

Catalonia is governed by the Statute of Autonomy (Estatut d'Autonomia) which dates from 1979, in accordance with the Spanish Constitution approved at the end of 1978. The statute is a basic charter for the Catalan community that endows Catalonia with its own Parliament and makes Catalan the official language. The political institutions of the autonomous community, its areas of competence and its relations with the Spanish state are all bound by an organic law. The government of Catalonia is centred around the *Generalitat*, which is composed of a parliament of 123 members elected through universal suffrage, a board of advisors and a legal council. The executive of 12 ministers is led by the president of the *Generalitat*.

The *Generalitat's* areas of competence are far-reaching. They cover the domains of culture, tourism, health, sports, education,

---

Political songs

What is known as *Nova Canç Catalana* ('New Catalan Song') originated in 1961 thanks to the *Els Setze Jutges* group. In the beginning it was influenced by French songs, notably those by Georges Brassens, and then it became a very popular style of its own. Raimon, the Valencian singer, was among the most original performers when the movement started.

'New Song' then moved on to other areas, including jazz (Núria Feliu), light modern music (Salomé), ballads and popular poetry (Guillem d'Efak) and pop (Pau Riba). Other singers (Joan Manuel Serrat) have moved into the bilingual (Catalan/Castilian) field or sing openly political songs (Xavier Ribalta). The two leading figures are Francesc Pic de la Serra, who gives middle-class society some sharp and subtle criticism, and Lluis Llach, who belongs to the new-wave movement of the popular, modern version of 'New Song'.

public works and so on. The community also has its own police force although certain institutions, such as the judiciary and the military, remain under the responsibility of the Spanish state.

THE PEOPLE

It may be futile to try to draw a typical character portrait of the Catalans — Miguel de Cervantes praised their courtesy, integrity, hospitality and sense of honour, while Dante mocked their covetousness. Nevertheless, they are a proud and unique people and the ups and downs of Catalan history have reinforced these characteristics. Possibly because their identity has so often been denied, the Catalans have worked hard at preserving their culture and protecting their 'national spirit'. This can now be done under the patronage of an autonomous government and with the help of the town councils.

The Catalans still give priority to ethnic identity and allegiance over any social, cultural or economic identification with the Spanish state. Their language is the central binding factor, guaranteeing the historical and cultural continuity of Catalonia. Anxious to assert their individuality, they resist national attempts at integration and centralization and proudly reject the political and cultural supremacy of Madrid. Catalonia has set itself up as a lively national community with a strong character. The return to autonomy, the re-establishment of the *Generalitat* and the official recognition of the Catalan tongue have opened up new perspectives for the people. During Franco's dictatorship, Catalan identity suffered severe repression and over the last few years the community has striven to re-establish itself, living through a period of intense nationalism — to the point of becoming isolationist. However, Catalonia is now taking up the European challenge and defying its old rivals: Madrid, Bilbao and Seville. Open to commercial and cultural exchange, stimulated by competition from Madrid, the inventive, enthusiastic Catalans are working towards a healthy competitive economy by encouraging private and public enterprises. As at the dawn of the century when they were the first in Spain to vaunt the benefits of the Industrial Revolution, the first to build steamships, railways and locomotives, so today they are on the cutting edge of progress and innovation.

Not only active from an economic point of view, Catalonia is also an influential and dynamic cultural centre. The thirst for renewal, which came to the fore with the *Renaixença*, (see p. 62) and Modernism, has continued to express itself throughout the 20th century. Contemporary inventors and creators are following the illustrious example of their predecessors (Picasso, Dalí, Miró, etc.) to whom Catalonia has dedicated many of its museums. As well as being the headquarters for Spain's publishing industry, Barcelona today leads a number of aesthetic movements in the realms of architecture, design, painting and music.

Along with this creative vivacity the Catalans have managed to keep their traditions and festivals alive. Saints' feast days arouse terrific interest in town and countryfolk alike while the traditional *sardana*, originally a sun dance, is enjoyed by both

Men and women, young and old, gather in a public plaza to dance the Sardana; joining hands in a circle they move with precise steps to the sounds of the cobla.

young and old. Furthermore, the Catalans can be proud of their unique handicrafts, with numerous workshops specializing in ceramics, lacework, tapestry and glassware.

Most of Catalonia's population is centred in the towns, where the atmosphere is lively — especially in the larger ones and most of all in Barcelona. The capital has a feverish, ardent, bubbling air about it, reflected in its bustling streets, numerous bars, the juxtaposition of classic and postmodern styles, and the population mix. It's as though the Catalans have invented a new kind of urban culture with Barcelona as its resplendent model.

Lluís Llach, spokesman

Lluís Llach is one of the most popular singers in Catalonia today. He began to sing in 1967 before joining the *Els Setze Jutges* group the same year. The members were politically committed artists who sang in Catalan. Lluís Llach has given concerts in countries all over the world and has made numerous records in Spain and in France. In 1985 he performed in the FC Barcelona stadium to an audience of 100,000 people. His songs relate the collective Catalan story with lyrical and rhythmic freedom tinged with romanticism.

BARCELONA: OLYMPIC CITY 1992

Baron Pierre de Coubertin, president of the International Olympic Committee from 1896 to 1925, wrote the following on November 19, 1926 after a stay in Barcelona: 'Since the flowers and farewell you organized for us, we've spent some interesting pleasant days but we often miss Barcelona and will be so happy to be with you there again. I think this will be around the 30th of November. Then we'll be able to enjoy the warm Olympic atmosphere that reigns in Barcelona, the city's enthusiasm for sport and its rightful wish to organize the Olympic Games...'

Barcelona submitted its candidature for the organization of the Olympics games of 1924, 1936, 1972 and 1992. This persistence finally won it the recognition it needed, and the city obtained the honour of holding the 1992 games.

The Olympic Games project is centred around four zones in Barcelona covering an estimated area of 346-519 acres/ 140-210 hectares. This space includes various sports facilities for competition and training as well as parks, gardens, entertainment areas, public buildings, cultural centres and an Olympic Village. Of the 24 scheduled competitions, 19 take place within a 3.1 mi/5 km radius right inside the city itself.

Foremost among the four Olympic zones is Montjuïc hill and stadium. The entire hillside (a landscaped park) has been developed and includes a sports palace and swimming pool. Next, the area around Diagonal Avenue has the most extensive sports equipment, benefited from the amenities of FC Barcelona (football club) and the Reial Polo Club. The third zone, the Vall d'Hebron, hosts the track, cycling, handball and archery competitions. The fourth zone, the Parc de Mar along the seafront, is the site of the Olympic Village. It stretches along passeig Maritim parallel to the sea and is sheltered by a large park. The architects Bohigas, Martorell and Mackay are responsible for the project, and a competition has been held for the building of a monumental fountain on the site. Other facilities are located in Barcelona's suburbs (Bardalona, Terrassa, Sabadell and Granollers) while two of the Olympic sites are well outside the town. The first is Lake Banyoles, 73 mi/118 km away, and the second the marina of Palma de Majorca. Finally, the river slalom competition takes place on the Valira near La Seu d'Urgell.

Cobi, Olympic mascot

Cobi is a sheepdog with three hairs on the top of his head which, like his eyes and mouth, are highly expressive, according to his mood. When he is angry, for example his hairs knot together in a spiral. He is the symbol of all the Olympic disciplines and can adapt his pose to the sport. Cobi was designed by the Valencian artist, Xavier Mariscal, who published his first comic book in 1974. Mariscal designs fabrics and furniture. He is also an interior decorator and has exhibited in many different countries.

In the past the city has been transformed by international events: the Parc de la Ciutadella is a permanent reminder of the Universal Exhibition and the whole Montjuïc area was built up for the International Exhibition of 1929. Today, with the Olympics, Barcelona will once again be transformed. Those most concerned with these changes, of course, are the local inhabitants, who've decided to contribute to the metamorphosis of their town. This is apparent in the city's slogan *Barcelona, posa't guapa!* Barcelona, make yourself beautiful!

CATALAN ART

ANTIQUITY

The Palaeolithic Age in Catalonia, covered the period from the early Stone Age to about 6000 BC. The oldest human remains discovered in the region date from about 300,000 BC. In 1971, an adolescent skull was found in the cave of Arago (Tautavel, in Roussillon, now part of France). Cave paintings characteristic of this era have been found throughout the Levante region of the Spanish peninsula. Among the best-known are those of the Roca dels Moros del Cogul in Les Garrigues (not far from Lleida). The most famous scene depicts a dance of nine women around a naked man painted black.

The Neolithic Age (between 6000 and 2500 BC) was a period of technical transformation during which ceramics, fabrics and polished stone appeared, as did the first primitive urban settlements, such as Roc d'en Serdinya in Sant Genis de Vilassar.

Between 1800 and 700 BC, with the Bronze Age, the arrival of central-European Hallstatt civilizations brought progress to the settlements and during the Iron Age (700-500 BC) colonies were set up by Mediterranean people, mainly Phoenicians and Greeks. Apart from iron, the era was marked by the use of coins and the development of writing.

Archaeological finds indicate the presence of Phoenician and Etruscan traders in Catalonia during the first half of the 6th century BC. The major event of Antiquity in the region, however, was the arrival of the Phocaeans at Empuries in the 8th century BC, where they founded a town known as Palaiapolis (today, Sant Marti d'Empuries). Little remains of ancient Empuries — a temple dedicated to the Greek god of healing, Asclepius (Aesculapius), and another to Zeus Serapis. The famous statue of Asclepius, the largest Greek sculpture of the western Mediterranean, belongs to a much later period, and certainly does not predate the 3rd century BC.

Historical sources testify to the variety of peoples who lived in Catalonia at the end of the Iron Age, and contributed to the evolution of Iberian art and culture. The Ilergets, for example,

The Catalans are justifiably proud of Joan Miró (1893-1983), a native of Barcelona; this original poster was created for an exhibition devoted to his works.

occupied the area around Lleida, the Laietans that of Barcelona and the Ausentans that of Vic. A typical Iberian village of the time was fortified, constructed on high ground, often with wide paved streets and houses built to a rectangular plan. Among the most interesting are those of Ullastret, El Molí d'Espigol in Tornabous (Urgell) and Castellet de Banyoles in Tivissa (Ribera d'Ebre). The treasury in Tivissa contains silver objects from the third century, testifying to the influence of classical precious metalwork on local artists.

THE ROMAN ERA

The long process of Romanization began in 218 BC with the arrival of the Romans at Empuries. Catalonia has many monuments from Roman times: city walls, bridges (Martorell), triumphal arches (the Berà arch near Tarragona), aqueducts (Taragona, Pineda de Mar), theatres, amphitheatres and arenas (Tarragona), temples and city monuments (Barcelona, Empuries), and grand funeral monuments (Scipio Tower in Tarragona).

Sculpture and mosaic art of the period were orginally marked by an Italic style that gave way in time to a provincial one. Museums in Barcelona and Tarragona house many such works.

Among the main vestiges of palaeo-Christian art are the basilicas of Empuries, Sant Cugat del Vallès and Terrassa, the Tarragona necropolis and the Barcelona basilica and baptistry. The funeral monument in Centcelles (Tarragona), probably built as a mausoleum for a member of the imperial dynasty, goes well beyond the ambitions of local art and belongs rather to the stylistic tendencies of Rome.

THE MIDDLE AGES

Examples of pre-Romanesque architecture can be seen in Roussillon (once part of Catalonia, now in France) in the churches of Saint-Martin-de-Fenollar and Saint-Michel-de-Cuxa. These edifices are characterized by horseshoe arches, the result of a combination of traditional local and Mozarabic styles. (The latter was developed by Christians living in Muslim territory under Moorish rule). During this period the remarkable monasteries of Sant Joan de les Abadesses and Ripoll were founded. Ripoll became the royal pantheon for the Counts of Barcelona.

Throughout the early Middle Ages, when reformist work was being carried out by religious Christian orders, there was a real need for the building of new monasteries, which, in turn, left their stamp on rural and urban life.

EARLY ROMANESQUE ARCHITECTURE

The fall of the Umayyad Caliphate of Cordoba in the 11th century opened the way for Catalonia to take part in the reconquest of the peninsula and to benefit from the various battles led in the name of the holy crusade. From an architectural point of view, the period was characterized by the sober traits of early Romanesque art; naves were enlarged, bell towers built and roofs vaulted.

The major work of the time was the church of Sant Vincent de Cardona, consecrated in 1040. All the elements of early Romanesque art can be seen here; in the church's proportions, its unadorned simplicity, and its Lombard-style arcading. One of the features of the period was the increasing number of large monastery libraries; that of Ripoll was especially fine. This epoch heralded the beginning of the great blossoming of 12th-century Romanesque architecture and sculpture.

ROMANESQUE ART

On March 6, 1151, Count Ramon Berenguer IV granted the Cistercian monks of Fontfroide (in France) the right to build monasteries in Catalonia. As a result, the large edifices in Poblet and Santes Creus (see p. 181) came into being. This second period of Catalan Romanesque art also saw the beginnings of the Seu d'Urgell cathedral (see p. 160), the church of Sant Cugat del Vallès (see p. 133) and the Girona cathedral (see p. 150) as well as the cloisters of Saint-Pierre-de-Galligants and the work of the Master of Cabestany, both in present-day France.

During the 12th century, frescoes and wood paintings reached their most majestic expression epitomized in the famous miniature Bibles of Ripoll and Rodes, and the paintings from the churches of Sant Climent and Santa Maria in Taüll. Paintings like these, once dispersed among little half-abandoned churches in the Pyrenees, have fortunately been saved and now form a unique collection in the national *Museu d'Art de Catalunya* in Barcelona.

At this time, a school of sculpture was evolving in Ripoll (see p. 142), a tradition inherited from Cuxa and Serrabone (in France) whose influence spread over a large part of the country. Work was being done on the magnificent Ripoll monastery church portal and in the Romanesque gallery in the cloisters. During the 13th century, architecture became increasingly grandiose and went through a transitional period when ribbed vaults replaced barrel vaults, spreading into aisles and ambulatories. Building began on the Seu Vella de Lleida and continued on the monasteries of Poblet and Santes Creus.

GOTHIC ART

Catalonia developed its own variant of Gothic architecture. The most common type in towns is a church with a single aisle and pointed vaulting, like the churches of Santa Maria del Pi and Sants Just i Pastor in Barcelona (see p. 101). The cathedrals of Barcelona and Girona and the church of Santa Maria del Mar in Barcelona were all built at this time.

The flowering of city architecture went hand in hand with the urban revival of the time and was partly due to greater prosperity through trade. The palace of the *Generalitat* (1276) in Barcelona and the Town Hall (1372) with its assembly chamber for the *Consell de Cent* are jewels of medieval urban architecture. The royal palace in Barcelona with its Tinell room and the palace of the Kings of Majorca in Perpignan (France) are fine examples of court architecture. Some of the main municipal edifices of the period include shipyards, hospitals and exchange buildings.

Catalan Gothic painting benefited from the wealth of middle-class tradesmen and was influenced by Mediterranean trends in art. The important pictorial heritage from the period can be seen in the museums of Barcelona, Vic and Solsona. Among Gothic painters, Ferrer Bassa, Ramon Destorrents and the Serra brothers all brought Italian influences to the Catalan tradition. Lluis Borrassà introduced the International Style which was intensified by Bernat Martorell. Finally, Flemish trends were added by artists like Lluís Dalmau and especially Jaume Huguet.

RENAISSANCE AND BAROQUE ART

Political decline was accompanied by a lack of artistic creativity. During the 15th century, buildings were still constructed in the flamboyant style but when the Italian Renaissance came to Catalonia, the region, which by this time had lost all political and commercial initiative, could only play a secondary artistic role with the exception of a few isolated cases. One of them was the sculptor Damià Forment, a native of Valencia, who produced some outstanding works, including the altarpiece in Poblet (1527).

The presence of a great many foreign painters resulted in a remarkable variety of trends. But it was only with the profusion of church retables and the Baroque style, exemplified by the Dalmases Palace courtyard and the Betlem church in Barcelona, that Catalan art could make its mark on European art. The 17th century was dominated by a new Baroque spirit which combined architecture, sculpture and painting to form an integral, visual entity. A good example of the influence that the Italian art of the Counter-Reformation had on local artists can be seen in the façade of the Tortosa cathedral. The façade of the Girona cathedral, which is designed like an altarpiece, also belongs to this movement. Among civic buildings of note, mention should be made of the convalescent home of the Sante Creu hospital in Barcelona. Notable artists included Francesc Ribalta from Solsona whose remarkable work was highly influenced by Caravaggio.

During the reign of Felipe V in 1700 a number of buildings reflected the official stamp of Bourbon architecture. The best example could well be the arsenal building of the citadel in Barcelona, the present seat of the Catalan Parliament. Also of note is the university of Cervera, designed by Francesc Montagut, which was opened to replace the one in Barcelona during the period of Catalan repression under the Bourbons. Finally, the church of Mercy in Barcelona displays a fine synthesis of Baroque and Rococo styles.

Detail of a niche from the door of the monastery of Santes Creus; built in the 13th century, the edifice contains splendid architectural elements from various periods up until the Renaissance.

THE 19th AND 20th CENTURIES

The 19th century brought with it the industrial power and wealth that was so sorely needed to revive the arts. French Classicism left a few traces, such as the Virreina palace in Barcelona (1773). The arrival of neo-Classicism brought a new spirit to Catalan art. Buildings from this period in Barcelona include: the new façade of the Exchange (1774), Els Porxos d'en Xifré (1836), the Teatro del Lliceu (1848) and the Plaça Reial (1848). The architect Elies Rogent designed the university of Barcelona (1863-1874) and with great energy directed the rebuilding of the monastery at Ripoll. The two artists who perhaps best

---

Ricard Bofill

Ricard Bofill is a Catalan architect, born in 1939, who is particularly well-known in France for his work in Marne-la-Vallée, Paris and Montpellier. The work produced by his office or *taller d'arquitectura* (architecture workshop) is marked by a return to classical shapes. It also bears the stamp of his reflection on the way a monument should be integrated into an urban framework. He has two large projects in Barcelona — the reorganization of the airport and the National Theatre of Catalonia, the centre of new urban planning on the plaça de les Glòries Catalanes.

---

represent the close of the 19th century were the painters Marià Fortuny (1837-1874) and Ramon Martí Alsina (1826-1894).

A new era of splendour began with the Art Nouveau style (1900) which in Catalonia took the name *Modernisme*, as defined by Eugeni d'Ors (Xenius). In spite of the fact that he kept some distance from the movement, Antoni Gaudí is considered its founder and most representative architect. Using traditional materials in his unique style, he created the Parc Güell and the Sagrada Familia in Barcelona (see p. 121) as well as numerous houses.

Lluis Domenech i Montaner (1850-1924) built the Palace of Catalan Music in Barcelona, one of the masterpieces of Modernism. Sculpture was meanwhile being given new life by artists like Josep Llimona (1864-1934) and Aristide Maillol (from Roussillon). Modernism became popular thanks largely to the decorative arts that flooded the market.

Contemporary Catalan art flourished with the painter Isidre Nonell, the sculptor Pau Gargallo and the early works of Joan Miró, Pablo Picasso and Josep Clarà. But in the second quarter of the 20th century, Catalonia suffered a massive exodus of artists to Paris. Picasso, Dalí and Miró were followed by Manolo Hugué, Fenosa, Julio González and the ceramist Artigas (see 'Barcelona-Paris' p. 76). In the post-war period, apart from work by Ramon Rogent, little artistic activity came to light before 1947.

In 1948, the artists Tharrats, Cuixart and Tàpies formed the *Dau al Set* group. Antoni Tàpies, who moved in the same circle as the surrealist Miró (see p. 117), was soon to stand out with his collages of unusual materials, tending towards informal artistic expression. The novelty of his art lay in the building up of texture on his canvases with thick applications of different substances. In 1951 he systematized his research on matter and introduced real objects into his painting. He has explained his artistic process in books, essays and articles (as in the *Pratique de l'art,* 1970). A Tàpies foundation is presently being set up in Barcelona.

New projects in architecture are being carried out by Xavier Busquets, Oriol Bohigas (see p. 133), Antoni Bonet and Josep Antoni Coderch (see 'Trade Towers', p. 123). The break with abstract art asserted itself in 1963 when the Jordi Gali and Albert

Gaudís Casa Milà on passeig de Gràcia, built between 1905 and 1910, is known as La Pedrera for its imagery that is reminiscent of the mountainous landscape of Catalonia.

Porta group introduced a new realism that closely followed the work of another team, Guinovart and Rafols Casamada. The architect, Eusebi Sempere, who uses kinetics in his work, also deserves mention.

In the field of sculpture, the artist Subirachs started with an approach sometimes likened to that of Henry Moore, then moved into the domain of symbolic abstract art before recently inheriting the task of continuing Gaudí's Sagrada Familia. Andreu Alfara has been leading the way in geometrical kinetics and Suzana Solano, with her metal work heralding a mobile, innovative type of architecture of pure shapes, is representative of the most recent trends in Catalan art today.

MUSIC

Liturgical dramas and different types of hymns appeared from the 10th century onward, a time when Ripoll and Sant Cugat del Vallès were important centres of music. The polyphonic mode (music in parts, each with an independent melody) came into being in the 11th century, thanks to musical transcripts made by monks — especially those of Ripoll. Court music was popularized in the 12th century by Catalan and Provençal troubadours, yet it was in the 14th century that the court of the kings of Aragon in Barcelona became famous through its musical refinement. Pedro IV the Ceremonious, Juan I and Martin the Humane all favoured keen musical exchanges with Europe. Similarly, religious music in the cathedrals of Barcelona and Tarragona and in the monasteries of Santes Creus, Poblet and Montserrat was experiencing a particularly brilliant period, as can be seen in the *Llibre vermell* of Montserrat, transcribed at the end of the 14th century. It marked the transition from *Ars Antica* to *Ars Nova* and illustrated the sacred dances of the time. The royal chapel continued to thrive under the patronage of Alfonso the Magnanimous, Juan II and Fernando the Catholic.

Numerous surviving 16th-century documents contain lists of organists and choirmasters though not always manuscripts of the music they played. On the death of Fernando the Catholic, the royal choir and orchestra was disbanded and many musicians were pressured to devote themselves to religious music. Noteworthy musicians from the period include Francesc Tovar, who published a book on practical music in 1510 and was one of the first theoreticians of modern music, and Joan Carles Amat, who wrote the earliest known guitar treatise in 1586.

The situation was to change at the beginning of the 18th century with Italian influences and a new taste for oratory. Italian opera came to Barcelona when the court of Carlos II was set up. Among the best-known Catalan musicians at the time were Joseph Duran, Miguel Terraidelles, Antoni Soler of Olot, Manalt of Girona, and Anselm Viola and Narcis Casanoves, who belonged to the Montserrat school. Favourable links with Italy continued into the beginning of the 19th century thanks, mainly to the influence of Rossini.

After triumphing in Madrid, the *zarzuela* (a musical play with songs and dances) was also appreciated in Barcelona and the

---

Cinema

Though renowned today, Catalan cinema has expressed itself with difficulty throughout its history because the professional language in use since the appearance of talking films has been Castilian. The first productions date from 1896 with Fructuós Gelabert. Since then Catalonia has followed the general development of European cinema and has often been influenced by French trends. Pere Portabella and Antoni Ribas are among the best-known directors today. Over the last few years several film festivals such as those in Barcelona and Sitges have gained international recognition.

---

guitar became the most popular musical instrument. At the same time the *sardana* dance (see p. 152) was undergoing change with the reorganization by Pep Ventura of its *cobla*, a group of wind instruments and small drums.

The *Renaixença* (Renaissance) brought new impetus to the musical world. The most eminent figure was Joseph Anselm Clavé, best-known for his popular choral works. From then on, orchestras and choirs became widespread, and demand grew for music teaching and opera buildings, the best example of which is the 1847 opera house (Liceu) in Barcelona. The end of the century was marked by the founding of the *Orfeo català* by Lluis Mallet and Amadeu Vives in 1891.

Among the most illustrious names of the 20th century, mention should first be made of the generation of 1908 that included Millet, Vives, Nicolau and Pujol, and which was centred around the newly inaugurated palace of Catalan music and the *Orfeo català*. Well-known composers of the 1920s include Frederic Mompou and Eduard Toldrà, while the major figure in the domain of the *sardana* was Joaquim Serra.

Members of the civil war generation, such as Xavier Monsalvatge, who founded the Manuel de Falla Circle in Barcelona around 1947, have all demonstrated the vitality of Catalan music, which continues to assert itself today in the performances of artists such as Carles Santos. Very special mention must be made of the internationally famous cellist, composer and conductor, Pau (Pablo) Casals (1876-1973), and one of his best-known works, *El Pessebre.*

CATALAN LITERATURE

A DISTINCTIVE LANGUAGE AND EXPRESSION

At the end of the 12th century, popular literature began to develop in the form of 'troubadouresque' poetry, written not in Catalan, the spoken language, but in Provençal, the poetic and literary medium.

The oldest surviving Catalan text in verse is the *Chansó de Santa Fé* (1054-1056) by an anonymous author from either Saint-Michel-de-Cuxa or Saint-Martin-du-Canigou (both in present-day France). Recent research has proved that epic poetry and verse existed prior to 1038, and flourished in the 13th century with the works of Guerau de Cabrera, Guillem de Berguedà and Cerverí de Girona (1250-1280).

Catalan literature blossomed with the economic prosperity and political expansion of the 13th century. One of the most eminent writers of the time was Ramon Llull, author of more than 200 works. Mention should be made of his poem *Desconhort (Despair,* 1285), the *Llibre de contemplació (Book of Contemplation),* the *Llibre d'Amic e Amat (Book of the Lover and the Beloved)* and *Blanquerna,* a portrait of society which preceded Chaucer's *Canterbury Tales* by almost a century. Apart from the *Chronicle of Jaume I,* medieval Catalan literature produced other great historical chronicles like those of Bernat Desclot, Ramon Muntaner and Pedro the Ceremonious.

GOLDEN AGE AND DECLINE

Catalan literature reached its Golden Age in the 14th century, with a work by Francese Eiximenis, a Franciscan friar who wrote a large encyclopaedia of Christian knowledge *(Lo Crestià),* and Anselm Turmeda (1352-1432), considered to have introduced modern literature to Catalonia with his *Disputa de l'ase.*

The great Catalan classics remain *Lo Somni,* by Bernard Metge (1340-1413) and *Tirand lo Blanch,* by Joanot Martorell (1413-1468). Praised by Cervantes, the latter blends realism with adventure, not unlike Cervantes' *Don Quixote.* Along with *Curial e Güelfa,* by an anonymous author, it is among the first great modern novels.

Poetry was encouraged by the founding of the *Jocj Florals* (poetry contests) in Barcelona in 1395. Proponents of what was known as the Catalan school of lyric poetry included Jaume March, Ausias March and Jordi de Sant Jordi. Andreu Febrer wrote the first translation of *The Divine Comedy* in verse; Catalan translations of various classics already existed, including the tragedies of Seneca, works by Petrarch and Cicero, and the Vulgate (Latin versions of the Bible).

Catalonia's brilliant literary output temporarily slackened during a period of unsettling political events and economic decline when the Court and the nobility were transferred to Castile. Nevertheless, Catalan remained the language spoken by the people. Catalan literature was adversely affected but not entirely abandoned; the philosopher Joan Lluis Vives, poet Pere Serafi and Francesc Vicent Garcia, known as the 'Rector of Vallfogona', all produced important works during this period. There also remain works that give historical accounts of life in Barcelona, such as the *Canço del comte Arnau.*

THE ROMANTIC 'RENAIXENÇA'

Aided by Romanticism, the cultural and literary movement of the *Renaixença* developed in the early 19th century, beginning with *Oda a la Pàtria,* written in 1833 by Bonaventura Carles Aribau: 'It matters little what fate has misled me to look closer at the towers of Castile if my ear no longer hears the songs of the troubadours and if there is no awakening of noble memories in my heart. It pleases me to still speak the language of those learned men who filled the universe with their customs and their laws; the language of the strong who overcame kings, defended rights and avenged insults.'

The *Jochs Florals* were won in 1877 by Jacint Verdaguer for his epic poem, *Atlàntida*, the first great poetical work of modern Catalonia. Other writers such as Joan Maragall, Santiago Rusinol, Serafí Pitarra and Angel Guimerà added to the glory of Catalan letters and drama. Guimerà's play, *Terra Baixa (Lowlands),* was translated into several languages. Catalan periodicals began to appear, among them *Lo Vertader català* (1843), *Calendari català* (1864), *Lo Gai Saber* (1864), *Lo Tros de Paper* (1865) and *L'Esquella de la Torratxa,* which ran to four editions and had a circulation of 16,000.

THE 20th CENTURY

Three events marked Catalan literature in the early 20th century — the Congress of the Catalan Language in 1906, the reinforcement of the Institute of Catalan Studies in 1911 and the spelling norms laid down by Pompeu Fabra in 1913 that gave the language grammatical unity, making it a modern language for general use.

The first third of the 20th century was a period of splendour for Catalan literature; the official status of the language encouraged many authors. Among literary figures of note from this period were Josep Carner, Guerau de Liost, Josep Maria Lopez-Picó and Carles Riba.

The intellectual world suffered a hard blow following the coup d'état in Madrid by General Primo de Rivera (see p. 43) in 1923. The use of Catalan was banned, first from schools and universities and later from publishing houses. Then arose the problem of reconciling the difference between the purer literary Catalan and spoken Catalan, which was tinged with Castilian. The use of Catalan as a liturgical language became widespread from 1965 onwards, after the Vatican II council.

The fate of post-war literature in Catalonia was linked to the specific conditions of the country at the time. People continued to write but were either not published at all or had their work published elsewhere. While some began writing in Castilian, others, exiled or not, remained faithful to their language. Catalan poetry was written almost clandestinely, in a kind of internal exile. Nonetheless, several literary prizes were created to reward the efforts of these poets. Mention should be made here of a prize that was awarded over 25 years in Cantonigròs (near Vic) from 1944 to 1968. Since those days its jury has become itinerant. The first literary prize after the war was the Joanot Martorell in 1947 which became the Sant Jordi prize in 1960. In 1969, a prize called the *Gran Premi d'Honor de les Lletres Catalanes* was awarded to a writer whose works as a whole were particularly dedicated to Catalan culture.

A renewed general interest in Catalan literature appeared between 1959 and 1962 and the poets broke their silence. Several themes recur frequently in their work: the quest for freedom and justice, the awareness of oppression, international struggle and solidarity. The leaders of this generation are Pere Quart (also known as Joan Oliver) and Salvador Espriu, a poet and short story writer whose *Llibre de Sinera* was adapted for the stage under the title *Ronda de mort a Sinera*. Espriu bears a strong influence on contemporary Catalan literature. Foix, Brossa, Joan Colomines and Gabriel Ferrater figure among the most popular poets, while Francesc Vallverdú is representative of the more politically committed trend in poetry. The first *Festival Popular de Poesia Catalana*, held in Barcelona on April 25, 1970, was a tremendous success.

Like the rest of literary production in Catalonia, the novel in the second half of the century has been strongly affected by the defeat of the civil war and is suffering from reduced readership, partly due to the low rate of population growth in the region. With *La Plaça del Diamant*, Mercè Rodoreda went beyond national boundaries and had the book translated into several languages.

Today's most renowned novelists include Maria Aurèlia Capmany, Llorenç Villalonga and Joan Sales. Josep Pla writes portraits of his country while Terenci Moix is known for breaking all literary conventions. A realist trend is currently emerging with authors such as Joseph Maria Espinàs, Baltasar Porcel and Estanislau Torres. Finally, Joan Fuster is the current spokesman for Valencia.

An important step towards the normalization of Catalan language and literature was taken in 1969 with the publication of

The Catalan language

Catalan is a Romance language which stems from Latin. It is spoken in Spain throughout the region of Catalonia and the Balearic Islands and Valencia, and outside Spain in the French region of the *Pyrénées-Orientales* and in the town of Alghero in Sardinia. *Rousillonais* (spoken in Roussillon in France) and the languages spoken in Valencia and the Balearic Islands, form a coherent, idiomatic whole. According to Article 3 of the *Estatut d'Autonomia,* 'the Catalan language is the official language of Catalonia as Castilian is the official language of the whole Spanish state'. The recognition of Catalan as the official language has contributed to its use in schools and establishments of higher education. Catalan literature is currently experiencing a remarkable boom with more than 4500 books published a year, and it is crossing frontiers with Spanish, English and French translations of classics from the Middle Ages such as those by Ramon Llull, Bernat Metge and Ausiàs March as well as works by contemporary writers such as Josep Carner, J.-V. Foix and Joan Perucho.

Catalan is also gaining recognition in the world of drama; the majority of plays staged in Barcelona are in Catalan. Apart from national television, which broadcasts some of its programs in Catalan, Catalonia has its own autonomous channels. Catalan is used commonly in everyday life as well as in judicial and administrative fields. Catalan is today a living, flourishing language.

the first volume of the Great Catalan Encyclopaedia. In addition, the number of writers using Catalan has increased since the language was declared official for use in everyday life throughout the region. Finally, in 1989, the Cultural Commission of the European Parliament added Catalan to the list of official languages used in Common Market institutions.

THEATRE

Like other literary domains, the theatre lived through a low period in the early postwar years. The crisis of the official theatre that authorities set up after the war worsened after the 1950s. However, Catalonia found its own direction and in 1955 the *Agrupació Dramaticà* was formed in Barcelona. This was followed by the *Escola d'Art Dramàtic Adrià Gual* in 1960, founded by Maria Aurèlia Capmany and Ricard Salvat to train future generations of actors. In 1962, the *Theatre experimental català* was opened to stage performances that would introduce the public to foreign avant-garde drama. Joan Oliver, who sharply satirizes middle-class society in his comedies, together with Manuel de Pedrolo and other playwrights, produces plays that fit in well with the spirit of postwar Catalan drama: works that concentrate on an experimental approach to theatrical expression, less intended for the general public. Today, Catalan drama is well-known abroad thanks to the success of Josep Maria Flotats and the young *Fura dels Baus* company.

BARCELONA

Barcelona, *cap i casal de Catalunya* ('head and cradle of Catalonia'), is a capital in the fullest sense of the word, by virtue of its history, modernity and cosmopolitan way of life. While to the sun-worshipper of the 1960s Barcelona may have been just a brief stopover, today's visitors discover a capital that has regained the splendour it had at the beginning of the century; Barcelona is once again a fashionable city bursting with culture and business, a place to savour and explore.

When Cervantes' Don Quixote arrived in Barcelona on St. John's Eve, he was delighted by the sea and the bustle of the streets, and was regaled by the sound of 'oboes, kettledrums and morrice-bells', as well as the 'sweet martial music' that rang out from clarions and trumpets aboard the galleys in the harbour. After a series of inimitable adventures, he defined the city in these immortal words: 'The treasure house of courtesy, the refuge of strangers, the hospital of the poor, the country of the valiant, the avenger of the injured, and the abode of firm and reciprocal friendships, unique in its position and its beauty.'

A HISTORY OF BARCELONA THROUGH ITS ARCHITECTURE

In pre-Roman times Barcelona was the centre of a region called *Laietana.* The new Augustan town was built around a place known in later centuries as *Mons Taber,* the present Gothic quarter. The colony was given the title of *Colonia Iulia Augusta Faventia Paterna Barcino* and was endowed with an orderly urban plan. The forum was situated in the north-east corner of the present plaça de Sant Jaume. Finally, there were walls around the town which were rebuilt in late Antiquity.

The first documents of the Christianization of the town date from the end of the 4th century when Bishop Pacià headed the community. The first cathedral and baptistery have been preserved in what is now the basement of the town's History Museum, underneath the present cathedral. The old edifice has three aisles and the baptistery contains a polygonal baptismal font.

Antonio Gaudí marked the architecture of Barcelona with his highly distinctive and imaginative style; much of the latter period of his career was spent on the construction of his most renowned masterpiece, the church of La Sagrada Familia — unfortunately unfinished at his death.

Barcelona served as the provisional Visigoth capital in the 5th century before it moved to Old Castile. The Visigoth kingdom collapsed with the arrival of the Muslims in 720. However, Barcelona did not remain Muslim for long; in 801 the Franks, under Louis the Pious, made it the capital of the Spanish March, a frontier zone of the Carolingian Empire. The march was divided into earldoms, Barcelona quickly gaining supremacy over the others.

Throughout the Middle Ages, the history of Barcelona was one and the same as that of the entire Catalan region. This section briefly reviews the main stages of the area's urban and architectural development.

By the end of the 12th century, Barcelona had spread well beyond its Roman walls (as the church of Sant Pau del Camp testifies) and during the reign of Jaume I the Conqueror (1213-1276), when the kingdom was expanding into the Mediterranean, a second wall was built. This was enlarged in the 14th century under Pedro III the Great, followed by the construction of the most majestic part of the Royal Palace (the Saló de Tinell) and the monumental shipyards. Under the earlier rule of Alfonso II and Jaume II (during the last quarter of the 13th century and the first third of the 14th) the town had been enriched by the building of a number of Gothic churches, thanks to the blossoming of new religious orders, and a healthy economy aided by maritime expansion. Under Juan I (1387-1396), patron of the arts and literature, Barcelona was renowned for the sophistication of its court. During the reign of his successor, Martin the Humane (1396-1410), the last of the dynasty of Barcelona, the Hospital de la Santa Creu was constructed. The medieval city was built from the prosperity brought about by the trade that maritime conquests engendered rather than from the spoils of the conquests themselves.

During the 14th and 15th centuries the most gifted artists received commissions from the Court and the main religious orders. For inspiration, these artists looked to their counterparts in southern France and Provence, or to Italy.

The Renaissance reached Barcelona through exchanges with Naples, which was annexed to the kingdom by Alfonso V the Magnanimous (1416-1458). A good example of this style is the Palau de la Generalitat. When the Court moved to the centre of Spain under Fernando II the Catholic (1452-1516), Barcelona was kept in the background and was therefore less affected by the consequences of Spain's conquest of America.

During the War of Spanish Succession, Barcelona took sides with Archduke Charles of Austria against the pretender, Philippe de Bourbon. Upon his victory in 1714, after more than a year's siege, the French prince imposed humiliating conditions on the town. In order to keep an eye on the newly conquered city he destroyed a whole district and built a citadel (Ciutadella) in its place. A new classical style of architecture slowly began to emerge, evident in some of the buildings inside the citadel. However, from an artistic point of view, 18th-century Barcelona was discreet; architectural creation advanced on a small scale. The last period of the Counter-Reformation is manifest in churches like Sant Felipe Neri, Sant Agustí Nou and the basilica of Mercè. On the other hand, several palaces testify to the wealth of some of Barcelona's citizens who invested in beautiful buildings: Palau Sessa-Larrard, Palau de la Virreina, Palau Moja and Palau March. The church of Sant Miquel del Port and the Horta maze, designed on the initiative of the Marquis of Alfarràs with references to the gardens in Versailles, are examples of a style midway between Baroque and Classicism. All this contributed to what was to become in the 19th century the promenade par excellence, the Ramblas.

The first half of the 19th century was marked by the gradual demolition of the walls that had hitherto prevented Barcelona from expanding. The municipality decided upon a grandiose plan known as the *Eixample*, that was to link Barcelona to other towns in the inland plain and also to occupy any unused territory stretching to the gates of the city. Designed by the architect Cerdà, the plan was to build a grid pattern of streets, all a minimum of 66 ft/20 m wide, broken only by two large diagonal avenues. It was one of the most ambitious examples of urban planning in the 19th century and one of the major factors in the revival of the capital.

Meanwhile, the new wealth of the epoch was accompanied by a romantic rediscovery of Catalonia's medieval past and in the case of Barcelona, its former metropolitan role. By the end of the century the Cathedral was completed with the addition of its façade and tower, and the new university was built in a resolutely Roman style. Its architect, Elies Rogent, also restored the famous Roman style abbey-church at Ripoll.

At the same time, a type of architecture was developing that made extensive use of metal; markets, prestigious industrial buildings such as the Montaner i Simon printing works and, with the arrival of the railway, train stations were all built of metal. The monument (1882-1886) dedicated to Christopher Columbus was one of the more impressive constructions of the period.

The Universal Exhibition in Barcelona (1888) marked the beginning of the artistic movement known as *Modernisme* (see p. 64). Barcelona became an important arts capital with painters such as Casas, Nonell, Miró and Picasso, as well as many lesser-known people in all the decorative arts, who met the extraordinary challenge created by *Modernisme.*

At the end of the first quarter of this century, the architectural trend known as *Noucentiste* looked to models in Mediterranean Renaissance architecture or to styles of central European monuments. This resulted in works that contrasted with the exaggerated profusion of *Modernisme* by a return to a more academic style, although the effect was still ornate (the Coliseum cinema is a good example). This period was marked by the development of the plaça de Catalunya and more especially by the International Exhibition of 1929. The whole of Montjuïc hill was landscaped for the event and much of this development can still be seen today. The most innovative aspects of that monumental work have been highlighted recently by the rebuilding of Ludwig Mies van der Rohe's German pavilion. Although the Exhibition took place during the military dictatorship of Primo de Rivera (1923-1930) — which influenced the choice of

---

Barcelona-Paris

Cultural and artistic relations between Barcelona and Paris since the 19th century have replaced the former ties with Rome. A certain cultural affinity and the quest for artistic references and models are among the factors contributing to the interest of Spanish artists in French art. The journey by the greatest mid-19th-century Catalan painter, Marià Fortuny (1838-1874), initiated exchanges between the two cities. Catalan *Modernisme* looked to Montmartre for inspiration: Ramon Casas (1866-1932) and Santiago Rusiñol (1861-1930) met Degas and Erik Satie. Isidre Nonell (1873-1911) admired the work of Toulouse-Lautrec, Richard Canals (1876-1931) was influenced by Renoir, and Pidelaserra (1877-1946), with his Parisian cityscapes, brought Impressionism to Catalonia. Among the Catalans who became famous in Paris were Anglada-Camarasa (1891-1959), Xavier Gosé (1876-1915), Josep Maria Sert (1876-1945) and Salvador Dalí (1904-1988). The best known, of course, is Picasso (1881-1973), who made his début in Catalonia and Barcelona before settling in Paris. In the French capital, Picasso hosted the best Catalan artists, from Manolo Hugué to Joan Miró, Pau Gargallo, Julio González and Apel.les Fenosa. In return, French artists such as Picabia spent time in Barcelona. Today these exchanges continue with such artists as Tàpies and Bofill.

---

architecture — the idea had been conceived well before this time by the *Mancommunitat* (see 'Catalonia in the Past', p. 43).

In the 1930s, during the period of political autonomy and up until the end of the civil war, Barcelona's architecture tuned into the political and cultural atmosphere of the European scene: Art Deco (as in the Casal Sant Jordi on carrer de Pau Claris 81), Le Corbusier (Josep Lluís Sert building on carrer de Montaner 342-348) and Bauhaus (Astona building on carrer de Paris 193-199). The Government of the *Generalitat de Catalunya* was originally responsible for important social projects such as the *Pla Macià* (Macià Plan, named after the president). It also developed workers' housing projects in collaboration with Le Corbusier (passeig Torras i Bages 91-105). However, the first years of Francoism were characterized by a deliberate rejection of modern architecture and, it must be said, a period of mediocrity from which only rare exceptions managed to escape. It wasn't until the middle of the 1950s that new experiments were given international recognition (J.A. Coderch) and not until the 1960s and 1970s that innovation was widely applied by teams of architects. Happily over these past few decades there has been terrific architectural development, especially in the upper part of town. Traditionally, this turning point is symbolized by the Miró Foundation (1972-1974) designed by Josep Lluís Sert. Since the return of democratic institutions, Barcelona has benefited from a new economic climate.

The capital has been transformed in recent years not only by numerous restorations but also by the naming of streets in Catalan, as opposed to Spanish, the sign of a certain change in attitude. Urban planning and architecture, resolutely taken in hand by the municipal authorities, centres around the 1992 Olympic Games which, following the example of the great exhibitions of 1888 and 1929, will leave a lasting mark on the city.

Reptilian representations in metal were a common theme in Gaudí's work: this dragon adorns the entrance to the Finca Güell, the estate of Gaudí's main patron.

SOME OF THE GREAT MODERNIST ARCHITECTS

The word *Modernisme* covers a vast artistic movement in Catalonia that took place in the late 19th and early 20th centuries. It developed during the same period as Art Nouveau in France and Belgium, the Modern Style in Great Britain and Jugendstil in Germany. All these styles coincided with the Belle Epoque, reaching their apogee in 1900 and dying out by World War I. They reflected the scientific and technical revival of the time, the economic prosperity and social restlessness, as well as the cultural creativity which produced Symbolism in literature and Wagnerism in music. Catalan *Modernisme* was integrated into the romantic movement called *Renaixença*, which strove to restore the Catalan language and literature.

The Catalan architecture of the period adopted both new techniques and new industrial materials, and often drew upon building styles of the country's past. *Modernisme* is characterized by the importance given to curved, asymmetric, sinuous lines, as well as foliage embellishments (such as leaves, fruit, flowers, intertwining stems and so on). It is also marked by the use of many different colours and the decorative arts (ceramics, stained glass, metal). Finally, it reflects an intense interest in all aspects of drawing and graphic art.

Cerdà's far-sighted project *(Eixample)* to enlarge the town of Barcelona gave rise to the building fever of the new middle class, who wanted to compete in the exuberance of their street façades. Today in Barcelona there are over one thousand classified buildings from this period including churches, shops, public facilities, industrial buildings, private houses and apartment blocks. *Modernisme* quickly spread to other towns in Catalonia but the impressive number of restored buildings of great artistic value in Barcelona most certainly justifies a visit to the capital.

Antoni Gaudí (1852-1926)

Gaudí's prestige is immense. He began as an architect in 1878, working mainly in Barcelona under the patronage of the Güell family. When he undertook the Sagrada Família, his major work, he decided to live on the building site and devote his entire life to the project. Gaudí favoured decor achieved through the breaking up of shapes and minimum use of straight lines, giving a surprising, curving, organic effect. His work often appears as Expressionist and in some cases is strongly marked by religious symbolism.

His works: Casa Vicens (p. 121), Pavellons de la Finca Güell (p. 119), Palau Güell (p. 110), Casa Calvet (p. 123), Bellesguard (a country house outside Barcelona), Casa Batlló (p. 120), Casa Milà (*La Pedrera*, p. 121), La Sagrada Família (p. 120). You can also visit the Collegi de les Teresianes, a religious school completed by Gaudí (carrer de Ganduxer 85-87, off map II, B1. Access: buses 14, 16, 22, 58 and 64).

Lluís Domènech i Montaner (1850-1923)

He was an architect (1873), director of the school of architecture in Barcelona (1901), politician, historian and archaeologist. His work represents the rationalist trend of *Modernisme* in architecture with the use of new materials and advanced technology, which he adapted to the industrial and decorative arts. From the formal point of view, he was anchored in the artistic past of his country. You can visit his buildings in Barcelona, Reus, Canet and Olot.

His works: Castell dels Tres Dragons (p. 114), the Montaner i Simon printing house (p. 122), the Hospital de Sant Pau (p. 120).

Josep Puig i Cadafalch (1867-1957)

As well as being an architect (1891), and a student of Domènech i Montaner, he was also an art historian, politician and president of the Catalan *Mancommunitat* from 1917 to 1923. His interest in medieval architecture influenced his own work, in which he made great use of Gothic shapes enriched with an abundance

of decorative plant motifs. He worked in Barcelona, Mataró,
Argentona, Viladrau, Montserrat and Sant Sadurní d'Anoia.
His works: Casa Martí - Els Quatre Gats (p. 85), Casa Amatller
(p. 121), Casa Macaya (p. 121), Casa Quadras (p. 120), Casa
Terrades (p. 121), Casa Serra (p. 121).

PRACTICAL INFORMATION

Telephone area code: **93**.
Map coordinates refer to the maps pp. 6-7, 8-9.

Accommodation

See p. 21 for an explanation of hotel classification.

▲▲▲▲▲ **Ritz,** Gran Via de les Corts Catalanes 668, 08010, II, D2,
☎ 318 5200. 167 rooms. Restaurant. Classical-style palace built at
the beginning of the century.

▲▲▲▲ **Arenas,** carrer Capita Arenes 20, 08034, off map,
☎ 204 0300. 59 rooms. Parking. Located in one of Barcelona's
residential areas. Luxurious.

▲▲▲▲ **Calderon,** rambla de Catalunya 26, 08007, II, C2,
☎ 301 0000. 161 rooms. Restaurant, parking and swimming pool.
Known as the hotel where football players retire to before big
matches.

▲▲▲▲ **Colón,** avinguda Catedral 7, 08002, I, C2, ☎ 301 1404.
161 rooms. Restaurant. Splendid position just opposite the
Cathedral. A fine hotel and meeting place particularly appreciated for
the quality of its service.

▲▲▲▲ **Condes de Barcelona,** passeig de Gràcia 75, 08008, II, C1-2,
☎ 215 0616. 100 rooms. Restaurant and parking. Set in a
magnificent Modernist building.

▲▲▲▲ **Condor,** via Augusta 127, 08006, off map, ☎ 209 4511.
78 rooms. Restaurant and parking. Given its luxury, the prices are
very reasonable.

▲▲▲▲ **Duques de Bergara,** carrer Bergara 11, 08002, II, C2,
☎ 301 5151. 56 rooms. Restaurant. It has a majestic hall dating
from the turn of the century.

▲▲▲▲ **Ramadá Renaissance,** ramblas 111, 08002, II, C2,
☎ 318 6200. 210 rooms. Restaurant and parking. Has recently
been done up and is very expensive but it does face the famous
Ramblas!

▲▲▲ **Atenas,** avinguda de la Meridiana 151, 08026, off map,
☎ 232 2011. 165 rooms. Restaurant, parking and swimming pool.
Inexpensive for its category.

▲▲▲ **El Casal,** carrer Tapineria 10, 08002, I, C2, ☎ 319 7800.
36 rooms. Located in the heart of the Gothic quarter. From the bar
you can see the Cathedral towers.

▲▲▲ **El Castillo,** circumval. lació, 08830, off map, ☎ 661 0700.
48 rooms. Swimming pool, tennis courts and garden. Friendly hotel,
pleasantly situated in the green belt outside Barcelona. 20 minutes
by train from the city centre.

▲▲▲ **Cuatro Naciones,** ramblas 40, 08002, II, C3, ☎ 317 3624.
34 rooms. Parking. This was one of the most renowned hotels in
Barcelona in the 19th century when a number of famous figures,
such as the French author Stendhal, used to stay here.

▲▲▲ **Gótico,** carrer Jaume I 14, 08002, I, C2, ☎ 315 2211.
68 rooms. Comfortable and ideally situated in the heart of the
Gothic quarter.

▲▲▲ **Mikado,** passeig de la Bonanova 58, 08017, off map, II, B1, ☎ 211 4166. 66 rooms. Restaurant and parking. Apartments with hotel service.

▲▲▲ **Monte Carlo,** rambla d'Estudis 124, 08002, I, B1, ☎ 317 5800. 81 rooms. Parking. There is a fine Art Deco reception room which, when lit up, can be admired from the Ramblas.

▲▲▲ **Oriente,** ramblas 45-47, 08002, II, C3, ☎ 302 2558. 142 rooms. Built on the site of a former Franciscan convent, Santa Bonaventura, of which the 17th-century cloister is now the main reception room. The hotel itself has been in existence since 1842 and the artists who frequented it made it famous. Nineteenth-century decor.

▲▲▲ **Villa de Madrid,** plaça Vila de Madrid 3, 08002, I, C1, ☎ 317 4916. 28 rooms. Parking. Very reasonable for its category. Right in the heart of the old town.

▲▲ **La Cartuja,** carrer de Tordera 43, 08012, II, D1, ☎ 213 3312. 10 rooms. In the Gràcia district with a quiet little garden.

▲▲ **Lider,** rambla de Catalunya 84, 08008, II, C1-2, ☎ 215 5065. 29 rooms. Accommodation of the *hostal* type.

▲▲ **Lleó,** carrer de Pelai 24, 08001, I, B1, ☎ 318 13.12. 63 rooms. Restaurant. Ideal for keen shoppers as it is right in the commercial centre of town.

▲▲ **Rossinyol,** avinguda Joan Borras 64, 08190, Valldoreix, off map, ☎ (93) 674 2300. 40 rooms. Set well away from the noise and bustle of town (12 mi/19 km). Garden. Very reasonably priced.

▲▲ **Torelló,** carrer Ample 31, 08002, I, C3, ☎ 315 4011. 72 rooms. Parking. Inexpensive for its category.

▲ **Nouvel,** carrer de Santa Anna 20, 08002, I, C1, ☎ 301 8274. 76 rooms. Charming hotel a stone's throw from plaça de Catalunya and the Ramblas.

▲ **Park Hotel,** avinguda Marquès de l'Argentera 11, 08003, I, D3, ☎ 319 6000. 95 rooms. Restaurant and parking. Not far from the Parc de la Ciutadella.

Entertainment and leisure

Beaches

Platja de la Barceloneta, passeig Marítim, no number, Ciutat Vella, off map. Metro: Barceloneta and Ciutadella (line 4); buses: 17, 39, 45, 57 and 64. Bars, showers, public baths and changing rooms.

Platja de la Mar Bella, passeig Calvell, no number, San Martí. Metro: Poble Nou (line 4). Bars and showers.

Bowling

Bolera Pedralbes, avinguda Doctor Maranón 11, 08028, off map, ☎ 333 0352. Metro: Zona Universitaria (line 3); buses: 7 and 15. *Open 10am-1:30am.*

Boliche, avinguda Diagonal 508, 08006, off map, ☎ 237 9098. Buses: 6, 7, 15 and 27. *Open 6pm-2am.*

Bowling Center AMFF, carrer de Sabino de Arana 6, 08028, off map, ☎ 330 5048. Metro: María Cristina (line 3). *Open 11am-1:30am.* Free introductory class for beginners.

Music and dance

For information on concerts, whether classical, jazz or folklore, call the **Amics de la Música** (Friends of Music), ☎ 302 6870. For dance performances, especially Barcelona's contemporary ballet productions, call 322 1037.

Parks and gardens

For general information on Barcelona's parks and gardens call: (93) 424 3834.

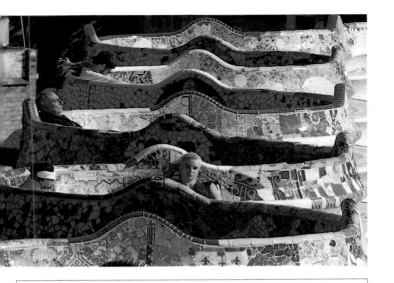

Parc Güell (1904-1914)

The park was originally planned to be a kind of garden city where the architecture would be integrated into the natural surroundings. There were to be houses, restaurants, shops and schools. However, ten years after work began, the death of Eusebio Güell, the banker who had commissioned and financed the project, meant that Gaudí could not finish it. Nevertheless, what you see today vividly expresses the inventive, Baroque spirit of the architect's genius. The area known as the Greek Theatre, supported by 86 columns, was intended to be a covered market. It is flanked by a long undulating bench — mainly the work of Josep-Maria Jujol — that rises up the hillside above the town in a series of ceramic curves. The fountains are multi-coloured mosaics, as is the enormous dragon that welcomes you up the monumental staircase. Lining some of the pathways are knobbly leaning columns that melt in with the trees. A description, however, does not do justice to the park: go there for a stroll and the garden masterpiece will speak for itself.

Castell de l'Oreneta, near the Pedralbes monastery, entrance on carrer de Montevideo, off map. Buses: 22 and 64. A ruined castle in a 37-acre/15-hectare park. A miniature train tootles through the park in the morning on Sundays and holidays.

Parc Cervantes, at the end of avinguda Diagonal, entrance on avinguda Diagonal near carrer Advocat Ballvé, off map. Metro: Zona Universitaria (line 3); bus: 7. There are 245 varieties of roses.

Parc de la Ciutadella, entrance on passeig de Pujades or passeig de Picasso, II, D3. Buses: 14, 36, 39, 40, 41, 42 and 51. There is a zoo, a lake and also some greenhouses (see p. 114).

Parc Güell, in the north of the Gràcia district, entrance on carretera del Carmel or carrer d'Olot, off map. Metro: Lesseps (line 3), quite a long walk from here; bus: 10. This world famous park was designed by Gaudí.

Parc del Laberint, beside the Horta velodrome, entrance on passeig de la Vall d'Hebron, off map. Buses: 26, 27 and 73. The gardens were designed in the 19th century. There is a maze.

Parc de Montjuïc, on Montjuïc hill, entrance on avinguda de la Reina Maria Cristina, II, A2. Metro: plaça d'Espanya (lines 1, 3); buses: 61, 101 and 201. Amusement park, museums and a cactus garden.

Turó del Putxet, entrance on carrer de Manacor, off map. Buses: 22, 26, 28 and 58. Meteorological observatory.

Theatre

Poliorama, rambla 115, I, B2, 08002, ☎ 317 7599. Former public baths, now the headquarters of the Josep M. Flotats theatre company.

Romea, carrer de Hospital 51, I, B2, 08001, ☎ 317 7189. Drama centre for the *Generalitat de Catalunya.*

Teatre Lliure, carrer de Montseny 47, off map, 08012, ☎ 218 9251. The company concentrates on progressive, experimental drama.

Festivals

Epiphany: Late afternoon on January 5 the Three Wise Men and their cortège disembark at the Moll de la Fusta. This sumptuously attired group then leads a procession through town to the huge delight of children and their parents who crowd along the streets to watch. Those children who have written to the Three Wise Men several weeks beforehand, now wait in great excitement: during the night of January 5 to 6 the Three Wise Men send their emissaries with presents to be put on the balconies of each house, tucked inside shoes neatly arranged in rows.

Feast of St Joseph: March 19 is a widely celebrated day in Barcelona and throughout Catalonia when traditionally, *crema catalana cremada* (caramelized Catalan cream) is eaten.

Palm Sunday, *(Diumenge de Rams)*: During the week prior to Palm Sunday you can buy delicately crafted objects *(palmes* and *palmons)* made from young palm fronds. Children have them blessed on Palm Sunday in memory of the palm branches strewn on the ground during the entry of Jesus into Jerusalem.

Feast of St George (Sant Jordi): On April 23 the patron saint of Barcelona is celebrated as is the appearance of the first roses. This is also considered a special day for books and lovers. A rose competition is held in the courtyard of the Palau de la Generalitat. In honour of the day of the book, Barcelona's streets (especially the Ramblas) fill with bookstands selling works for all ages and all budgets.

Easter: This is the occasion for a procession of dwarves and giants or 'big heads' *(caps grossos),* while a 'dancing egg' *(l'ou cóm ballá)* is placed in the fountains of the Cathedral cloister and the Casa de l'Ardiaca. In the afternoon a solemn, ceremonial procession passes through the streets near the Cathedral led by the monstrance displayed on the throne of King Martin.

Verbena de Sant Joan: On June 23, the eve of Midsummer's day, the beginning of the summer solstice is celebrated and the town lights up with bonfires and fireworks.

Verbena de Sant Pere: On the feast of St Peter (June 29) the boat processions organized by experienced sailors are the occasion for landlubbers to put to sea for the first time.

Festa: On August 15, a procession is held in the Gràcia district in honour of Sant Medir, with floats and riders who distribute delicacies in the streets and on the squares. The local inhabitants bring along tables and chairs to sit outside. They sometimes organize collective meals before going off to dance the *harbanera.*

Festa: On September 24, to honour Our Lady of Mercy, patron saint of the town, there is a Montjuïc fountain show combining water, music and fireworks. Jubilation throughout the entire town centres around artistic, sports or religious events. As there are so many to choose from it is best to consult the festival schedule printed each year.

All Saints' Day: In memory of an ancient custom in Roman times when ritual meals were taken over tombs, on November 1, chestnuts are eaten along with *panellets,* small cakes made of almonds, pine nuts, sugar and honey.

Christmas: The festive season begins with the fair of St Lucy on

December 13 when the Cathedral square and the square in front of La Sagrada Família fill up with hawkers selling such indispensable items for cribs as ornamental figures, moss collected in woods, and bark from cork trees.

Innocents' Day: This is celebrated on December 28 with tricks rather like those for April Fools' Day; jokes are the order of the day, including the ever-popular custom of sticking little paper figures onto people's backs.

Food And Drink

There are countless numbers of restaurants in Barcelona; bars too, for that matter!

The following list is selective, designed to help hurried visitors find something easily when it's time to eat. For a wider choice than this guide allows, get a copy of the *Barcelona Bar, Guia illustrada de bars*, published by the Town Hall and available in bookshops and kiosks. Or try the *Guía del Ocio* which publishes an up-dated list each week of the restaurants, cafés and bars available, taking seasonal variations into account.

Restaurants

See p. 4 for an explanation of restaurant classification. In the following addresses, the letter (P) means that parking is availiable.

♦♦♦ **Agut d'Avignon,** carrer de Trinitat 3 (intersects carrer d'Avinyó 8), Ciutat Vella, Barceloneta, Gothic quarter, I, C2-3, ☎ 302 6034. *Open 1-3:30pm and 9-11:30pm.* In a street made famous by Picasso's painting *Les Demoiselles d'Avignon*. Traditional Catalan and Basque dishes.

♦♦♦ **Cal Pinxo,** platja Sant Miquel 10, Ciutat Vella, Barceloneta, Gothic quarter, II, D3, ☎ 310 4513. *Open 12:30-4pm and 8:30-11:30pm.*(P). One of Barceloneta's most typical fish restaurants.

♦♦♦ **La Dorada,** travessera de Gràcia 44-46, Sant Gervasi, off map, ☎ 200 6322. *Open 1-4pm and 8pm-midnight.* (P) Nautical decor in the long dining rooms. All manner of fish and seafood. Favourite lunchtime haunt of businessmen.

♦♦♦ **Eldorado Petit,** carrer de Dolors Monserda 51, Sarrià, off map, ☎ 204 5153. Expensive cuisine. Cabbage au gratin stuffed with seafood was served to members of the Olympic Committee in 1985 to convince them of Barcelona's merit as candidate to host the Games!

♦♦♦ **Finisterre,** avinguda Diagonal 469, Eixample, off map, ☎ 239 5576. *Open 1-4:30pm and 8:30-11:30pm.* A chic restaurant frequented by the bourgeoisie for Sunday lunch. Fine international fare and several Catalan dishes.

♦♦♦ **Florian,** carrer Bertrand i Serra 20, Sant Gervasi, off map, ☎ 212 4627. *Open 1-3:30pm and 9-11:30pm.* By drawing on ideas from the heart of traditional Mediterranean cuisine, Rosa Grau produces daringly imaginative meals to the great delight of gourmets.

♦♦♦ **Giardinetto Notte,** carrer de la Granada del Penedès 22, Eixample, II, C1, ☎ 218 7536. *Open 8-11pm.* Frequented by artists and entertainers.

♦♦♦ **Jaume de Provença,** carrer de Provença 88, Eixample, II, B1, ☎ 230 0029. *Closed Sun evening, Mon and in Aug.* Jaume Barques, one of the best chefs in Barcelona, successfully combines modern cuisine with traditional Catalan cooking. The simplest country products go together wonderfully with the most delicate dishes.

♦♦♦ **Neichel,** avinguda de Pedralbes 16 bis, Pedralbes, off map, ☎ 203 8408. *Closed Sun, holidays, Christmas, Holy Week and Aug.* Masterly subtle cuisine. Jean-Louis Neichel is one of Barcelona's stars in the field of gastronomy.

♦♦♦ Via Veneto, carrer de Granduxer 10-12, Turó Parc, off map, ☎ 200 7044 and 200 7024. *Open 1:15-4pm and 8:45-11:30pm.* (P). Impeccable service. Champagne cockscombs are one of Barcelona's musts.

♦♦ Antigua Casa Sole, carrer de Sant Carles 4, Barceloneta, I, C3, ☎ 319 5012. *Open 1-2pm and 8-11pm.* Excellent fish dishes cooked in traditional style.

♦♦ Can Culleretes, carrer Quintana 5, Barri Gòtic, I, C2-3, ☎ 317 6485. *Open 1:30-4pm and 9-11pm.* (P). Catalan cuisine. The speciality is *porquet* (pork) *a la catalana.*

♦♦ Carboner, carrer Ample 46, Port, I, C3, ☎ 315 2260. *Open 1-4pm and 9-11:30pm.* Simple, friendly, popular restaurant with varied Catalan cuisine. Daily clientele, crowded on Sundays.

♦♦ Los Caracoles, carrer dels Escudellers 14, Casc Antic, Ciutat Vella, I, B-C3, ☎ 302 3185. *Open 1pm-midnight.* Probably the best-known restaurant in Barcelona, thanks in part to its unique decor. You should try their speciality, the snail casserole *(caracoles).*

♦♦ Casa Leopoldo, carrer de Sant Rafael 24, El Raval, I, A-B2, ☎ 241 3014. *Open 1-4pm and 9-11pm.* Country-style restaurant in the Chinese quarter. Very reasonably priced home cooking; seafood slightly more expensive.

♦♦ Duran Duran, carrer d'Alfonso XII 39-41, Eixample, II, B-C1-2, ☎ 201 3513. Seasonal cooking; the menu adapts to what's available in the market. Classical background music, ideal for a romantic dinner.

♦♦ Il Fiorino, carrer Cornet i Mas 45, Sarrià, off map, ☎ 205 3017. Delicious Italian food. Reserve beforehand — the restaurant is often full.

♦♦ La Garrotada-2, Ntra Sra de los Desamparados 59, Hospitalet, Sants-Montjuïc, off map, ☎ 249 3097. Delicious seafood and famous 'tomato bread'. Difficult to find a free table.

♦♦ Maharaja, carrer d'Entença 137, Eixample, II, B1, ☎ 422 3460. Good mutton curry and excellent *lassis.* Delicious, authentic Indian specialities.

♦♦ Orotava, carrer del Consell de Cent 335, Eixample, II, C2, ☎ 302 3128 and 302 4397. *Open 1-4pm and 8pm-midnight.* (P). Don't miss the renowned traditional game dishes.

♦♦ Els Quatre Gats, carrer Montsió 3 bis, Casc Antic, I, C1, ☎ 302 4140. *Open 1:30-4pm and 9pm-midnight.* Good Catalan cuisine. Frequented by Barcelona's painters at the turn of the century.

♦♦ Xix Kebab, carrer de Còrsega 193, Eixample, II, C1, ☎ 321 8210. The best Lebanese restaurant in town. Their sweet cakes come from Cleopatra, a Syrian confectioner's.

♦ Agut, carrer d'En Gignas 16, Barri Gòtic, I, C3, ☎ 315 1709. *Open 1-3:45pm and 9-11:45pm.* Wonderful decor. Traditional Catalan dishes served here since its founding, 80 years ago.

♦ Can Solé, passeig de Colom 17, Ribera, I, B-C3, ☎ 302 6174. *Open 1-4pm.* A family-run bar and restaurant with a terrace. Lunch is good and inexpensive. Popular, simple dishes.

♦ La Carreta, carrer de Balmes 358, Eixample, off map, ☎ 211 4196. Copious South American dishes at reasonable prices.

♦ Claudio's, carrer de Casanova 94, Eixample, II, C2, ☎ 323 5987. *Open 1-4pm and 8pm-midnight.* Italo-Argentine specialities, mainly meat and pasta.

♦ Montseny, carrer de la Princesa 29, Casc Antic, I, D2, ☎ 319 7084. *Open 8am-8pm.* Unusual, modest restaurant that produces meals cooked with regional products freshly bought from neighbouring markets.

♦ **Recó d'en Pep,** carrer de Grunyi 5, Casc Antic, I, D2. Self-service buffet, ideal if you're in a hurry. Charming, romantic medieval decor.

♦ **La Taula d'en Bernat,** carrer de la Canuda 41, Casc Antic, I, D2, ☎ 301 1052. *Open 1-4pm and 8:30-11:30pm.* Vegetarian dishes as well as Catalan cuisine.

Bars

Armarcord, passeig de Gràcia, in 'La Pedrera', Gaudi's famous Casa Milà building, II, C1.

Boadas, carrer dels Tallers 1, II, C2. Here you can taste Barcelona's best cocktails in an elegant setting.

Café de l'Opera, rambla dels Caputxins 74, II, C3. One of the last of the old cafés to have preserved its original decor of wood panels and mirrors. A typical Ramblas venue frequented by a colourful crowd.

Gimlet, carrer de Riu 24, off map (Bibera district). Frequented by wealthy bohemians who enjoy a good drink.

K.G.B., carrer l'Alegre de Dalt 55, off map. A trendy place both day and night with a music-bar, avant-garde art exhibitions, rock concerts and a discotheque.

Linea 6-25, carrer E. Granados 54, II, C1. Basketball fans will be delighted with the gymnasium decor, video clips and professional American basketball games shown on a giant screen.

El Llantiol, carrer de Riereta 7, I, A2 (in the old quarter). Theatre and cabaret performers as well as magicians and conjurers. You can even have your palm or cards read.

Nick Havanna, carrer Roselló 208, II, C1. Delectable cocktails. A huge place with a 'machine' interior design; a must.

El Paraigua, carrer Pas de l'Ensenyança 2, I, C2 (in the old quarter). 1900s decor and classical music in the basement. One of Barcelona's authentic classics.

Pastis, carrer Santa Mónica 4, Ramblas, I, B3. 40-year-old establishment with French music and *chansonniers*.

Patio Andaluz, carrer de C. Fastenrath 14, off map. Immense establishment with a garden. A lively place to witness the different cultures that rub shoulders in Barcelona. The local youth create the atmosphere by drinking, singing and clapping hands, but groups break up quickly and a stranger is always welcome to continue the party.

El Quatres Gats, carrer Montsió 5, I, C1. A classic meeting place. Designed by Puig i Cadalfach. At the beginning of the century artists such as Picasso, Casa and Rusiñol used to get together here. Today the bar exhibits work by contemporary painters.

Sisisi, avinguda Diagonal 442, where it crosses passeig de Gràcia, II, C1. Designer decor. Good cocktails served in a relaxed atmosphere.

Snooker Club, carrer de Roger de Lluria 42 (opposite the Ritz), II, D2. A bar with a large billiard table. The entire room was designed around the table and the club won the FAD (Association for the Promotion of the Decorative Arts) decor prize.

La Xampanyeria, carrer de Provença 236, Eixample, II, C1. The best 'cellar' in town. Catalan champagne (*cava*) is served here along with a variety of other drinks; it is well worth a visit.

Zig-Zag, carrer de Plató, off map. Barcelona's most 'in' bar. Good music.

Zurich, plaça de la Catalunya 1, I, C1. Barcelona's most cosmopolitan central café. The terrace is a great place for watching the world go by.

Cafés with a terrace

Bar Pinocho, in the Boqueria market, I, B2. When Barcelona's late-nighters need a little sustenance to keep awake they come here for such specialities as *tallat* and grilled *ensaïmades*.

Dos Torres, via Augusta 300, off map. Situated in the upper part of town. You have a choice between a terrace or a garden with its impressive palm trees. Tanned faces and smart clothes in a pleasant atmosphere.

Los Italianos, Ramblas 70, I, B2. Enjoy delicious Italian ice cream as you watch the passers-by.

Partycular, avinguda del Tibidabo 6, off map. A former chalet now converted into a cocktail bar. You can sit either inside or in the garden; whichever you choose, you enter through an unusual tunnel.

Plaça Reial, I, B2. Numerous cafés around the square - you can't tell where one ends and another begins. Favourite haunt for beer lovers and an ideal place for an aperitif.

Late-night bars

Ars Studio, carrer d'Atenes 27, off map. The avant-garde gather here.

Boliche, avinguda Diagonal 510, off map. A large bar with a bowling alley.

Café de las Artes, carrer de Valencia 234, II, C2. Very trendy and always packed.

La Cova del Drac, carrer de Tuset 30, II, C1. Jazz club with good music and a warm and friendly atmosphere.

Gimblet, carrer de Santaló 46, off map. Sophisticated cocktails for a discriminating clientele.

Marcel, carrer de Santaló 44, off map. Fashionable bar with eclectic customers.

Metropol, passeig Domingo 3, II, C1. Stays open very late. The decor is pure post-Modernism.

Mirablau, avinguda del Tibidabo, off map (right at the top). Magnificent view of the whole town and beyond to the sea. The hillside is invaded at weekends, with traffic sometimes brought to a complete standstill.

Network, avinguda Diagonal 616, off map. Sophisticated decor and a select clientele.

Ticktacktoc, carrer de Roger de Llúria 40, II, D1. Several rooms - bars and billiards - eagerly frequented by Barcelona's trendy crowd.

Universal, carrer de Marià Cubi 184, off map. Cultural atmosphere for the sophisticated set. Great punch.

Getting around Barcelona

Plaça de Catalunya, the social hub of the city, forms a link between the old town and the newer 19th-century district of Eixample. Leading from the square are the Ramblas which form the main street which runs down to the harbour marking the boundary of the Roman and medieval town, more commonly known as the Gothic quarter (Barri gòtic). The seafront to the east ends in Barceloneta, a former fishing district.

Passeig de Gràcia is Eixample's main street. This district is laid out in a grid pattern that at first glance may seem rather monotonous but has advantages.

Useful information to know about Barcelona:

● streets are usually one-way, with a few exceptions (wide avenues).

● the direction of the traffic alternates street by street.

● most streets keep the same name for the entire length, the main exception being the Ramblas, which changes name five times; nonetheless, everyone refers to the street under the general term 'Ramblas'.

● streets have even numbers on one side and odd numbers on the other. Streets running parallel to the sea have their even numbers on the side of the street nearest the sea.

● Barcelonans often use the sea or Tibidabo (the mountain) as points of reference. For instance, when arranging a meeting on plaça de Catalunya they will specify whether it's to be on the 'sea' side or the 'mountain' side of the square.

• In Eixample, houses on street corners usually have two numbers, one for each street, which may cause some confusion. Places can often be located using the names of both streets; the 'Pedrera' for instance is at passeig de Gràcia-Provença.

If you get lost, remember the saying, *'Preguntant la gent s'entén'* ('By asking, we understand one another'). Barcelonans will be pleased to help you and it may be the ideal opportunity for you to practice your Catalan or Spanish — unless you get a direct answer in English, which sometimes happens.

Bicycle
The following companies rent bicycles:

Bicitram, avinguda Marques de L'Argentera 15, 08003, I, D3, ☎ 204 3678. Tandems are also available.

Viatges Langarica, carrer de Pelai 60, 08001, I, B1, ☎ 302 3097 (in summer).

Bus
Barcelona has a good network of buses that covers the entire town. Night buses, however, are few and far between.

There are different booklets of tickets available, valid for a number of journeys (generally 10). One is the T1 which gives access to Barcelona's buses as well as to the metro, the blue tramway (Tibidabo), the Montjuïc funicular railway and Catalan railways (FFCC) city lines. These booklets can be bought in metro stations, Savings Banks and in several special sales outlets, including plaça de Catalunya (carrer Bergara and carrer Rivadeneyra), Universitat metro (access on carrer de Pelai) and ronda de Sant Pau 43.

Various buses link the town to its outer suburbs. Prices vary according to the distance and you can buy multiple-journey tickets on some lines.

The EA bus line runs to the airport from plaça d'Espanya. EN buses take over at night. Buses run approximately every half-hour (less frequent at night) and the journey takes about three-quarters of an hour.

Tourist bus: Line 100 runs a circular bus tour which takes in the most interesting parts of town. You buy a day ticket allowing you to stop as often as you like. The service operates from June to September, every day, every half-hour. The ticket includes the use of the Montjuïc cableway, the blue tramway and the funicular railway to Tibidabo. You can also buy a 3-day pass at a reduced price. The tour stops at the following places: plaça del Palau, plaça Sant Jaume, plaça de Catalunya, passeig de Gràcia, La Sagrada Família, avinguda del Tibidabo, Camp Nou, Estació de Sants, Poble Espanyol, Zona Olimpica, Montjuïc park and plaça del Palau (subject to change).

For information on buses and other public transport, ☎ (93) 836 000. *Open 7:30am-8:30pm or 8am-2pm on Sat.*

Microbus service for the handicapped: for information, ☎ (93) 352 5450.

Car
Barcelona suffers from extremely dense traffic, especially during the rush hour (8-9:30am, 12:30-2:30pm, 3:30-4pm and 6:30-8pm). If you have to be in the centre at these times you will be far better off taking the metro or walking

Today only a few of the streets still have their old cobble stones; most have been paved. If you drive a motorbike you should pay particular attention to the former tramway lines as these cause numerous accidents.

Barcelona has an inner ringroad (beltway), the *1er cinturó de Ronda* and a large outer one, the *II cinturó*, currently under construction. You can also by-pass the town completely by continuing along the highway that runs from the French border to Girona, Tarragona and beyond.

Parking

All the big hotels have private parking available. There are also guarded underground parking areas in the following streets and squares: avinguda de Pau Casals, off map II, B1, passeig de Gràcia, II, C1, plaça de Catalunya, I, C1, plaça de Castelló, off map, II, C1, plaça de la Garduna, I, B2, rambla de Catalunya, II, C2, plaça Urquinaona, I, C1, plaça Doctor Ferrer i Cajigal, II, C1, passeig de Lluís Companys, II, D2, and avinguda de la Reina Maria Cristina, II, A2. Because of the high incidence of vandalism and car theft, it is advisable to use one of the parking areas whenever possible.

Car rental

All the major international car rental agencies have offices in Barcelona. Prices vary little from one to the next but do change according to the season. You are best advised to approach a company that also operates in your own country.

Atesa, carrer de Balmes 141, 08008, II, C1, ☎ 237 8140, telex: 51197. Airport: 302 2832.

Avis Rent-a-Car, carrer de Casanova 209, 08021, II, C1, ☎ 209 9533, telex: 54030. Airport: 241 1476.

Europcar, carrer del Consell de Cent 363, 08006, II, C2, ☎ 317 5876. Airport 317 6980.

Hertz, carrer de Tuset 10, Entlo. 3, staircase D, 08006, off map, ☎ 237 3737, telex: 53037. Airport: 370 5752.

Godfrey Davis, carrer de Viladomat 214, 08029, II, B2, ☎ 239 8401, telex: 52291.

Ital, travessera de Gràcia 71, 08006, II, C1, ☎ 201 2199.

Regente Car, carrer d'Aragó 382, 08009, II, D1, ☎ 245 2402, telex: 52691.

Totcar, carrer de la Infanta Carlota 93, 08029, off map, ☎ 321 3754.

Metro

Open weekdays 5am-11pm, 5am-1am on Saturdays and evenings before holidays, 6am-1am Sundays and holidays.

The metro network covers almost the whole town and outskirts such as Badalona, l'Hospitalet and Santa Coloma de Gramanet.

A T2 booklet of tickets gives access to the metro, the blue tramway (Tribidabo), the Montjuïc funicular railway and Catalan railways (FFCC) city lines.

Always keep your ticket handy as inspectors can ask to see it at any time.

The four metro lines are colour-coded: L1 (red), L3 (green), L4 (yellow) and L5 (blue). In some stations (Passeig de Gràcia, Sants) you can change to connect with suburban or inter-city trains.

Taxi

This is a practical means of transport except during the rush hour. There are a lot of taxis and they are easy to find. All twin-coloured, black and yellow, they display a green light when free. You can hail them wherever you like, particularly on street corners. They take a maximum of four passengers and charge extra for luggage. Pets are not always welcome; you pay extra for them too.

Other transport

Blue Tramway (from avinguda del Tibidabo to Tibidabo funicular railway).

Cable-car (from Miramar-Montjuïc to Torre Jaume and on to Torre de Sant Sebastià-Barceloneta). ☎ 241 4820.

Golondrines boats cross the harbour from Portal de la Pau to Escullera (jetty).

Horse-drawn carriages (tourist itinerary) can be hired in Ciutadella park.

Montjuïc cableway (from the amusement park to Montjuïc castle), ☎ 256 6400.

Montjuïc funicular railway (from Paral.lel metro station to the amusement park), ☎ 256 6440.

Tibidabo funicular railway (from plaça Tibidabo to Tibidabo amusement park), *6:50am-8:40pm,* ☎ 256 6400.

Vallvidrera funicular railway (the *Generalitat* FFCC station in Vallvidrera). *6:45am-10:15pm weekdays (every 15 minutes) and 7:15am-10:30pm weekends and holidays (every half hour).*

Guided tours

Many travel agents offer guided tours of the town in buses with guides who speak English (and other foreign languages). Among them are:

Julià Tours, ronda Universitat 5, 08007, II, C2, ☎ (93) 317 6454/ 318 3895.

Pullmantur, Gran Via de les Corts Catalanes 635, 08010, II, C2, ☎ (93) 317 1297/318 0241.

Nightlife

Nights in Barcelona can be as busy as the days. In certain districts, like the popular Ramblas, life goes on day and night without interruption. You'll be fascinated by the variety of people out walking and the number of things to do.

Discos and dancing

Bikini, avinguda Diagonal 571, II, D1, ☎ 230 5134. Live music on Tues and Wed, variety shows every Thurs, Junior disco on Sun mornings. Non-stop salsa dancing in one of the rooms. Mini-golf every day from 5pm to dawn.

Cibeles, carrer de Còrsega 363, II, C1. Dance hall. Salsa on Thurs.

Otto Zutz Club, carrer de Lincoln 15, off map, ☎ 238 0722. Difficult to get past the door without a membership card. Nevertheless, it's one of the trendiest places in the Catalan capital. Early in the morning a neighbouring croissant bakery serves the night-birds their 'suppers'.

La Paloma, carrer del Tigre 27, I, A1. A popular dance hall in the old town.

Studio 54, avinguda del Paral.lel 64, I, A3. Ranks among the latest in big international discos.

Zeleste, carrer dels Almogàvers 122 in Poble Nou, II, D2. Several different scenes and events. You can have a drink, listen to a concert (classical, jazz or rock) or simply dance.

Variety shows and music halls

El Cordobés, rambla dels Caputxins 35, I, B2. Andalusian flamenco shows (*tabloas flamencos*). Performances from 10pm to midnight and midnight to 2am.

Romeria, carrer de la Diputació 180, II, C2. Runs along the same lines as El Cordobés. Also has performances of *sevillanas*, rumbas and Spanish dances.

Scala Barcelona, passeig de Sant Joan 47-49, II, D2, ☎ 232 6363. A large establishment with a restaurant (four set menus and also service à la carte) and a revue with more than 60 performers at 8:15pm and again at a quarter past midnight.

Los Tarantos, plaça Reial 17, I, B2, ☎ 317 8098. Flamenco performances from 10pm to 2am.

Organizing your time

If you have two days or more, the suggestions in this section should help you organize an itinerary. This said, don't hesitate to wander off and explore the town yourself, you'll then get a better idea of the mood and spirit of the city.

For a long exploration of Barcelona, aim to get up early but don't expect to visit any public buildings before 9am as most are not open before ten.

One-day visit

The itinerary we suggest if you have just one day includes visits to the tourist sites which really shouldn't be missed. As for transport, try walking through the old town and taking a taxi or bus to go to Montjuïc or La Sagrada Família.

Morning:

Plaça de Catalunya

Cathedral and cloisters

Plaça del Rei: Saló del Tinell, chapel of Santa Agata, Museu d'Historia de la Ciutat

Plaça Sant Jaume: Casa de la Ciutat-Ajuntament, Generalitat

Ramblas: Palau Güell, Museu Marítim

Montjuïc: Museu d'Art de Catalunya

Lunch in Barceloneta or in the Gothic quarter.

Afternoon:

Parc de la Ciutadella

Santa Maria del Mar

Carrer de Montcada: Museu Picasso

Palau de la Musica Catalana

Passeig de Gràcia

La Sagrada Família and Hospital de Sant Pau

Evening:

Plaça Reial — Ramblas

Barcelona by night: dinner, cabarets, bars, Chinese quarter.

Two-day visit

If you have at least two days in Barcelona, the suggestions in this section should help you organize an itinerary.

Day one:

In summer we recommend you begin with part A of the itinerary and in winter with part B (Montjuïc) so that you can take full advantage of the panoramic views of the city. In both cases it is advisable to get up early but double check museum opening times.

A. Plaça de Catalunya

   Gothic quarter and Museu Marès

   Ramblas

   Hospital de la Santa Creu

   Palau Güell

   Museu Marítim

B. Montjuïc: Fundació Joan Miró

   Museu d'Art de Catalunya

   Poble Espanyol

Day Two:

A. Plaça de Catalunya

   Eixample - Passeig de Gràcia

   La Sagrada Família

Avinguda de Gaudi
Hospital de Sant Pau
Lunch: Tibidabo or Barceloneta
B. Monestir de Pedralbes
Avinguda Diagonal or Parc de la Ciutadella
Zoo.

Shopping

Barcelona has a multitude of shops. Among them are the most prestigious names in Spanish and European fashion. Business is focused along the town's two main axes, the first in the city's real centre, the popular area around the plaça de Catalunya and the Ramblas, and the second, which is more elegant and luxurious, in the Eixample district along avinguda Diagonal and around plaça de Francesc Màcia.

Around plaça de Catalunya

You could begin a shopping trip along **carrer de Pelai,** I, B1, where you will find numerous shoe shops selling Spanish-made footwear of excellent value. Barcelona's department stores are nearby — **El Corte Inglés** (plaça de Catalunya) and **Galerias Preciados** (avinguda Portal de l'Angel). The streets in this quarter are generally extremely crowded during the afternoon. The area around the **Cathedral** , I, C2, and up to the church of **Santa Maria del Mar,** I, D2-3, is where you will find antiques and second-hand books. Shops selling arts and crafts such as plates multi-coloured fans, ceramics, and hand-decorated papier-mâché figurines and masks, are concentrated in the Ribera district around Santa Maria del Mar.

In the area bordering on the **Ramblas** and in most tourist sites, souvenir shops of all types abound. These sell everything from reproductions of La Sagrada Família to Catalan *barratina*, or even Flamenco and castanet dancing dolls (neither of which actually belong to Catalan tradition).

Near the harbour, below **passeig d'Isabel II,** I, CD3, bazaars sell electrical appliances, watches, cameras, video equipment and so on at absolutely unbeatable prices. Be cautious, however, as articles are often sold without a guarantee.

Eixample II, BC1-2

In this chic area you will find haute couture, jewelers, furriers, shoe-makers, designers, decorators and prestigious art galleries.

Among the main shopping arcades is **Boulevard Rosa** (fashion and accessories) which gives onto rambla de Catalunya and passeig de Gràcia 55. Beside it at passeig Gràcia 55 is **Gremi d'Antiquaries de Barcelona,** a group of distinguished antique shops. This is the ideal place to find an exquisite present when you are in a hurry but it lacks the charm of traditional antique shops.

Aramis, rambla de Catalunya, II, C2. Classic fashion. This is where King Juan Carlos shops.

Artespaña, rambla de Catalunya 75, II, C2. Arts and crafts from all over Spain.

Baguès, passeig de Gràcia 41, II, C1. Classic and modern jewelry set in the magnificent Casa Amatller.

Adolfo Dominguez, passeig de Gràcia 59, II, C2. One of the internationally known Spanish designers. His creations have a sober contemporary look.

Grog, rambla de Catalunya 100, II, C2. Everything from leather to silverware by the most up-to-date designers.

Loewe, passeig de Gràcia 35 and avinguda Diagonal 510, II, C1 Tasteful leather goods with a distinctive style. You pay for the quality.

Tocs, carrer del Consell de Cent 341, II, C1. The place to go for cultural pastimes, parlour games, books, music, video and electronics. An attractive post-modern bar-style setting with non-stop video clips.

Torrents, Gran via de les Corts Catalanes, II, C2, between passeig de Gràcia and rambla de Catalunya. Very good shoemaker.

Vinçon, passeig de Gràcia 96, II, C2. Gifts and decorations.

Art galleries

Some of Barcelona's largest art galleries are located in **carrer del Consell de Cent,** II, C1-2, between carrer de Balmes and carrer de Pau Claris. Apart from these modern Eixample galleries and the older ones in Barri Gòtic, mention should be made of those setting up in the old market area (El Born), a district that is currently being completely transformed.

Dau al Set, carrer del Consell de Cent 333, 08007, II, C1, ☎ (93)301 1236. Large exhibitions of 20th-century artists for contemporary art lovers.

Estol, carrer del Consell de Cent 286, 08007, II, C2, ☎ (93) 302 7530. This large space exhibits the work of several contemporary artists at a time.

Galeria Ignacio de Cassaleta, rambla de Catalunya 47, 08007, II, C2, ☎ (93) 301 0636. Retrospectives of painters and also presentations of contemporary artists. Comfortable setting.

Galeria Joan Prats, rambla de Catalunya 54, 08007, II, C2, ☎ (93) 216 0290. A pioneer of the avant-garde in the 1960s. Presents the latest trends in the art world.

Galeria Maeght, carrer de Montcada 25, I, D2. This famous gallery (a subsidiary of the one in Paris) is set in a fine palace and exhibits works by established artists.

Galeria René Métras, carrer de Consell de Cent 331, 08007, II, C1, ☎ (93) 302 0539. Work by important 20th-century painters in addition to examples of the latest trends in art.

Kreisler, carrer de València 262, 08007, II, C1, ☎ (93) 215 7405. Small gallery which exhibits naive and surrealist work.

Metronom, carrer Fusina 9, 08003, I, D2, ☎ (93)310 6162. A gallery that expanded in 1984 when it set up in an abandoned market, it is part of a foundation that plays an important role in supporting contemporary art and cultural life through fashion shows, comic strips, photography, films, contemporary music, video, an arts library, and so on.

Sala Gaspar, carrer del Consell de Cent 323, 08007, II, C1, ☎ (93) 318 8740. A prestigious gallery (Picasso exhibited here) in a majestic setting that continues to welcome work by good artists.

Sala Pares, carrer Petritxol, 08002, I, B2. A well-known gallery that supported Impressionists and Catalan painters at the end of the last century. This now refurbished hundred-year-old establishment exhibits work by young artists and the latest trends in figurative art.

Markets

Barcelona's main flea market, **Encants** ('Enchantments') is situated on plaça de Les Gloriès Catalanes (entrance on carrer del Dos de Maig, off map I, D2) and is *open all day Mon, Wed, Fri and Sat.* Bear in mind that for the best deals, however, it is preferable to go in the morning.

There are also a number of fairs and weekly markets. Here are some of the main ones:

An **antique market** is held on Fridays in front of the Cathedral, I, C2.

A big **paper-trade and second-hand book market** is held on Sunday mornings at the Mercat de Sant Antoni (carrer del Comte d'Urgell, ronda de Sant Pau, carrer de Tamarit, I, A1). Not to be missed if you are interested in holy pictures, old postcards, collections of magazines, calendars, second-hand books and so on.

A **coin and stamp market** is held on Sunday mornings in plaça Reial, I, B2

Many buildings from the Modernist period have been restored and classified.

Sports

See p. 32 for a list of golf courses in Catalonia.

Sailing and water-skiing
Catalan Sailing Federation, passeig de Manuel Girona 2, 08034, off map, ☎ 203 3800.
Catalan Speedboat Racing Federation, avinguda de Madrid 118, 08028, II, A1, ☎ 330 4757.
Catalan Water-skiing Federation, address and telephone number as above.
Real Club Marítimo e Náutico de Barcelona, Moll d'Espanya, 08003, I, C3, ☎ 315 1805, 315 0007 and 315 1161.
Spanish Water-skiing Federation, carrer de Sabino de Arana 30, 08028, off map, ☎ 330 8903.

Sports Calendar

The following are the major sporting events. Note that the dates are subject to change.

January: International Hockey Tournament (*Reial Club de Polo de Barcelona*).

February: Costa Brava Car Rally.

March: Marathon of Catalonia.

June: 'Els Corte Inglés' race; International Eurhythmics Trophy (Sports Palace).

July: 24-hour Montjuïc Motorbike Race; 'Barcelona Town' athletics meeting.

August: Joan Gamper Football Trophy (Nou Camp); Barcelona-Perpignan cycle race.

September: *Volta ciclista a Catalunya*: Tour of Catalonia; The *Mercè* Trophy: regattas in the harbour; Swimming across the harbour.

October: *Generalitat* Polo Trophy; Grand Barcelona baseball prize; International Montjuïc bicycle climb.

November: Bicycle festival.

December: Joaquim Blume memorial of international gymnastics; Advance Paris-Dakar motor rally.

Soccer

Soccer is the most popular sport in Barcelona, hence its importance in social life and in the media. Catalan soccer rivalry is divided between the town's two teams, F.C. Barcelona and R.C.D. Español. Supporters of the first are known as *els Cules*, and supporters of the second *els Periquites*. The first team is without doubt the most popular; according to a slogan it is much more than just a club — it was in fact often the pretext for nationalist gatherings under Francoism. Today the 'Nou Camp' or 'Camp del Barça' stadium is one of the largest in the world, with 120,000 seats. During the soccer season (September to May) the two teams play alternate matches in their home stadiums on Sunday afternoons or Saturday evenings.

Swimming

The following is a selection of swimming-pools:

Bernat Picornell, avinguda del Estadi 34, Sants-Montjuïc, II, A2, ☎ 325 9281. Metro plaça d'Espanya, line 1; bus 61. *Open June 1-Sept 15*. An Olympic, open-air pool.

Folch I Torres, plaça Folch i Torres, Ciutat Vella, II, B3, ☎ 241 0122. *Open Mon-Fri 11:30am-1:30pm*. An indoor pool in the old town.

Marítim piscina, passeig Marítim, no number, II, D3, ☎ 309 3412. *Open Mon-Fri 7am-9pm*. By the sea.

Useful Addresses

Airlines

Air Algeria, passeig de Gràcia 83, 08008, II, C2, ☎ 216 0008.

Air France, passeig de Gràcia 63, 08008, II, C2, ☎ 215 2866.

Alitalia, avinguda Diagonal 403, 08008, II, C1, ☎ 238 0424.

British Airways, passeig de Gràcia 59, 08007, II, C2, ☎ 215 2463.

Iberia, plaça d'Espanya, 08004, II, A2, ☎ 325 7358.

Lufthansa, passeig de Gràcia 83, 08008, II, C2, ☎ 215 1015.

Pan American World Airways, rambla de Catalunya 26, 08007, II, C2, ☎ 301 0358.

Sabena, passeig de Gràcia 78, 08008, II, C2, ☎ 215 4732.

Swissair, passeig de Gràcia 44, 08007, II, C2, ☎ 215 9150.

Tunis Air, carrer del Consell de Cent 308, 08007, II, C2, ☎ 317 1749.

TWA, passeig de Gràcia 55, 08007, II, C2, ☎ 215 8188.

Banks
Banks are open Mon-Fri 8:30am-2pm; Sat 9am-12:30pm.
Banca Catalana, passeig de Gràcia 84, II, C2 ☎ 215 0071.
Banca de Bilbao, plaça de Catalunya 5, II, C2, ☎ 302 3200.
Banco de Sabadell, passeig de Gràcia 36, II C2, ☎ 302 2721.
Banco Español de Credito, plaça de Catalunya 10, II, C2, ☎ 301 9200.
Indochina and Suez Bank (Indosuez), carrer de Balmes 150, II, C2, ☎ 217 9000.
Banque de Paris et des Pays Bas (Paribas), avinguda Diagonal 427 bis-429, II, C1, ☎ 201 4133.
Banque Nationale de Paris (BNP), carrer d'Entença 321, II, B2, ☎ 321 5900.
Barclays Banks, passeig de Gràcia 45, II, C2, ☎ 215 5444.
Chase Manhattan Bank, avinguda Diagonal 632, II, C1, ☎ 201 2122.
Crédit Agricole (CNCA), passeig de Gràcia 2, II, C2, ☎ 317 7716.
Crédit Commercial de France, carrer de Balmes 89-91, II, C2, ☎ 253 8005.
Crédit Lyonnais, carrer de Londres 102, II, B1, ☎ 200 0311.
Deutsche Bank, passeig de Gràcia 111, II, C2, ☎ 218 2835.

Consulates
Canada, via Augusta 125, 08007, II, C1, ☎ 209 0634.
Great Britain, avinguda Diagonal 477, II, C1, ☎ 322 2151.
Ireland, Gran Via Carles III 94, off map, ☎ 330 9652.
United States, via Laietana 33, I, C2, ☎ 319 9550.

Emergencies
Ambulance service, ☎ 329 7766 and 300 2020 (24-hour service).
Barcelona Health Service Information, ☎ 318 2525. (24-hour service).
Doctor service, ☎ 212 8585.
Evangelical Hospital, carrer de les Camèlies 15, 08024, ☎ 219 7100.
Hospital Clinic, carrer de Casanova 143, 08026, II, B1, ☎ 323 1414. Emergency service, ☎ 254 2580.
Hospital de Sant Pau, carrer de Sant Antoni M. Claret 167, 08025, off map, ☎ 236 4120. Emergency service, ☎ 235 5555.
Nurse service, ☎ 417 1994.
Oxygen service, ☎ 235 4040.
Red Cross Hospital, (hospital de la Creu Roja), carrer de Dos de Maig 301, 08025, off map, ☎ 235 9300.
Road accident emergency service, ☎ 092.

Intercity buses
Autocares Barcelona, carrer de Felipe II 35, off map, ☎ 340 8748.
Autocares Burell, carrer de Galileo 300, 08014, II, A1, ☎ 239 4456.
Autocares Canals, carrer d'Urgell 239, 08011, off map, ☎ 230 7816.
Autocares Julià, ronda Universitat 5, 08006, II, C2, ☎ 302 2486.
Autocares Molist, carrer de Numància 63, 08015, II, A1, ☎ 230 1041.
Autocares Pullmantur, Gran Via de les Corts Catalanes 635, 08010, II, D2, ☎ 318 0241.
Empresa Casas, Gran Via de les Corts Catalanes 669, II, D2, ☎ 232 6658.
Empresa Sagales, plaça de Tetuàn, II, D2, ☎ 231 2756.

Police stations with interpreters

Ample (English, German, French and Italian), carrer Ample 23, I, C3, ☎ (93) 318 3689. *Open Mon-Fri 10am-8pm; Sat 3-10pm.*

Audiencia, (English, French and Italian), via Laietana 49, I, C2, ☎ (93) 302 6325. *Open Mon-Sat 9am-9pm.*

Hospital (English, French and German), carrer Doctor Dou 4, I, B1, ☎ (93) 302 6772. *Open Mon-Sat 9am-8pm.*

Sant Gervasi (English, French and German), carrer de Copèrnic 54, off map, ☎ (93) 201 2700. *Open Mon-Sat 9am-3pm.*

Universitat (English and French), carrer de Mallorca 213, II, C1, ☎ (93) 254 4343. *Open Mon-Sat 9am-3:30pm.*

Tourist Information

Barcelona Fair, plaça de l'Univers, II, A2, ☎ 325 5235. *Open 10am-8pm.*

Barcelona Harbour (Moll de la Fusta), II, C3, ☎ 310 3716. *Open 9am-3pm. June-Sept 8am-8pm.*

Estació Barcelona Central-Sants, II, A1, ☎ 410 2594. Open *8am-8pm.*

Estació Barcelona Terme-França, II, D3, ☎ 319 2791. *June-Sept 8am-8pm.*

Tourist information telephone (24-hour service): ☎ 010 (if you are in Barcelona) or (93) 318 2525 (if you are calling from outside Barcelona).

Tourist Office, Gran Via de les Corts Catalanes 658, II, C2, ☎ 301 7443. *Open Mon-Fri 9am-7pm; Sat 9am-2pm.*

Street names: reflections of Barcelona's history

If you look at a map of Barcelona you will find a mosaic of ancient and modern names, some of them geographic, others historical, some enigmatic and many with ambitious, exuberant or even presumptuous connotations.

In the days when streets had no precise names, they were identified by distinctive characteristics of the surrounding landscape; carrer dels Arcs, for instance, took its name from the Roman aqueduct that ran along it.

Other streets took their names from various trades: carrer Argenteria for the street where one found the silversmiths, and carrer Llibreteria for the street of the book printers, for example. It is said that during the Middle Ages the blind could find their way around, thanks to the sounds or smells of the different crafts.

Streets were occasionally named after geographical zones such as Torrent. Others, such as Vigatans and Manresa refer to the areas (Vic, Manresa) where the merchants originated. Sometimes names were taken from plants and trees, such as the plaça del Pi (Pine Square). Other streets refer to important public or private buildings. In this way the Cathedral and Episcopal Palace gave rise to names like del Bisbe (bishop), del Paradis, de la Pietat and dels Capellans (priests).

Most of the old streets, however, were named after important men or families who lived there, as is the case with Avinyó, Miró, Rauric and so on.

The names mentioned above originated spontaneously, but from the 18th century onwards, with the creation of new districts, more carefully selected names were also given. This was true of Barceloneta and, during the 19th century, of Eixample. In 1864, the names thought up by Victor Balaguer in a state of romantic euphoria were a grandiose tribute to the glory of Catalan history. Some examples of his project remain today: Parlament, Cortes, Diputació, Consell de Cent (government institutions), Provença, Rosselló, Còrsega, Nàpols, Sicilia, Sardenya (states belonging to the Catalan-Aragonese crown), count Borrell, Ramon Llull (historical and literary personalities), Viladomat (a painter), and Balmes and Aribau (illustrious members of the romantic *Renaixença* movement).

Travel Agents
American Express Viajes, passeig de Gràcia 101, 08008, II, C2,
☎ 2170070. Telex: 59092 AMXCO E.
Central de Viajes, carrer de Muntaner 53, 08011, II, C2, ☎ 3233211.
Telex: 51217 CVIA E.
Viajes Iberia, avinguda Diagonal 523, 08029, II, C1, ☎ 3226462.
Telex: 99450 IBERO E.
Viajes Melià, passeig de Gràcia 6, 08007, II, C2,
☎ 3178900/3024574. Telex: 54746 MELIA E.
Wagons-Lits Viajes, carrer de Roger de Llúria 36, 08009, II, D2,
☎ 3187975/3012835. Telex: 97263 CRBA E/99566 CRBA E.

GETTING TO KNOW BARCELONA

THE GOTHIC QUARTER AND THE OLD TOWN

Around the Cathedral *** I, C2
You will find the city's most important historical monuments dating from
the Roman era to the Middle Ages in this area. The heart of antique and
medieval Barcelona is demarcated by the **Roman walls** beside the
Cathedral. The present walls date from the end of the 3rd to the
beginning of the 4th century — modifications of the Augustan
constructions. More than 50 towers from the period have been identified,
as have four gates that gave access to the ancient Roman town, via two
large streets — the *cardo* and *decumanus*, which ran north to south and
east to west, crossing the central square or forum (plaça de Sant Jaume).

The itinerary begins at **plaça Nova,** I, C2, where remains of Barcelona's
past provide a counterpoint to one of the town's most contemporary
works: the two Roman towers flanking the **Portal del Bisbe** (the Bishop's
gateway) face the **College of Architects★★** with engravings in cement by
Picasso. The square itself dates from the end of the Middle Ages. The
semicircular Roman towers were modified in the 16th century and to the
right, the Baroque façade of the **Palau Episcopal,** built in 1784 by Jaume
Mas, closes off the square.

The Cathedral square is flanked by important monuments marking the
transition from the Middle Ages to the first Renaissance (as distinguished
from the romantic 19th-century *Renaixença*) which was late in coming to
Barcelona. To the left is a house known as **la Canonja** (chapter-house) or
Casa de la Pia Almoina, begun in the middle of the 15th century and
enlarged a century later. Opposite you will see the **Casa del Degà** (the
dean's house) which backs onto the **Casa de l'Ardiaca,** built in the 14th
century and cut back in 1420 to make room for the Cathedral square.
The present façade, begun in 1448, was restored at the beginning of this
century. The courtyard is typical of Barcelona, with its palm tree
stretching up to the first floor (which is reached by a fine external
staircase). Built in the Gothic style by Lluís Desplà before 1510, it has
housed the town's historical archives since 1919, as well as the **History
Institute of Barcelona,** founded by the historian and archaeologist,
Agusti' Duran i Sanpere. *(Open Mon-Fri 9am-9pm, Sat 9am-1pm).*
Access to the archives is restricted.

The Cathedral (La Seu)★★ I, C2
Cathedral open 7am-1:30pm and 4-7:30pm. Museum open 9am-1pm.
The main façade of the Cathedral hides its modernity behind a doorway
suggesting the Middle Ages; it was in fact built during the 19th century.

The **Chapel of Santa Llúcia** (facing the Casa de l'Ardiaca on the corner of carrer del Bisbe) is late Roman, dating from after the middle of the 13th century. Originally separate from the Cathedral it now opens on to the cloisters. Note the Roman doorway with columns and capitals — one of the few vestiges of ancient Rome preserved in Barcelona.

The Cathedral **cloisters** (one of the most romantic spots in the city) serve as an oasis of peace for local inhabitants and tourists alike. The Gothic galleries with their pointed arches surround a garden of palms, orange and magnolia trees, and a central pool on which float contented geese. Building began in the 14th century with the chapels and the wings adjacent to the Cathedral and carrer de la Pietat; the rest of the structure dates from the 15th century. Up until the 18th century, most of the chapels served as burial places for the families who had contributed to the building.

One of the chapels houses the **Museu Capitular** where you can see paintings by Catalan artists from the Gothic and Renaissance periods. There is a particularly lovely *Pietà* — the major work of Bartolomé Bermejo from Córdoba, who created it between 1480 and 1490. There are also altarpiece panels: *St Bernardino* and *The Guardian Angel* by Jaume Huguet, and *St Martha* and *Santa Eulalia* by Ramon Destorrents. Other exhibits include works by Sano di Pietro, Jaume Serra and Pere Serafí.

Among the traditions associated with the Cathedral cloisters is the popular dancing egg which, during Easter, is placed atop the fountain and sustained in the air by water pressure. Another tradition is in commemoration of the blind who used to gather here on December 13, the feast of Santa Llúcia, to receive alms from passers-by.

The remains of the palaeo-Christian **basilica** and **baptistery** are underneath the present Cathedral (access through the Museu d'Historia de la Ciutat). Work on the Gothic Cathedral itself began in 1298 under King Jaume II and Bishop Bernat Pelegrí. The oldest parts are in the northern arm of the transept, through which you can pass to see the outside of the **Sant lu doorway** with its carved relief work. The apse was built by Jaume Fabre between 1317 and 1338 and, like the transept, was endowed with Gothic arches before the end of the 14th century. Building was interrupted in 1422.

The Cathedral has three aisles and an ambulatory around the apse. This has pointed arches with carved, polychrome keystones (recently restored). Chapels characteristic of Gothic Catalan architecture fill the side aisles between the buttresses.

Beneath the choir, in the sunken **crypt of Santa Eulalia,** is the white alabaster sarcophagus of the saint—the work of a Pisan artist that dates from around 1325. The choir enclosure was begun in 1517 by the sculptor Bartolomé Ordónez. Note the pulpit and the magnificent Canons' choir **stalls,** created by the sculptor Pere Ça Anglada, who began them in 1399, and by Macià Bonafè who finished them about 1460.

The former chapter-house, now the **Chapel of the Holy Sacrament,** is to the right as you enter from the main door. It was built by Arnau Bargués at the beginning of the 15th century and has a starry, octagonal vault resting on ribbed squinches (corner supports). Note also the tomb of St Oleguer and the famous 15th-century *Christ of Lepanto* which is believed to have been mounted on the prow of the boat belonging to Don Juan of Austria during the Battle of Lepanto (1571) and which, according to legend, pivoted about to avoid being hit by bullets from the Turks.

Stop in one of the chapels on the right to see the Gothic sarcophagus of Ramon de Penyafort that was taken from the former church of Santa Caterina. Then visit the Cathedral **treasury** in the sacristy. The famous missal of Santa Eulalia, illuminated by Destorrents at the beginning of the 15th century, is exhibited here. You can also see the gilt silver Gothic throne believed to be that of Martin I the Humane which, like the Gothic monstrance, is taken out for the Corpus Christi procession.

Leave the Cathedral through the cloisters and the **Porta de la Pietat**. This

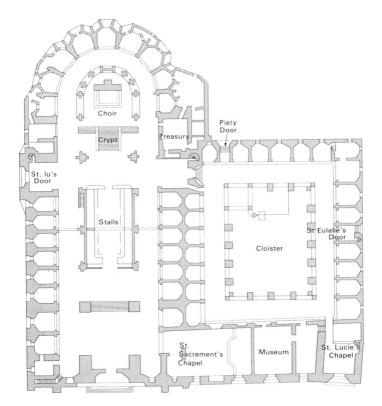

BARCELONA: THE CATHEDRAL

is adorned with a wooden sculpture depicting the donor kneeling at the feet of the Virgin, and dates from the beginning of the 16th century. Once out in the street you will see a series of 14th-century Gothic houses restored in 1929.

Continuing your walk you come to carrer del Paradís. At n°10, the *Centre Excursionista de Catalunya*, you will see four Corinthian columns and their entablature preserved on a podium. They once belonged to the Roman Temple of Augustus which stood on the summit of *Mons Taber*, the hill of the ancient Roman town.

Plaça de Sant Jaume I, C2

This was the heart of both the antique and medieval town — the old forum and market place where the *cardo* and *decumanus* once crossed. The square was the nerve centre for the social and political life of the town. Today, the *Generalitat de Catalunya* and the Town Hall or *Ajuntament*, face each other across the square.

The **Palau de la Generalitat** is on the 'mountain' side of the square *(visits by request, 10am-6pm. April 23, open from noon)*.

The palace has a Gothic entrance on carrer del Bisbe. The doorway was built in 1416 by Marc Safont and decorated in 1418 by Pere Joan Aliot de la Font.

The institution of the Catalan *Cortes* (or Parliament) dates from the reign of Jaume I (1213-1276) but its organization into three sections (ecclesiastic, military and secular) wasn't accomplished until 1283 under Pedro the Great. Pedro the Ceremonious instituted a restricted permanent Parliamentary body called the *Generalitat de Catalunya* and it was in order to house this new institution that the present palace was built in the first half of the 15th century. Climb the large exterior staircase up to the Gothic **chapel of Sant Jordi*** (St George); both staircase and chapel were designed by Marc Safont in the early 15th century, and the chapel is considered the finest example of Catalan architecture in the Flamboyant Gothic style. The interior was modified and enlarged in 1620 with richly worked vaults, a dome and the suspended capitals without columns that are typical of 17th-century architecture in Barcelona. Inside, there is a 15th-century statuette of Sant Jordi, patron saint of the city, and one of the symbols of the *Generalitat.*

Opposite the chapel is the attractive **Orange Tree Courtyard** built in the 16th century. The two main palace buildings open onto this courtyard. The first is the **Saló Daurat** (Gilded Room) with a beautiful ceiling painted and gilded at the end of the 16th century. The decoration also includes ornamental ceramic tiling and tapestries from the same period. The second, the **Saló de Sant Jordi** (St George's Room), is a very large room divided into three aisles, with vaults and a cupola surmounting the transept crossing. Pere Blai was responsible for the project and the room dates from 1596. The paintings on the walls depicting historical scenes date from 1928. This was where the Republic was proclaimed and today, from the balcony overlooking the square, the President of the *Generalitat* makes public speeches. The façade was begun in 1597 with marble from Genoa and recalls the Farnese palace in Rome. The statues date from the 18th century.

Facing the Generalitat is the **Ajuntament*** (Town Hall) or **Casa de la Ciutat**. In the 13th century, when Barcelona's inhabitants obtained recognition of their privileges, the king appointed a few citizens to represent the town. Later the number of councillors in the municipal Assembly reached 100 — giving rise to the famous Consell de Cent (Council of the Hundred). Today's main façade — a neo-Classic monument by Joan Mas opposite the Generalitat — dates from 1845; the Gothic façade on the side of the building in carrer de la Ciutat is an elegant 14th-century construction.

On entering the building from plaça de Sant Jaume behind the old Gothic doorway, you will see the remains of the room where official documents were compiled. It has an interesting ceiling dating from the beginning of the 15th century. A black marble staircase built in 1926 leads up to the main floor. Its walls are decorated with paintings by Miquel Viladrich illustrating passages from *Canigó,* a poem by Mossèn Jacint Verdaguer. Opposite the staircase is the old façade of the Saló de Cent (council chamber) with a 14th-century doorway and 17th-century sculptures. To the right is the gallery of the Gothic courtyard.

The **Saló de Cent** was built in three stages beginning with a magnificent Gothic construction (1369-1407, completed in 1525), wide semicircular Roman arches and a wooden ceiling decorated in the 14th century. This phase was followed by Baroque work from 1628 to 1684 and finally by modern additions consisting of the two last bays, the furniture and most of the paintings. A door on the right leads into the **Public Meetings** room built in a neo-Gothic style during the second half of the 19th century. In the former **office** of the mayor there are paintings by Xavier Nogués (1874-1941) done in 1929, illustrating 19th-century scenes of Barcelona.

Next to it is the **Reception Room** with a ceiling painted by Pei, an artist from the Modernist era. Opposite is the **Private Meetings** chamber decorated by Ricard Canals. Between 1960 and 1965 several rooms nearby were decorated by such well-known painters as F. Galí, Josep Obiols, Ramon Rogent and Antoni Tàpies. The former **Chronicle Chamber** that adjoins the black marble staircase has a dramatic mural decoration by Josep Maria Sert (known for his work on the Vic cathedral) consisting of panel paintings depicting scenes from Catalan expeditions to the Orient in the 14th century. The **chapel** next door is a treasury of academic sculptures by Monjo.

The Town Hall is adorned with many sculptures, among them Josep Llimona's *Sant Miquel* in the hall near the main staircase. Josep Clarà's *La Puixança* (Allegory of Strength) and Subirachs' *Matèria-Forma 8* stand beneath the staircase gallery, while Josep Clarà's *La Deesa* (Goddess) and Frederic Marès' *La Primavera* (Spring) can be seen behind the old Gothic doorway.

The Ajuntament was enlarged in the 19th century when an annex was added to the back façade (the Casa Nova). In 1982, the **Municipal Information Office** was set up to the left of the main entrance and decorated with vault frescoes by Ràfols Casamada.

Around the Royal Palace I, C2

Your itinerary could continue down carrer d'Hèrcules, which ends at the small **plaça Sant Just,** and its church. The square dates back to earliest Christian antiquity and was traditionally the burial place of the first martyrs. The Gothic **fountain** (1367) by Joan Fiveller was altered in the neo-Classic era. At the end of bajada Caçador the large **palace of the Countess of Palamós,** where the governor-general of Catalonia lived at the end of the 15th century, was built over the Roman wall and preserves some Roman and Gothic remains. During medieval times it was the largest private palace in Barcelona and today it houses the Acadèmia de Bones Lletres. On the square itself you will see the church of **Sants Just i Pastor** which was rebuilt in the Gothic period (14th-15th centuries) when it belonged to the Royal parish. Inside, near the apse, the chapel of Sant Feliu contains an **altarpiece** begun in 1525 by the Flemish sculptor, Jean de Bruxelles and painted by the Portuguese artist, Pero Nuñez.

By taking carrer Llibreteria you eventually reach **plaça del Rei,** the noblest of Barcelona's medieval squares. The Palau Reial Major (Royal Palace) stands at the end of the square with the palatine chapel or Capella de Santa Agata on the right and the former Palau del Lloctinent (Lieutenant's Palace), now the Archives of the Crown of Aragon, on the left. Opposite the Royal Palace, the Casa Clariana-Padellàs houses the Museu d'Historia de la Ciutat.

The present **Palau Reial Major** dates for the most part from the 14th century. *(Open Mon 3-8pm; Wed-Sat 9am-8pm; Sun 9am-1:30pm.)* It originated earlier, at the end of the 10th century and the beginning of the 11th, when a first palace for the Counts of Barcelona was built not far from the former Visigoth palace.

The main palace façade is a monumental structure with large arches connecting the buttresses. The 16th-century mirador on the upper part known as King Martin's watch-tower has five tiers of superimposed arches. The monumental entrance to the palace leads directly to the Throne Room or **Saló del Tinell;** the name refers to a display shelf of luxurious crockery. It's an impressive room (108 ft/33 m long, 56 ft/ 17m high) with six semicircular Roman arches supporting a wooden ceiling in the central part of the room and vaults at the ends. Building took place from 1359 to 1362 under Pedro the Ceremonious. Nineteen alabaster statues of the 11 Counts of Barcelona and the eight successive kings adorn the Throne Room, built by Master Aloi between 1342 and 1350. The room has been the setting for many historical events from the time when the *Cortes* met here in the 1370s to 1461 and 1472, when it was used as a chapel of rest by the Prince of Viana and his father, Juan II. Legend has it that this was also where Christopher Colombus first met the Catholic monarchs on his return in 1493 from his first trip to the Americas.

The wall paintings in the antechamber were found in the main room. They date from about 1300 and illustrate scenes from the life of Barcelona's high society at the beginning of the Gothic era, treating two essential aspects: warfare and court life.

From the Saló del Tinell you pass onto a loggia overlooking the courtyard which served as the palace orchard in the Middle Ages. Then you enter the **Capella de Santa Agata***. This chapel replaced the former

11th-century oratory and was built onto the oratory wall in 1302 for Jaume II and his wife Blanche d'Anjou. Work was directed first by Bertran Riquer, then by Jaume del Rei and finally by Pere Oliva. The chapel consists of a single nave punctuated by three semicircular transversal arches supported by buttresses covered in fine wood. Leading off from the side walls are the king's and queen's staircases which extend to the choir and the royal chambers. If one of the monarchs fell ill, he or she could attend services directly from the palace by means of a window in the wall behind the choir. Originally, the only access to the chapel was through the palace. The doorway now facing the square dates from the 15th century.

Between 1338 and 1355 the **Queen's chapel** was built near the altar. It was dedicated to St Nicolas and adorned with a carved decoration by Jaume Cascalls. Under Martin I another chapel was built near the entrance, inside a tower in the Roman wall. Sitting imposingly on the main altar is the famous *altarpiece of Constable Pedro of Portugal* (1464-1466), the work of the painter Jaume Huguet. The *Adoration of the Magi* in the centre is considered one of the most important paintings of the Gothic period. The *Crucifixion* is depicted on the upper part; on the wings you can see the *Annunciation* and the *Nativity*; the *Resurrection* and the *Ascension* in the middle; *Pentecost* and the *Dormition* at the bottom.

Casa Clariana-Padellàs is a 16th-century Gothic edifice standing opposite the Royal Palace on the other side of the square. It belonged to a wealthy merchant and, when via Laietana was being built, it was moved stone by stone from the old carrer dels Mercaders (Merchants' street) to its present position. Its courtyard has an open staircase and a gallery of Gothic arches supported by small columns typical of large houses built in the transition period between the late Middle Ages and the Renaissance. Today it houses the History Museum, **Museu d'Historia de la Ciutat** (see 'Barcelona's Museums', p. 131).

The **Palau del Lloctinent*** (Lieutenant's Palace) stands opposite the chapel of Santa Agata. You enter the building from carrer dels Comtes de Barcelona. Today the palace houses the Archives of the Crown of Aragon. In 1547, when the Corts Catalanes (Parliament) approved the project for an annex to the Royal Palace, work went ahead under Antoni Carbonell and was most probably finished ten years later. The three façades of the palace with their subtle mixture of Gothic and Renaissance styles are typical of Catalan architecture of the first half of the 16th century. The square courtyard inside, with two floors of arches supported by Tuscan columns, belongs to the Renaissance period, as does the staircase. The carved door on the ground floor dating from 1975 is by Subirachs.

Continue along carrer dels Comtes de Barcelona past the St Yves doorway of the Cathedral and you come to the former palace orchard, now an Italian-style courtyard. From here you can enter the **Museu Marès** (see 'Barcelona's Museums', p. 131).

Come back towards the Cathedral square and turn right into carrer Tapineria (the name comes from '*tapins*' meaning shoes, as this was where the cobblers once worked) for a walk alongside the ancient walls. You arrive in **plaça del comte Berenguer el Gran** dominated by an equestrian statue of the Count Berenguer by Josep Llimona. Here you will admire whole sections of the Roman and medieval walls that have been restored carefully.

The Santa Maria del Mar district I, D2-3

By following the ancient city walls you reach plaça de l'Angel, I, C2, where you cross via Laietana into another part of old Barcelona.

Carrer Argenteria leads into the heart of what was the artisan quarter during the Middle Ages. Traces still remain in the names of the streets: Argenteria (silversmiths), Mercaders (merchants), Sombrerers (hatters), Mirallers (mirror cutters), Espaseria (swords), Vidrieria (glassworkers),

A taste for decorated façades marked the architecture of Barcelona from the 18th century until the Modernist movement at the beginning of the 20th century.

Formatgeria (cheese makers) and so on. Carrer Argenteria ends at the small plaça Santa Maria in front of the church of Santa Maria del Mar.

Known as the 'Cathedral of the Ribera district', **Santa Maria del Mar**** is one of the most important Gothic churches in Barcelona. It was begun by the architect Berenguer de Montagut in 1329 and finished unusually quickly in 1384. It is the symbol of the economic and political power of the district in the Middle Ages, when merchants and shipowners grew rich through Catalonia's Mediterranean expansionism. The church was built to commemorate the conquest of Sardinia by the Catalans. It is a homogenous, gracefully proportioned building and one of the few major Gothic monuments to have been finished according to the original plan. The façade bears the characteristics of Catalan Gothic architecture: the importance of horizontal as opposed to vertical lines, massive buttresses, and the predominance of solid wall over gaps or openings. The splayed doorway retains sculptures on the tympanum and statues on either side of St Peter and St Paul. Several modifications on the upper part of the façade have not detracted from the whole. These include the 15th-century rose window, the north tower finished in 1496 and the south one only completed in 1902.

The interior of Santa Maria del Mar is a wonderful example of the Mediterranean Gothic Architectural style. Three extremely high aisles (121 ft/37 m) give it the impression of a vast church-hall. The slender octagonal columns are such light supports they in no way break the spacial unity of the whole. The church has some highly valuable stained glass from the beginning of the 15th century such as the *Ascension* in the Santa Maria chapel and the window in the St Raphael chapel where the large *Last Judgement* by Senier Desmanes dates from 1494. Equally important from an art history point of view is the rose window of the *Coronation of the Virgin*.

There is a **Parish Museum** at nº 6 carrer Sombrerers (*open 10am-1pm, 3-7:30pm.*)

Behind Santa Maria del Mar you come to **passeig del Born** which, from the 13th to the 17th century, was a place for public holiday celebrations, jousts, tournaments, processions, carnivals and fairs. **Carrer de Montcada*** begins from here and, thanks to its fine palaces, illustrates more than any other street the aristocratic aspect the quarter had from the Middle Ages to the end of the 18th century. Immediately to the right is a small street, carrer Mosques ('street of the Flies'), the narrowest street in Barcelona. All along carrer de Montcada you will see the smooth austere façades of palaces adorned here and there with delicate carvings, saving their grandeur and richness for the interior courtyards, staircases, balconies and galleries. The street is a living museum demonstrating the way Barcelona's residential quarters developed through the Gothic, Renaissance and Baroque styles. The wealth of these fortified constructions corresponds to the period (mainly in the 15th century) when Catalonia experienced rapid maritime expansion and economic growth. When the sea routes were changed to the Atlantic, the wealthy families of Barcelona entered a period of economic decline; nonetheless, many continued to live in the palaces along this street until the last century.

There are four main palaces:

● **Casa Cervelló-Giudice**, at nº 25, is a 15th-century palace that was altered in the 16th century. It has one of the most beautiful façades in Barcelona with its Gothic bearing and large windows adorned with 17th-century balconies. Originally the residence of the Cervelló family — important members of the Catalan nobility — it passed into the hands of the Giudice, a family of traders from Genoa who settled in Barcelona in the 18th century. Today the palace houses the Maeght Gallery.

● **Palau Dalmases**, at nº 20, opposite the above palace, is the result of a revamping in the 17th century which retained little of the original 15th-century Gothic residence other than the chapel, preserved on the main floor. It is, however, a good example of Barcelona's Baroque architecture — especially the courtyard staircase. Today the palace houses an organization that promotes Catalan culture.

● **Palau dels Marquesos de Llió**, at nº 12, is a 14th-century edifice rebuilt by the Marquis of Llió in the 18th century. Some Gothic elements, such as the courtyard, have been preserved as well as some of the 16th-century alterations. Today, along with the neighbouring Palau Nadal, the palace houses the Rocamora collection of textiles, costumes and lace in its **Museu del Tèxtil i de la Indumentaria** (see 'Barcelona's Museums', p. 131).

● **Palau Berenguer d'Aguilar,** at nº 15, stands opposite the above. Although it has maintained elements from the 13th and 14th centuries, this palace is mainly 15th-century. It was commissioned by Joan Berenguer d'Aguilar and may have been built by Marc Safont, an architect who worked on the Generalitat palace. The courtyard and the interior are particularly noteworthy with 13th-century wall paintings illustrating the conquest of Majorca. The municipality of Barcelona bought the palace in 1953 and, after restoring it (1960-1963), installed the Picasso museum. The museum has spread to the **Palau de Castellet,** the palace next door (nº 17), which has a sumptuous 19th-century neo-Classical salon, and to the **Palau Meca** (nº 19). (See 'Barcelona's Museums', p. 132).

In the middle of the 19th century, the upper part of carrer de Montcada was crossed at right angles by the newly built carrer de la Princesa. Once you've crossed carrer de la Princesa continue to carrer Carders where at nº 2 you will see the **Marcús chapel**. It is one of Barcelona's few preserved Roman churches and was originally built as the chapel of a hospital for the poor. Financed in the second half of the 12th century by Bernardí Marcús, a merchant, it has suffered from excessive restoration as well as from alteration along neo-Classical lines during the 19th century.

If you wander through these little streets in a northerly direction you will eventually reach carrer Sant Pere més Alt and, on the right, the plaça Sant Pere with the church of **Sant Pere de les Puel.les,** I, D1. Founded by the Visigoths and members of the Carolingian dynasty, you can see remains of the latter period in the chapel of St Saturn. The Gothic portal dates from the 15th century; otherwise the church has undergone extensive modern repairs.

From here walk left all the way along carrer Sant Pere més Alt to the corner of carrer Amadeu Vives. Here you will see the exuberant **Palau de la Música Catalana,** built between 1905 and 1908 by the architect Lluís Domènech i Montaner. It is one of Barcelona's most spectacular Modernist buildings. A temple to the Catalan art of music, it replaced the former concert hall and headquarters of Orfeó Català, installed there since 1891. Domènech i Montaner undertook the construction of the new building with great creative liberty while retaining the symbolic significance the palace would take on. The use of a laminated iron structure resting on a set of isolated stanchions left not only the walls but also the central part of the building free from all supporting constraints. This meant that there was room for an unparalleled profusion of ornamentation including panes of stained glass. Some of the ornamentation, such as the inverted cupola in the main room, are striking in their originality. The wealth of decoration is extraordinary; Domènech called upon all the minor art forms of the time, including mosaics and tiles, and integrated them into his architecture. There is also a large collection of sculpture, both inside and outside the palace. Among these works is a group by Miquel Bray evoking the concept of the popular song and an arch symbolizing popular and classical music. The stage *Muses* by Eusebi Arnau represent national music, and the work by Gargallo to the left of the stage is an evocation of Catalan song.

Continuing on to via Laietana, look to the right and, on the corner of carrer Jonqueres, you will see the headquarters of the **Caixa de Pensions,** by Enric Sagnier — another Modernist building, this time in neo-Gothic style (1914-1917). At n° 50, on the corner of plaça Lluís Millet, the former **Corporació dels Velers o de la Seda** (Guild of Drapers and Silk Merchants) narrowly escaped demolition in 1913 when via Laietana was being built. The building dates from 1758-1763 and the decorative engravings were redone during the restoration of 1931.

By taking carrer Comtal opposite, then carrer Amargós to the left, you come to carrer Montsió. At n° 3 bis, you will see one of the first houses by Puig i Cadafalch (1895-1896) in which he developed his personal interpretation of models from the Middle Ages. The famous bar, **Els Quatre Gats** (the Four Cats) on the ground floor, is where artists such as Casas, Nonel, Picassa and Utrillo used to gather and exhibit their work.

If you continue along the street you reach avinguda Portal de l'Àngel and, on the left, carrer de Santa Anna which leads to the church of the same name (n° 27-28). In 1141 the Order of the Holy Sepulchre was founded here and a monastery was built together with the collegiate church of **Santa Anna.** This benefited from a general alteration in the 15th century mainly with the building of the cloisters and the chapter house. By following carrer Rivadeneyra from this point, you can return to plaça de Catalunya.

Les Demoiselles d'Avignon

Picasso studied in Barcelona where he settled in 1895 and consequently took part in the artistic movements of Catalonia until he moved to Paris in 1904. He is the best-known painter of the 20th century with strong ties to Paris and Barcelona, each of which have a museum of his work. Picasso kept in close touch with the Catalan capital throughout his life.

One of the artist's most famous works, *Les Demoiselles d'Avignon* (1907), now hangs in the Museum of Modern Art in New York. It illustrates a group of women paradoxically hiding their nudity yet simultaneously flaunting themselves through their postures. An inspired, mysterious work, it is considered a masterpiece of modern painting. The name does not derive from the town in the south of France but rather from carrer d'Avinyó in the old town of Barcelona. During the 19th century, some of the stately medieval and classic mansions in the lower part of the street were converted into brothels. Their part in the history of art and the origin of Cubism has not often been stressed; it is from them that Picasso drew his inspiration.

THE RAMBLAS

The Ramblas have become a symbol of the town. They make up Barcelona's liveliest street where the action is a non-stop, day and night affair. You will certainly find yourself wandering down the Ramblas at some time during your visit and will enjoy sitting at one of the outdoor café tables to watch the crowd pass by, and drink in the cosmopolitan atmosphere. The street can be written in the singular or in the plural and changes its name as well as its atmosphere with each new section. The Ramblas lead exuberantly down to the sea, reflecting the character of Barcelona in concentrated form. Serving at once as agora and salon, they are also an open-air market for a variety of goods ranging from the ordinary to the sophisticated — birds, flowers, books, newspapers, arts, crafts, and so on.

Before beginning the Ramblas itinerary from **plaça de Catalunya,** I, C1, you might want to stroll up carrer de Pelai and ronda Universitat to plaça de la Universitat, where the old university of Barcelona stands. It was built by Elies Rogent i Amat between 1860 and 1872 and is a good example of neo-Roman architecture. Its decorative borrowings from Byzantine and Islamic arts are in keeping with the European trends at the time. Today it houses a large library.

The Ramblas begin from plaça de Catalunya. As they head toward the harbour the name changes five times: rambla de Canaletes, rambla dels Estudis, rambla de Sant Josep, rambla dels Caputxins and rambla Santa Mònica.

It is said of the **Canaletes fountain,** which gave its name to the uppermost section of the Ramblas, that whoever drinks its water will either never leave Barcelona or will certainly come back. The groups of people crowding round it seem to be always discussing soccer, or, failing that, politics. If you would like to see the remains of a **Roman necropolis,** take carrer de la Canuda to the left to plaça Vila de Madrid, again on the left, where there are open monumental tombs.

Originally, the Rambla was a stream outside the fortified Roman town which marked the city's western boundary in the 13th century; the walls begun by Jaume I were built along it. During the 16th and 17th centuries, the building of numerous monasteries in the Raval district (between the antique city and Montjuïc) gradually transformed the stream into a well-used thoroughfare. However, its definitive form did not take shape until the early 18th century when houses were built over the ancient Gothic walls. Various 19th-century changes transformed the promenade into the bustling thoroughfare you will experience today.

The Rambla of the Birds I, B1

The upper section of the Ramblas is known as **rambla dels Ocells** (of the birds) because of its bird market. You may notice that it bends into a slight curve here, recalling the shape of the dried-out river bed.

Its official name, rambla dels Estudis, derives from the former university (Estudi General) which stood here from the 15th century until the beginning of the 18th century, when Felipe V did away with it. A Jesuit convent once took over the entire right side, but today all that remains is the **church of Bethlehem** (Betlem) built between 1681 and 1732. It has a semicircular apse and a nave flanked by side chapels. Once its chapels were endowed with rich wooden tribunes reserved for the aristocracy but these disappeared in the fire of 1936. The church exterior is characterized by a regular embossed pattern. Apart from the doorway giving onto the Rambla, the main portal — an example of typical Catalan Baroque style — is on carrer del Carme. The sculptures adorning it are of St Ignatius and St Francis of Borja.

The **Palau Moja** stands on the other side of the Rambla on the corner of carrer Portaferrissa. It has been carefully restored and now houses the Department of Culture of the Generalitat de Catalunya. Two architects, Josep i Pau and Pas i Dordal, were responsible for construction, which

The Ramblas form a continuous wide avenue, despite the changing names, that stretches from plaça de Catalunya to the harbour. Lined with cafés, shops and outdoor stands — many open day and night — this is undoubtedly the liveliest street in the city.

took place from 1774 to 1790. In spite of its many alterations this neo-classical building with its sober lines lends a monumental air to the Ramblas. The present building occupies the site of an earlier palace built against the ancient city walls in 1702. It was one of the first with windows cut directly into the wall. Once rebuilt it gained great popularity because of its painted façades. During the Napoleonic occupation it was the residence of Chebrun, the French Prefect in Barcelona. Inside, the main reception room is one of the town's most luxurious and retains on two levels a 1790 decor painted by Francesc Pla, known as El Vigatà.

The Rambla of the Flowers and its neighbourhood I, B1-2

The **rambla de Sant Josep** is perhaps the most characteristic of the ramblas thanks to its flower market (hence its sobriquet rambla de les Flors). Unfortunately, the old cast-iron kiosks of last century have given way to more mobile stalls, but the florists are just as lively and the colours in the market change exuberantly according to the season. The attraction of this particular rambla for Barcelonans is more than sentimental as it is said that the flower-sellers here are the most beautiful in town; the painter Ramon Casas found his best model here and later married her.

On the right, set back from the street is the **Palau de la Virreina***. Manuel Amat, viceroy to Peru, sent the plans for the residence from Lima in 1771 and building was completed in 1778. However, Amat died a few years after his return to Barcelona. As his wife continued to live in the palace it was dubbed 'the palace of the Vice-Reine' (Virreina). Inside, two wide symmetrical staircases rise up on either side of a large hall. The **Museu Gabinet Postal** is on the first floor *(open Mon-Sat 9:30am-2pm, 6-9pm; closed Sun and holidays)*.

Several yards further on you come to the most popular covered market in town, the **Mercat de Sant Josep** or **Mercat de la Boqueria.** It stands on the site of the former Discalced (bare-foot) Carmelites of St Joseph Convent (1593). The market was built in several stages between 1840 and 1914. Its architecture is typical of the iron structures covering large areas (such as markets and train stations) that were put up in the 19th century and the ironwork and coloured glass decoration at the entrance well illustrates the Modernist trend. A wander through gives you a glimpse of working life in Barcelona with the shouts of the sellers and the colours and smells of the different stalls. You can find everything here from the most common foodstuffs to the most exquisite delicacy. Beside the market, on the corner of carrer Petxina, is **Figueras,** an old grocer's-confectioner's decorated by Antoni Ros in 1902 and restored in 1986. It is another fine testimony to Modernist commercial architecture.

Before continuing up the rambla dels Caputxins you can take one or two excursions to either side of the Ramblas. If you take carrer de Hospital to the right you reach the former Hospital de la Santa Creu after leaving (on your left) the 1728 Baroque church of **Sant Augustí.**

The **Hospital de la Santa Creu*** consists of a group of buildings, the earliest of which dates from 1401. At the end of the Middle Ages this renowned establishment underwent a series of enlargements resulting in the building you see today. The hospital has been restored several times since 1929 and now houses a number of institutions including the Academy of Medicine, the Institute of Catalan Studies, the National Library of Catalonia and the Municipal Conservatory of Decorative Arts (Escola Massana) as well as various temporary exhibitions. You enter the complex through the 16th-century façade (carrer de Hospital 56) which has made use of some of the windows from the earlier Gothic hospital.

Beyond the cloister you reach a courtyard giving into carrer del Carme. On the right you will see the noble neo-classical façade of the **Academia de Medicina,** which has a curious circular room reminiscent of the days when surgery was performed here. On the left is the former convalescent home. This section of the complex was begun in 1629 and is known for its magnificent decoration of earthenware tiling carried out by the best ceramists of the day. The finest example is the artwork in the hall by Llorenç Passolas dating from 1680-1681. Blues, yellows and greens predominate in scenes illustrating the life of St Paul. The two-tiered cloister served as a model in the 17th century for numerous inner courtyards in the town. In this particular case the grandiose aspect of the whole has been set off by a spectacular decorative device: the back of the first floor of the cloister, opposite the entrance, opens onto a hanging garden. The staircase on the left hand side of the courtyard leads to the **National Library of Catalonia*** set impressively in Gothic naves on the first floor of the former hospital.

By taking carrer Junta de Comerç or carrer Robador you reach carrer de Sant Pau which crosses one of Barcelona's red-light districts (where it is advisable to guard your cameras, handbags and so on). At the end of carrer de Sant Pau you come to the church of the former monastery of **Sant Pau del Camp*.** Its name 'in the Fields' indicates that it was once a

The Institute of Catalan Studies

The Institut d'Estudis Catalans, an academic, scientific and cultural corporation, was founded on June 18, 1907, by Enric Prat de la Riba. Its principal aim is the study of all aspects of Catalan culture in addition to high-level scientific research.

A member of the International Academic Union since 1922, it returned in 1982 to its former premises in the convalescent home of the old Hospital de la Santa Creu in Barcelona. The Institute participates actively in Catalan cultural life with programs for research and international cooperation, and also plays a normative role in language matters. It is made up of various departments (History-Archaeology, Philology, Sciences, Philosophy and Social Sciences) and their subsidiary sections.

good distance from the town centre. It's a rare example of Barcelona's Roman architecture and retains large carved sections from the Visigoth era which have been integrated into the façade. The present edifice (built to a Greek cross plan) dates from the 12th century and is completed by a charming little Roman cloister with carved capitals.

Cross over the Rambla into carrer Cardenal Casanas and walk along to plaça del Pi which, together with plaça Sant Josep Oriol, looks onto the Gothic church of **Santa Maria del Pi**. The church was begun in 1322 and bears the characteristics of 14th-century Gothic Catalan architecture, namely a massive, impenetrable-looking exterior, a rectangular façade with a rose window and a finely-decorated doorway, and inside an impression of spacial unity created by a single nave lined with side chapels. The number of palaces lining the square outside testifies to the intense architectural activity of Barcelona's past. Carrer Petritxol opposite was a centre of artistic life at the end of the 19th century and during the first half of the 20th, thanks to Sala Parés, the first art gallery in town (1884) where the works of great Catalan artists from the turn of the century (including Rusiñol, Casas, Miró and Picasso) were displayed. The street is still lively with shops, art galleries and *granges* (Catalan tearooms and confectioners).

The Rambla of Entertainment I, B2

The walk down the Ramblas continues into **rambla dels Caputxins** (or rambla del Centre), the section of the street that has been used the longest as a promenade. Until 1775 the whole of the left side was taken up by a Capuchin convent, while on the right there was a Trinitarian convent and three colleges, namely those of the Carmelites, St Bonaventure and St Ange. In 1824, a perfectly straight street, carrer de Ferran, was built to connect the Rambla to the heart of the old town. Then in 1848 the buildings lining plaça Reial went up. In 1844, on the site of the former Trinitarian convent, the building of Barcelona's opera, the **Gran Teatre del Liceu★**, began under the architect Miguel Garriga i Roca. It was inaugurated in 1848 and, despite successive repairs, has managed to maintain both its 19th-century decor (especially in the main concert hall). *Individual or small group tours of up to 5 people: Mon-Fri at 11:30am and 12:15pm. Group reservations in advance for visits Mon, Wed and Fri, 10am-1pm. Length of visit: 30 mins. Information,* ☎ *(93) 318 9122.*

The **Hotel Oriente,** a short distance beyond, has preserved parts of the former St Bonaventure college.

Retrace your steps to the small square on the Ramblas known as **Pla de la Boqueria**; the ornamental ground mosaic in the central promenade is by Miró. **Casa Bruno Quadros**, on the corner of the Ramblas and carrer Casañas, is a neo-Egyptian-style building reflecting the taste for Orientalism which prevailed at the end of the 19th century. Its Chinese dragon dominating the square is a well-known landmark.

On the right in carrer Nou de la Rambla (nº 3-5) you will see the **Palau Güell****, now home of the Institut del Teatre and the **Museu de les arts de l'Espectacle**. It was built by Antoni Gaudí between 1886 and 1890 and marks the beginning of this renowned architect's most prolific period. After a look at the façade with its wrought ironwork (an insignia of Gaudí's style), don't miss the interior. Here you will admire the architect's approach to filling space and the care he took to integrate the decor and furniture with the architecture. All these have been preserved.

The palace was originally built as a town house for the Güell family (1886-1888). When designing it Gaudí devoted much attention to the organization of space, from the underground stables to the staircase and, most particularly, the extraordinary central room. This is covered by a parabolic cupola which juts out in a cone shape onto the terrace. It is surrounded by carved chimneys adorned with pieces of ceramic tiling.

Across the rambla dels Caputxins, at nº 74, is the **Café de l'Opera** which has retained its elegant style. On the same side of the Rambla, directly opposite carrer Nou de la Rambla, is the entrance to **plaça Reial*** (the Royal square). Built between 1848 and 1859, the square was inspired by French town-planning from the Napoleonic period. The architect Francesc Daniel Molina managed to integrate the large quadrangular space into the irregular layout of the old quarter.

With its palm trees and bars, its porticoed arcades, and its streetlamps designed by Gaudí to match the cast-iron fountain of the *Three Graces*, it is one of the most pleasant places in Barcelona. Recent restoration has given a boost to its role as a convivial and fashionable centre. The interesting alleyways connecting it to the rest of the town were given special attention by the builders. Passeig Madoz was given the design of a courtyard, passeig Colom that of a street, and passeig Bacardí (1856) has a romantic air about it with its glass and iron bridge. Not very long ago the square still had a lot of old shops and, today, on the corner of carrer del Vidre and carrer les Heures, there is a herbalist's shop known as the King's herbalist which dates from the Romantic period.

Return to the Ramblas and continue to **Pla del Teatre** where the town's first theatre was set up in the 16th century. Today the square is dominated by the monument dedicated to the founder of Catalan theatre, Frederic Soler, known as Pitarra, by the architect Falqués and the sculptor Querol (1900). Unfortunately, the old **Teatre Principal** at nº 27-29 has been partly altered.

The Rambla of the Harbour I, B3

As you walk down rambla Santa Mònica towards the sea you leave the **Barri Xinès** (Chinese Quarter) on your right. This area, one of the town's hot-spots, so often praised by writers, has lost some of its aura as a forbidden zone. Passeig Banca leads left to the **Museu de Cera** (Wax Museum, see 'Barcelona's Museums', p. 130).

This section of the Ramblas is dominated by the Christopher Columbus monument (see p. 34) and forms the approach to the harbour. It was once frequented by groups of sailors and fishermen but they have been replaced by street hawkers and young craftsmen who sell their products to passers-by. On the right are the remains of the former convent of **Santa Mònica**. Of particular note is the Baroque cloister. On the left (nº 8) you will see the **Palau March de Reus,** built in 1776, after the demolition of the last vestiges of the medieval walls, for Francesc March, a rich merchant from the town of Reus. The palace has been restored and is now the headquarters of the Generalitat's Department of Culture.

This itinerary can end here but is really preliminary to a longer one which begins at the foot of the Columbus monument and follows the seafront to the Parc de la Ciutadella.

The seafront I, B3

Barcelona's seafront is both part of, and yet at some distance from, the rest of the town, a characteristic which distinguishes it from other

A replica of the Santa María, one of the ships that sailed to the Americas on Columbus' 1492 voyage, can be visited at the nearby Museu Marítim.

Mediterranean ports. It is not the real harbour district in the true sense of the term as the seafarers have their own quarter, Barceloneta, beyond the harbour to the east. Furthermore, the adventure seekers, typical of other Mediterranean ports, are concentrated in the Barri Xinès (Chinese Quarter) slightly inland.

Throughout the 19th century Barcelona's seafront was one of the middle-class areas of town. Although the wealthy have since deserted it the whole district has kept the stately, orderly look which once secured its reputation. During Antiquity the town was situated quite a distance from the sea and it wasn't until the Middle Ages that the pools and swamps were developed. The harbour site was set up in its present position in 1474. Travelers arriving in Barcelona by sea at that time would have noticed immediately two Gothic markets (the Cloth Market and the Exchange Building) as well as the convent of St Francis and the shipyards.

At the end of rambla Santa Mònica you will see **Drassanes**, I, B3, a group of some of the best preserved medieval shipyards in the West. They were begun at the end of the 14th century, enlarged in the 17th and from the Middle Ages to the 18th century built a great many ships for the Catalan war fleet and for rich merchants. Ricard Bofill, a contemporary architect, has compared the Gothic architecture of the shipyards to the industrial architecture of the last century. 'I would call the industrial Gothic Drassanes the first great industrial edifice in Barcelona and a precedent to the wonderful factories built at the end of the last century. It should serve as an example to prove that architecture and industrial activity are not opposing terms; on the contrary, the point where they intersect has created the driving force behind the development of Mediterranean towns — towns designed not merely for habitation or just compartmentalized into zones but in which there is a mixture of buildings for residence, work, institutions and leisure'. (From *Edificios singulares de Barcelona* in *Divina Barcelona*, nº 2, 1988, p. 106.) Today the Drassanes house the **Museu Marítim** (see 'Barcelona's Museums', p. 132).

Opposite the Drassanes is the **New Customs House,** a colossal edifice built between 1896 and 1902 by Enric Sagnier.

The **Christopher Columbus Monument,** I, B3, stands on plaça Portal de la Pau at the point where the Ramblas and passeig de Colom meet. It's the most popular landmark in Barcelona, the Catalan capital's equivalent of the Statue of Liberty, built to commemorate the return of the great navigator after his discovery of America. It consists of a pedestal supporting a wrought-iron column crowned by a globe. A bronze statue of Christopher Columbus pointing seawards stands on top of this globe. Construction began in 1882 and was finished in 1886. The monument, by Gaietà Buigas, caused a sensation at the Universal Exhibition of 1888. The overall height is 197 ft/60 m, and the statue itself is 25 ft/7.5 m high. Inside the hollow pedestal and column there is an elevator that will take you up to the lookout point at the top. *Open — variable timetable — Easter, 10am-8pm; June 15-Sept 30, 9am-9pm; the rest of the year 10am-2pm and 3:30-6:30pm. Closed Jan 1 and 6, Dec 25 and 26. Information on group visits,* ☎ *(93) 302 5224.*

The harbour opens out at the foot of the monument, with Barceloneta to the left. It is one of the largest in the Mediterranean; it has a long, eventful history and is an inevitable stopover for major shipping lines. Its annual traffic exceeds 16 million tons. It has a good number of docks, a harbour station, sailing clubs and a well-equipped marina. You can interrupt your itinerary with a trip on one of the *golondrines* — small tourist motorboats opposite the Columbus monument that cross the harbour to the jetty and afford a good view of the town and Montjuïc hill. *Departures every half-hour 10:30am-1pm and 3-5pm in winter; 10am-8pm in summer. Information,* ☎ *(93) 310 0382.*

If you prefer an aerial view of town from the port you can take a cable-car from Barceloneta to Montjuïc. *Open Oct-June, Mon-Fri 11:30am-6pm; weekends and holidays 11am-6:45pm; in summer every day from 11am-9pm. Information,* ☎ *(93) 310 1344 and 241 4820.*

Passeig de Colom, I, BC3, has undergone recent change thanks to the development of Molls Bosch i Alsina (also known as Moll de la Fusta) by the architect Solà-Morales. It has two levels of promenade. Since its inauguration in 1988 it has attracted Barcelonans (especially the young) back to this part of town and at the same time has solved the tricky traffic problem on the seafront.

The group of sculptures by Francisco López known as *Hommage to the Catalan Mediterranean* makes new use of figures by Miguel Blai. Accompanying the group is a series of bronze sculptures by Bob Krier representing some of Barcelona's illustrious citizens.

Plaça Duc de Medinaceli, I, B3, was designed by Francesc Daniel Molina in 1844 and embellished with the first iron column cast in the town. This was integrated into the monumental fountain in 1851. Running past the back of the square in carrer Ample, now a working-class area that was one of Barcelona's aristocratic streets from the 16th to the 19th century. Carrer de la Mercè leads off from the middle of the square to the square of the same name upon which stands the **la Mercè★.** The curved Baroque façade of this church by Jaume Mas is adorned with sculptures by Carles Grau.

According to tradition, the Virgin Mary appeared in a dream to Sant Pere Nolasque, Sant Ramon de Penyafort and Jaume I, urging them to found a monastic order for the redemption of Christians captured by Muslim pirates. For this reason the Virgin of Mercy, patron saint of the town, is particularly venerated in Barcelona. In 1267 the new Order of Mercy, or Mercedarians, was given a first church on the site where the present edifice, built between 1765 and 1775, now stands. The church is Baroque with a single nave, side chapels, a barely protruding transept and a dome over the crossing. Its sumptuous decoration makes it one of the jewels of Counter-Reformation architecture. It has retained two important Gothic works — inside, a statue of *Our Lady of Mercy* by Pere Moragues dating from 1361 (the figure of the Child is a 15th-century addition) and outside (looking onto carrer Ample) the façade that once belonged to the Gothic church of Sant Miquel and which was brought here at the beginning of the 19th century. On the right-hand side you will see an attractive bridge connecting the church to the former convent built between 1639 and 1642 by the Santacana architects. You will have to go to passeig de Colom n° 14-16 to see the façade (1928), in the style inspired by the colossal Italian buildings erected at the time of Mussolini. Inside, is one of the most beautiful 17th-century cloisters in Barcelona.

By continuing along passeig Colom or carrer Ample (if you take this street, there is a fine 17th-century palace, the **Palau Sessa-Larrard,** at n° 28) you come to plaça d'Antoní López and the **Post and Tele-communications** building (Correus i Telègrafs). It was built by Josep Goday and Jaume Torres between 1914 and 1927 to close off via Laietana. Inside, the great hall with overhead lighting was adorned by the major Catalan painters and decorators of the first half of this century, namely Galí, Obiols, Labarta and Canyelles.

From the other side of via Laietana you will see the **Llotja** (Exchange building) which can be reached either by carrer Consolat del Mar or passeig d'Isabel II. Like most large medieval towns, Barcelona had an Exchange or a bargaining room for commercial dealings from at least the middle of the 14th century but it wasn't until the end of the century that a large, solid room, now partly preserved, was built under the patronage of Pedro the Ceremonious by the architect Pere Arvey. After a variety of problems the edifice was rebuilt according to neo-Classical taste at the end of the 18th century, and this is what you see today. The large Gothic room and the structure of the building were kept but the façades were standardized into a classic style and the other rooms were redecorated. Up until a few years ago the Llotja housed Barcelona's Fine Arts School from which most of the great Catalan artists of this century graduated; today it is the Produce Exchange.

In the middle of plaça de Palau (the name comes from the viceroy's palace, the Exchange building's counterpart) rises the monument to the **Spirit of Catalonia,** I, D3, dating from the Romantic period. On the top is a winged spirit symbolizing Catalonia. The middle section is adorned with personifications of the four Catalan provinces, and the four Catalan rivers, the Llobregat, Ter, Èbre and Segre are represented by four spouts of gushing water.

Facing the Llotja, but this time from the other side of passeig Isabel II, is a group of buildings known as the **Porxos** or Cases d'en Xifré (from the name of the wealthy patron who invested in them). These fine neo-Classical edifices built between 1838 and 1840 have a common façade divided into five parts, with a porticoed ground floor for shops and three residential floors above. Note the fine terra-cotta reliefs by Damià Campeny, illustrating allegories of Commerce and Industry as well as scenes from the conquest of America.

The **Duana Vella,** I, D3 (Old Customs House), stands opposite and completes the majestic layout of the square. Built in a neo-Classical style at the end of the 18th century, the Duana Vella's interest lies in its perfect state of preservation and its rich decoration.

The wall paintings inside evoke the ancient history of the town and the development of its trade. The paintings in the Deeds Chamber by Pere Pau Montanyà, among the most important neo-Classical works in Barcelona, allude to Carlos III's commercial policy, while the ceiling painting represents the *Apotheosis of the Monarchy*, with the King, the Church and Time all crushing Islam.

▬ *BARCELONETA AND PARC DE LA CIUTADELLA*

Barceloneta II, D3

After plaça de Palau, head for passeig Nacional which brings you into the working district of Barceloneta (Little Barcelona). This triangular section of town 'driven like a wedge into the sea' was entirely rebuilt in the middle of the 18th century by military engineers, which explains the neatness of its grid pattern. Originally, the houses built for sailors and fishermen consisted of only two storeys, but because of demographic pressure in the 19th century they were heightened. Today the district with its beaches and its narrow, overpopulated, perpetually seething streets is renowned for its fish restaurants. If you happen to be around when fish are being sold on the quays, you're in for a real show. The church of **Sant Miquel del Port** on plaça Barceloneta is contemporaneous with the original (18th-century) layout of the area. Your walk can continue to such other points of interest as **La Maquinista**, the **Aquarium** (passeig Nacional, *open 10am-2pm and 4-7pm*) and on to passeig Marítim.

Parc de la Ciutadella II, D3

Access: Metro: Arc de Triomf (line 1). Buses 39, 40, 41 and 51.

The **Ciutadella** was built in 1715 by Felipe V over part of the medieval quarter of Ribera. The King, taking his revenge on Barcelona's inhabitants for having resisted him so fiercely the year before, had the citadel built in the shape of an immense irregular pentagon. Hated by the townspeople because it symbolized various periods of military occupation, it was razed to the ground during the third quarter of the 19th century and today only the Governor's palace, the chapel and the arsenal remain. The vast space was used for the Universal Exhibition in 1888. The Parliament of Catalonia has its seat in the former arsenal. There is also a zoological park.

Before going into the park (there's an obelisk at the entrance), head west towards passeig Lluís Companys to see the **Law Courts** (Palau Justícia) and especially the **triumphal arch** which marked the entrance to the Universal Exhibition and added a ceremonial touch to the avenue (the continuation of passeig de Sant Joan). With its Mudejar influence (a style of architecture developed by Arabs living in Christian kingdoms) and the use of visible brick, the arch design broke free from the neo-Classical models generally adorned with a stucco covering. The Law Courts building, one of the first modern edifices in Barcelona, was built by Enric Sagnier and Josep Domènech i Estapà between 1887 and 1908. In the central part of the building is a large room renowned for its pink granite columns and iron arches. The painted decor is by Josep Maria Sert.

You enter the park through a gateway flanked by allegorical sculptures representing Industry and Commerce. To the right of passeig dels Til.lers you will see the former restaurant of the Universal Exhibition, the **Castells dels Tres Dragons**. This substantial building, an example of Catalan Modernism by Lluís Domènech i Montaner, is also made of red brick and rests on an iron structure. It is highlighted by ceramic decoration. The large space inside harmonizes with the neo-medieval aspect of some of the decoration (crenels, escutcheons and towers). Today the **Museu Zoologia** is housed here (see 'Barcelona's Museums', p. 131).

The walk continues left along winding paths through a landscape garden which leads to **plaça de la Cascada**. The monumental fountain here by the architect Fontsère was built between 1875 and 1881 with, during the first three years, the help of young Gaudí, who was studying architecture at the time. He worked in particular on the design of the rocks and some of the decoration. The monument combines classicism with free expression. From here you move on to a small romantic lake and then to the former parade ground (plaça d'Armes). Of the fortress itself there remain to the west the Governor's palace and the chapel, behind which rises an equestrian statue of General Prim, who bestowed the citadel on the town, and to the east, the former arsenal (restored) now the seat of the Catalan Parliament. The gardens in the centre of the grounds date from the beginning of this century. The pond is embellished with an important work, *Deconsol* (the Inconsolable), by the Catalan sculptor Josep Llimona.

The **Umbracle** greenhouse of tropical plants is a large brick and wood

Poble Espanyol, constructed for the 1929 International Exhibition, offers a synthesis of the regional architectural styles of Spain.

construction with iron columns. It stands in front of a neo-Pompeian edifice by Fontsère which today houses Barcelona's oldest museum, the **Museu de Geologia** or **Museu Martorell** and its mineralogical and palaeontological collections (see 'Barcelona's Museums', p. 130).

The **Hivernacle** (another greenhouse), aligned with the two preceding buildings, is by Josep Amargós and dates from 1884. It is an ideal place to take a break, with its attractive glass and iron structure (slightly earlier than the Eiffel Tower) and its recently restored multi-coloured decoration. It is now a pleasant setting for temporary exhibitions.

Parc de la Ciutadella is also the home of Barcelona's **Zoo**. *Open daily 10am-5pm in winter; 9:30am-7pm in summer. Information: ☎ (93) 309 2500. On Sun and holidays a special bus leaves plaça de Catalunya for the zoo every 45 mins, 10am-3:15pm.*

The zoo has more than 7,000 animals of over 500 species from all over the world. It is renowned for its collection of primates, the largest in Europe, among them the rare albino gorilla. There's also a special farm animal section for children.

Inside the zoological park there is a **fountain** crowned by a sculpture of the *Senyoreta del Paraigua* (Young Lady with Umbrella), a souvenir of the clothes fashion of 1888. Its originality lies in the fact that water spouts out from the ends of the umbrella ribs.

▬ *MONTJUÏC*

Access: Metro: plaça d'Espanya, II, A2. Buses: 9, 13, 27, 38, 50, 57, 61, 91, 111, 201, 605, EA, EN, NF and UC. Bus 13 is the only one that leaves from the town centre (Mercat de Sant Antoni). Buses 13, 61, 111 and 201 tour the hill. Cable-car: this is taken from the port (Moll de Barcelona or Moll Nou). Montjuïc funicular railway: from avinguda del Paral.lel (metro: Paral.lel, line 3) to avinguda de Miramar and the Montjuïc amusement park. *Open only Sat and holidays 11am-8:15pm in winter; daily noon-2:45pm and 4:30-9pm in summer.*

The hill between the town and the sea in the south drops 699 ft/213 m to the harbour and separates the Barcelona plain from that of Llobregat. It has been gradually transformed into a 541 acre/219 hectare park. In 1929 the International Exhibition was held here (some of the buildings for the event have since been converted into museums) and in 1972 the Joan Miró Foundation was opened.

Montjuïc hill has many sports facilities, including those for the 1992 Olympics and the stadium built for the 1936 Games (which in the end were held in Berlin).

Plaça d'Espanya, the departure point for Montjuïc, is at the intersection of Gran Via de les Corts Catalanes and the old road to Madrid. In the Cerdà project for Eixample, the irregular shape originally planned for the square was converted into the present circular shape for the International Exhibition in 1929. The fountain in the middle by J.-M. Jujol dates from this time. From the square you will notice the palace and other exhibition buildings as well as the two red brick towers marking the entrance. The most noteworthy monument adjoining the square is the impressive **bullring**, built between 1899 and 1900 by August Font. Its architectural style with horsehoe arches, bare brickwork, coloured ceramic tiling and so on, draws to a large extent on medieval design and Islamic culture. The bullring will be used to house the Teatre Iliure. The inside will be redesigned and the outer ring restored and preserved.

The itinerary we suggest for Montjuïc can be followed on foot (a very long walk), by car or bus. The gardens on the hill are the work of a French landscape artist, J.-C.-N. Forestier (1861-1930), who applied his theory on gardens as works of art to the development of the area in preparation for the Exhibition in 1929. 'Artist-gardeners', he said, 'leave in their work the mark of a hand that is both tender and authoritative but not tyrannical . . . in order to create places of rest, kingdoms of poetry.'

Remains of the 1929 International Exhibition

The monumental entrance from plaça d'Espanya up the hill offers the visitor a wonderful perspective on the terraces and cascades. Some of the structures built for the International Exhibition in 1929 still remain, notably the **Palau Nacional** which dominates the hill. The architect Cantallops restored the fountains on the side by eliminating obsolete constructions.

On either side of the avenue you will see facilities for Barcelona's annual International Fair. The development of this area by Bonet has resulted in a wide open space that each fair adapts to its needs. A sculpture by Josep Llimona inspired by the neo-Realism of the first half of the century has been integrated into the site.

The illuminated **fountain** by Carles Buïgas crowning the avenue is one of the most spectacular creations built for the Exhibition. Sound, light and water displays are given on holidays and other occasions.

Take avinguda del Marquès de Comillas to the right where you will see the **German Pavilion*** designed by the noted German architect, Ludwig Mies van der Rohe. This was dismantled at the end of the Exhibition but was described by the American architect, Philip Johnson, as one of the rare contemporary structures worthy of comparison with the work of the great architects of the past, and it was thus rebuilt on its original site in 1985 — a risky undertaking as the building was originally planned to be only temporary. The architects for this project included C. Cirici, F. Ramos and I. de Solà-Morales; the sculpture, *Nude Woman*, is by Georg Kolbe.

The **Poble Espanyol** a little farther up the hill, is a village that offers a condensed overall view of the different styles of Spanish architecture through its reconstruction of houses characteristic of each region, as well as through the better known monuments. There are also shops selling souvenirs and arts and crafts, and workshops where you can see the latter being made *(open 9am-7pm; restaurants and discos open until later)*. Payment for entering the village includes access to the following museums: **Museu d'Arts, Industries i Tradicions populars; Museu del Llibre i de les Arts Gràfiques** and the **Museu del Vi** (Wine Museum).

By taking avinguda dels Montanyans from here you come to the **Palau Nacional** which houses the **Museu Nacional d'Art de Catalunya** (see 'Barcelona's Museums', p. 132). Before going in take a look at the sweeping view of plaça d'Espanya and the rest of the town from the palace watch-tower.

The **Botanic Gardens** behind the Palau Nacional were laid out on the site of some former quarries and have a large variety of plant species *(open 9am-2pm and 4-6pm. Closed Sun)*.

Not far from the Palau Nacional is the **Palau Albéni,** now the town's residence for illustrious guests, and the **Joan Maragall gardens**. Beside them is the Olympic zone.

The **Fundació Joan Miró**** is in a modern construction on avinguda de Miramar, built between 1972 and 1974. It is one of the major works of Josep Lluís Sert, the architect also responsible for the Fondation Maeght in Saint-Paul-de-Vence in France and Joan Miró's house in Majorca, built between 1954 and 1955 (see 'Barcelona's Museums', p. 130).

There are beautiful panoramic views of town from avinguda de Miramar. The **Mossèn Jacint Verdaguer Gardens** off it specialize in bulbs and tubers (tulips, narcissi, water lilies and so on).

Montjuïc Amusement Park, II, B3, can be reached directly by the funicular from avinguda del Paral.lel *(open Sat and holidays noon-8pm in winter; Tues-Sat 6pm-midnight; Sun noon-midnight in summer. Closed Mon)*. Here you will find all manner of entertainment for old and young alike (big dippers, big wheel and so on). A monument to the Sardana dance stands at the entrance.

You can take a cable car from the amusement park up to the top of the hill and the **Castell de Montjuïc** which houses the **Museu Militar** (see

---

Joan Miró (1893-1983)

Barcelona truly belongs to Miró; his works are present everywhere from the airport to the Ramblas and even in advertising logos (the Caixa de Pensions or Savings Bank is an example).

Miró is the most famous Catalan artist after Picasso. During his life his work evolved through a series of styles from ingenuous, magic realism to surrealism and including, of course, the period in which he developed his playful coloured drawings for which he is perhaps most widely known.

Apart from painting, Miró also worked with ceramics and made some monumental sculptures.

'Barcelona's Museums', p. 132). You have a wonderful view of the town and port from here.

The **Mossèn Costa i Llobera Gardens** on the precipitous southern slope of the hill have a variety of exotic plants and one of the largest cactus collections in the world with over 500 species. There are also about 30 different types of palm trees. You feel, on this slope, as though you've entered another world.

Back on the hill, passeig de Santa Madrona leads to the **Museu Etnològic** (see 'Barcelona's Museums', p. 131) and the **Museu Arqueològic de Barcelona,** which is housed in one of the palaces built for the International Exhibition in 1929.

The **Teatre Grec,** located in one of Montjuïc's former quarries, was also built in 1929. It was inspired by the antique theatre of Epidaurus. Performances of ballet and modern dance, as well as plays, concerts and recitals are given here on summer evenings.

To return to the centre of town you can take carrer de Lleida which leads to avinguda del Paral.lel. This wide thoroughfare owes its name to the 41°44' north parallel of latitude with which it coincides. Known as Barcelona's equivalent of Paris's Montmartre district, this centre of nightlife and theatre, was particularly lively until the 1970s, but has since lost some of its influence although it is still the home of large theatres (Victoria), cabarets (Apolo, Arnau) and variety shows (Studio 54). See 'Nightlife', p. 89.

▬ *EIXAMPLE* II, BC1-2

Bordered by avinguda Diagonal and Gran Via de les Corts Catalanes, Eixample is the fashion district where smart shops, cafés and restaurants attract Barcelona's young trendies.

Up until 1859 Barcelona was completely enclosed by uneven walls, some dating from Antiquity, others from the Middle Ages. It was difficult to move out into the plain that stretched beyond the enclosure to Collserola and Mount Tibidabo. A year after most of the walls had been demolished, the town-planning project for a modern Barcelona, put forward by the engineer Ildefons Cerdà, began to take effect.

Cerdà planned a gigantic grid pattern with blocks of houses *(mançanes)* measuring 374 ft/114 m on the sides and streets 66 ft/20 m wide. He also included broad avenues such as Diagonal, passeig de Gràcia and passeig de Sant Joan for fast traffic. Cerdà's project was extraordinarily far-sighted and efficient for his time.

Plaça de Catalunya II, C2

Plaça de Catalunya (approximately 12 acres/5 hectares) was created at the turn of the century. It is the heart of Barcelona and is surrounded by large buildings, banks and shopping centres. Its statues, fountains and pigeons tend to disappear behind the streams of cars and people who crowd through the area all day long. It serves as a hub linking the Gothic Quarter and the Ramblas to Eixample, the Barcelona of 1900. Between 1925 and 1927 the square was adorned with sculptures (notably *Goddess*) by Josep Clarà.

Today **passeig de Gràcia** has replaced the Ramblas as the centre of urban life from every point of view — social, economic, artistic and commercial. During the first quarter of the century it was a residential street for the upper-middle classes as can be seen by the bourgeois houses still lining it. Passeig de Gràcia, is the setting for all sorts of processions and parades and still functions as a kind of bridge between the sea and the mountain. It follows a straight line along the old road that led from Barcelona to the village of Gràcia. Building the passeig took seven years (1820 to 1827); it was then a promenade bordered by gardens. At the end of the century theatres and other entertainment halls

An inviting forest of strangely shaped stone chimneys rises out of the roof of Casa Milà, one of Gaudí's many masterpieces.

began to be built here, an example being the Moorish-style façade on your right as you walk up the street between Gran Via de les Corts Catalanes and carrer de la Diputació.

Of the original fixtures in the street you can still see the amazing streetlamps by Pere Falqués and the white ceramic benches, good examples of the Modernist era's creations.

Casa Calvet (carrer de Casp 48), II, D2 , is the first of Gaudí's works in this itinerary. It has a Baroque influence (1898-1900) and marks the change towards a style that is completely free of historic references. You should go in to see the staircase, the furniture and the elevator, all designed by Gaudí.

Casa Golferichs (Gran Via de les Corts Catalanes 491), II, CD2 , was built between 1900 and 1901 by Joan Rubio i Bellvé (1871-1952), one of Gaudí's students. It's a fine example of a detached house in the Gothic style in which very careful use has been made of traditional materials. The house has recently been restored and now serves as an administrative centre for the district.

Casa Heribert Pons (rambla de Catalunya 19-21), II, C2, by Alexandre Soler i March (1873-1949) was built between 1907 and 1909 and shows the influence of contemporary Viennese architecture. There is a series of sculptures by Eusebi Arnau in the garden representing the *Muses*. The building has undergone thorough restoration and now houses the Economy Department of the *Generalitat of Catalunya*.

The section of passeig de Gràcia between carrer de Consell de Cent and carrer d'Aragó is called *Mançana de la Discordia* (Block of Discord), an allusion to the architectural rivalry that reigned in the area during the first decade of the century when the buildings were going up, and also to the contrast between them.

Casa Lleó Morera, II, C2, stands on the corner of carrer de Consell de Cent and passeig de Gràcia (n° 35). It was designed by Domènech i Montaner in a 1900s style with a decoration of plant motifs. Unfortunately, the ground floor has been partly impaired by shops. The building can be compared with another, **Casa Fuster** (passeig de Gràcia 132), by the same architect. The next two houses date from the Belle Epoque, drawing on the Louis XVI style.

Casa Amatller* (passeig de Gràcia 41), II, C1, by Puig i Cadafalch is neo-Gothic in style and has ceramic tiling (mainly on the upper part). Between 1898 and 1900 the architect added the present façade to the already existing structure. It has a gabled front sloped into steps on either side, a style that draws upon medieval architecture from northern countries, but also has intermediate window openings and a main doorway which derive directly from Catalan Gothic. Cadafalch altered the inner courtyard and the staircase and also designed the lamps, windows, floor-coverings, furniture and the ceilings on the first floor. The sculptor Eusebi Arnau made the fireplace. Today the first floor of the house is taken up by the Amatller Institute of Hispanic Art.

Casa Batlló*, II, C1, is at n° 43 on the same avenue. Gaudí altered the 19th-century building between 1904 and 1907 by modifying the façade and the stairwell. The wavy shapes on the façade are made of carved Montjuïc stone below and coloured ceramic tiles above. It is said of the house that the openings on the front resemble mouths, the columns bones and the roof the back of a dragon. Inside, the sinuous lines of the staircase up to the first floor continue into the rooms, the decoration on the walls, the doors, windows and fireplaces. Casa Batlló and Casa Amatller, which is next door, form probably the most famous pair of buildings in Barcelona.

By taking a short detour into carrer d'Aragó you will see, at n° 25, the **Montaner i Simon printing house,** one of the first Modernist buildings (1879-1886). Here Domènech i Montaner used a supporting structure of different metal components (cast-iron columns and steel beams) which, until then, had only been used for building markets or train stations. The result is a two-storey edifice giving onto a central space lit by a large skylight. Today the building houses the newly-created **Antoni Tàpies Foundation of Contemporary Art** (see 'Barcelona's Museums', p. 129).

Return to passeig de Gràcia and three streets further up, on the corner of carrer de Provença, you will see **Casa Milà**** (n° 92), II, C1, known as *La Pedrera* (stone quarry) and built by Gaudí between 1905 and 1910. One of the most spectacular buildings in Barcelona, it recalls the rock shapes on Montserrat mountain and has recently been restored. Go inside to see the courtyards and terraces where chimneys and ventilation funnels look as though they're dancing a strange ballet. Among the many original features of the building is the sculptured aspect of the balconies, and the unusual treatment of the ground floor. The front windows seem to have been carved out of the stone (hence the name *Pedrera*). The Casa Milà was the last concession Gaudí made to civil architecture before shutting himself away in La Sagrada Família (see p. 121).

Take rambla de Catalunya to **Casa Serra** (nº 126) by Puig i Cadafalch. This town house (1903) has been preserved thanks to the installation of the new headquarters of the Deputació of Barcelona. Puig i Cadafalch decorated the façade in Renaissance style.

Passeig de Gràcia is crossed by avinguda Diagonal which, as its name suggests, breaks up the uniformity of Eixample's grid pattern by cutting diagonally across it. It's the longest boulevard in Barcelona (7 mi/12 km) and divides the north-east part of town from the south-west.

Passeig de Gràcia ends in the old town of **Gràcia** which underwent town planning between 1860 and 1870. Here you will find narrow streets, little squares (plaça del Sol, plaça Trilla), shops and all kinds of small and medium-sized companies.

Casa Vicens on carrer de les Carolines 22 is one of Gaudí's earliest works (1883-1888). It's a residential villa decorated in Islamic style with stalactite ceilings and lovely wrought-iron railings. The delightful, exuberant decoration inside testifies to the care Gaudí took over even the smallest details. He designed both exterior and interior, linking the decor and architecture together harmoniously.

By returning to avinguda Diagonal you will be able to see three more buildings by Puig i Cadafalch. The first, **Casa Quadras** (avinguda Diagonal 373, carrer del Rosselló 279) is a fine mansion (1902-1904). Today the building houses the **Museu de la Música** (see 'Barcelona's Museum', p. 131). The second, **Casa Terrades★** or Casa de les Punxes (avinguda Diagonal 416-420, carrer del Rosselló 260-262) is a large apartment block (1903-1905) in which the architect resolved the problem of an irregular plan by building a sort of medieval fortress, with round towers in the corners, influenced by northern Gothic architecture. The third, **Casa Macaya** (passeig de Sant Joan 106) is a town house (1899-1901) centred around an inner courtyard and large staircase in the same way as Barcelona's palaces were designed in the Middle Ages. This is the home of the **Cultural Centre of the Caixa de Pensions** where temporary exhibitions are held.

La Sagrada Família★★★ II, D1

Passeig de Sant Joan is crossed by carrer de Mallorca on which stands Gaudí's unfinished masterpiece, La Sagrada Família. The expiatory temple (Temple Expiatori de la Sagrada Família) has become a symbol of the work of the great architect, of Barcelona and of the Modernist movement. A neo-Gothic project for the church by the architect Francisco de Paula Villar had already begun in 1882 before Gaudí took over in 1883. Although Gaudí was unable to intervene in the plan of the crypt as a whole — it was already under construction — he nonetheless created a grandiose project which he continually redesigned during the building of the church. Combining a soaring technique in the architecture with a decor of symbolic sculpture characterized by mystical references he planned three monumental façades, only one of which was finished. This was the Nativity façade (1891-1900) which has strong expressionistic overtones. The plan provided for 12 spires in honour of the Apostles, four others for the Evangelists, one for the Virgin Mary and one dedicated to Christ (over 558 ft/170 m). Every architectural detail refers to some element of the Catholic faith. Gaudí took the opportunity with this project to experiment with his own architectural inventions (such as parabolic arches without buttresses) and to carve the stone into a variety of shapes reminiscent of the natural world.

In 1952 a strong controversy arose between those who wanted to continue work on the church based on preserved drawings and plans by Gaudí, and others who thought it better to leave the masterpiece unfinished for fear of betraying the architect's genius. By opting for the first line of action, Barcelona follows in medieval tradition when cathedrals took centuries to build. Recently, the sculptor Josep Maria Subirachs has been given the responsibility of continuing the sculpture of the church.

The Nativity façade with its three doorways is an immense kind of sculpture which recalls, by its general layout, the façades of Gothic cathedrals. The sculptures illustrate episodes from the Old and New Testaments (the crib, Christ's childhood and so on). The relationship between the sculpture and the architecture is so intimate that it is difficult to see where one begins and the other ends. In order to appreciate the technical genius, plasticity and proportion of the façade, it is best to look at it from inside.

Subirachs began illustrating the Passion on the façade in 1986 and has committed himself to the project for 15 years. He accepted the commission stating that the Sagrada Família is the most important sculpture in the world: '... The work that Gaudí began ... is, for me, by one of the greatest artists we have ever had. I have also accepted because in this way I will be collaborating in a work that is a symbol of Barcelona.' Subirachs has complete freedom for his task: 'I'm executing a piece of personal work. However, I'm also taking the site on which it has to stand into consideration.'

You can go up to the top of the spires or visit the crypt and its museum where you can see diagrams and models of the church: *open daily 9am-6pm in winter, 8am-8pm in summer.*

Avinguda de Gaudí was planned at the beginning of the century and recently re-developed by the architect Quintana. The column-like streetlamps by Pere Falqués have been re-installed and sculptures by Apel.les Fenosa have been placed along it.

The avenue leads to the **Hospital de Sant Pau** (off map), by Domènech i Montaner. It's an immense complex built between 1902 and 1912 in accordance with the new theories of hygiene and health propounded at the beginning of the century. A series of detached pavilions have been arranged on either side of a central boulevard (placed at an angle to Cerdà's grid pattern) in an effort to integrate the architecture as much as possible into a vast garden. The pavilions are connected to each other and to the communal facilities by underground passages.

▬▬ *PEDRALBES AND THE DIAGONAL*

Access. Buses 22, 64 and 75.

This eclectic itinerary takes you a good distance from the centre into newly developed districts which are both rich in examples of the medieval period as they are in the various stages of Barcelona's more recent architectural projects. Here the university and the FC Barcelona stadium form a second focus of interest for the capital.

The Monastery of Pedralbes★★

The monastery of the Clare order founded in 1326 by King Jaume II and his fourth wife, the young Elisenda de Montcada, forms an ensemble of buildings, both monastic and royal.

The speed of construction gave the monastery great unity of style. The **church★**, a fine example of 14th-century Catalan Gothic architecture, has a wide single nave, a polygonal apse, and side chapels between the buttresses. On the right, near the choir, is the mausoleum of Queen Elisenda which probably pre-dates 1364, the year of her death. The royal statue on the tomb accompanied by incense-bearing angels has all the attributes befitting the Queen's station. It lies beneath a canopy illustrating two angels carrying her soul heavenwards.

The **cloisters** on three levels are an example of delicate monastic architecture with their slender columns, while the verdant inner **courtyard** is a peaceful oasis, a restful distance from Barcelona's bustling centre.

Some wonderful 14th-century wall paintings by Ferrer Bassa have been preserved in the **Chapel of Sant Miquel★★**. The panels are characterized by a dominant blue colour and have been arranged on two levels. Those on the upper level illustrate the *Crucifixion*, flanked by scenes of the *Passion of Christ*, while those on the lower level depict the *Virgin and*

Child in Majesty surrounded by angels, with scenes from the life of Mary on either side. The frescoes, which are in good condition, throw light on the courtly Catalan style of painting and its Italian influences.

The monastery **museum** in the chapter-house contains important collections of Catalan painting, sculpture, altarpieces and furniture from the 16th and 17th centuries. *Open 9:30am-2pm. Closed Mon.*

On leaving the monastery, take avinguda de Pedralbes toward avinguda Diagonal. On the right, the residential block at nº 46 carrer de Sor Eulàlia d'Anzizu, built between 1967 and 1973, is by Josep Lluís Sert and his team of architects. His first work in Barcelona after a long stay in the United States, it was somewhat misunderstood during construction and combines American elements with certain Catalan traditions.

To the left of avinguda de Pedralbes, at nº 33-35 passeig de Manuel Girona, you can see an interesting example of an 18th-century **Catalan farmhouse.** Return to the avenue and on the other side, at nº 7, you will see the gateway and pavilions at the entrance to **Finca Güell,** built by Gaudí between 1884 and 1887. This bears the stamp of Gaudí's Oriental influence, evident in the arches, the dome and the layout of the gardens. Note the spectacular dragon with open jaws on the wrought iron railings at the entrance. Today the buildings are the seat of the Gaudí Chair of the School of Architecture which has a specialized library and archive section.

The University

As you walk down towards avinguda Diagonal, you have a good view of the university halls of residence. Their installation here has enabled the transfer of most of the student population to the outskirts of town.

The **Law School** at nº 684 by G. Giràldez Dávila, P. López Iñigo and X. Subias Fages, dates from 1958. It drew a lot of attention at the time because it represented a break with post-civil war architecture. The relief illustration of *Law* on the doorway at the entrance was carved by Subirachs in collaboration with Cumella, a ceramist.

The **Palau de Pedralbes** a little farther along at nº 686, by E. Bona Puig and F. de P. Nebot Torrens, stands on grounds formerly belonging to Count Güell. The gardens were laid out in 1925 under Rubió i Tudrí, a Catalan landscape gardener. Work was completed for the International Exhibition in 1929. King Alfonso XIII had already taken to staying here in 1926 and later, the Republic gave the palace to the municipality. The Decorative Arts Museum was installed in 1932. Then in 1936 the palace was reconverted to a residence for the Head of State. It is being renovated once again in order to house the Cambó collection of paintings and the **Museu de Ceràmica** with its lovely medieval works (see 'Barcelona's Museums', p. 130).

'El Camp Nou' or Futbol Club Barcelona

This is located on avinguda de Joan XXIII and was built between 1954 and 1957. As the venue for sports and other large events, it draws huge crowds. Its popularity can be explained by the fact that it is a powerful club with over 100,000 members; *'El Barcelona és més que un club'* (The Barcelona FC is more than a club) as the saying goes. The stadium stretches over more than 7 acres/2.8 hectares and was originally built to hold 90,000 spectators. For the World Football Championships in 1982, it was enlarged to a capacity of 120,000 and is now Europe's largest stadium. Work was completed by the building of a *mini estadi* (mini stadium) across the road, linked to the main stadium by a bridge.

Trade Towers office blocks

The towered office blocks at nº 86-94 Gran Via de Carles III were built between 1966 and 1969 by José Antonio Coderch from Sentmenat, in collaboration with Manuel Valls. They are cylindrical edifices covered in smoked glass with a common curved base. Enveloping the exterior of each block is a kind of continuous wavy curtain wall that creates the impression of a single monument composed of several separate blocks. With Sert and Sostres, Coderch (1913-1984) was one of the founders of modern Catalan architecture. You can easily see his works in Barcelona — for example, the multi-storeyed building in Barceloneta (1952-1954), the residential block at n° 7 carrer de Johann Sebastian Bach (1957-1961) or the apartment buildings at 21-23 carrer de Raset and 22-32 carrer de Freixa (1968-1974). If you are interested in contemporary art and architecture, bear in mind that in 1962 Coderch also built the house and workshop of the painter Antoni Tàpies, a curious edifice with a sun visor at n° 57 carrer de Saragossa (near the top of carrer de Balmes).

▬▬ TIBIDABO

Access: avinguda del Tibidabo at the top of carrer de Balmes. You can get here with FC railways (Tibidabo station) or by bus (58, NB, 73, 17 or 22). Then take the blue tramway which runs every half-hour from 7:20am-9:20pm and finally, the funicular railway from plaça del Dr Andreu (from 7:30am-9:30pm). Or, if you are driving, take carretera de l'Arrabassada.

Tibidabo mountain, 1644 ft/501 m high, protects the town to the west and seems to be almost pushing it into the sea. Because of Barcelona's position between the sea and the mountain the town has been forced to stretch out along a north-south axis. Tibidabo is part of the Collserola heights, an area destined to become a large green zone. Its main interests are the amusement park and a fine view of the town and the sea. The origin of the name is biblical, deriving from the words of the devil in the Gospel according to St Matthew: *'Haec omnia tibi dabo si cadens adoraberis me'*, 'All these things will I give thee, if thou wilt fall down and worship me'.

The summit of Tibidabo became part of Barcelona's modern history in 1885 when St John Bosco climbed the mountain to dedicate it to the Sacred Heart. In 1888 Queen Maria Cristina, who was in the city for the inauguration of the Universal Exhibition, also took a trip to the top. The wooden neo-Moorish pavilion built to welcome her no longer exists. Visits to the mountain on a more regular basis did not begin until the turn of the century when a rich pill manufacturer financed the construction of the blue tramway and the funicular railway.

The blue tramway is the last tramway remaining in Barcelona. It used to run through a residential zone, and several mansions from this time still exist. As you ascend you will see **Casa Roviralta** on the left (n° 31), built by Joan Rubió i Bellvé between 1903 and 1913. It is known as *El Frere Blanc* because the grounds once belonged to the Dominicans. Due to its shape and the use of traditional materials it's an excellent example of the neo-Gothic Catalan style. It has recently been restored and today houses a restaurant.

The **Museu de la Ciència** and the **Planetari** are a little farther up on the left at n° 55 carrer de Teodor Roviralta (see 'Barcelona's Museums', p. 130).

The **Basilica of the Sacred Heart** was founded in 1902 and work began on it in 1909. It is a neo-Gothic edifice dominated by a monumental statue of Christ, built along the same lines as the great 19th-century French basilicas of Paris, Lyons and Marseille. The architect Enric Sagnier (1858-1931) undertook the work but was unable to finish it before his death. Building was further interrupted by the outbreak of civil war and was continued later by the architect's son. The sculptures on the doorway are by Eusebi Arnau.

Tibidabo Amusement Park

Open Jan-Mar and Oct-Dec weekends 11am-8pm; Apr-Sep 11am-8pm (10pm summer). From 2:30-4:30pm only about 50% of the amusements function. Admission charge. You can buy tickets granting limitless access to all the attractions.

This is one of the most popular places in Barcelona for children and parents, competing with Montjuïc's amusement park, which is more recent. Apart from all sorts of traditional entertainment (distorting mirrors, ferris wheel, big dippers and so on) there is also a modern super-slide with a ski lift, for the adventurous visitor, of course! The **Automaton Museum** contains fine examples of various 19th-century gadgets (see 'Barcelona's Museums', p. 130).

OFF THE BEATEN TRACK

The Horta Maze (El Laberint d'Horta)

Part of the interest of this particular maze is its good condition. Once located in the middle of the country but now in passeig de la Vall d'Hebron, off map II, D1, this 18th-century neo-Classical construction backs onto an old 14th-century cylindrical tower. Behind the house stretch the gardens, now open to the public. These were begun in 1791 by the owner himself, Marquis Joan Desvalls, then president of the Royal Academy of the Arts and Sciences of Barcelona. Ever since the Classical period, mazes have played an important part in the gardens of stately homes. The marquis wanted a maze and a series of gardens adorned with little Tuscan temples and a variety of statues. In spite of restorations during the Romantic period these remain the most noteworthy example of Barcelona's neo-Classical gardens. The theme of Love runs throughout.

The Water Board's neo-Moorish chalet (xalet)

This strange edifice stands at nº 4 plaça d'Alfons el Savi, off map II, D1. It was built for the Water Board in 1890 in the middle of an immense park bought by the Board to protect a reservoir. Today it belongs to the Town Hall and is one of the few examples of neo-Moorish architecture preserved in Barcelona. The building surrounds a central courtyard with a gallery supported by iron columns. The visit is especially worthwhile for the extraordinary arches on the main façade.

Barcelona once had a great many Moorish buildings, most of which have disappeared. At the turn of the century it was good form in middle-class houses to decorate one of the rooms, especially the front room, in an oriental style. One of the best examples of this trend in architecture is in the small town of Arboç del Penedès, between Vilafranca and Tarragona, where you can see the magnificent copy of the Giralda of Seville (see p. 172).

Bullrings, markets and shops

The **Plaça de Toros Monumental**, Gran Via de les Corts Catalanes 749, off map II, D2, the largest of Barcelona's two bullrings, was built between 1913 and 1915 by the architect Ignasi Mas. He freely adapted Islamic architecture to the walls of the ring by using red brick with blue and white ceramic tiles.

Barcelona has a number of markets that throw light on the architectural development of this type of iron construction from early influences of Baltard's famous Parisian central food market onwards. From the point of view of decoration most of the markets belong to the Modernist movement or to the period just prior. Markets of interest include: **Mercat del Born** (1876), the former central food market near the Parc de la Ciutadella, II, D3; the **Mercat de Sant Antoni** (carrer del Comte d'Urgell and carrer de Tamarit) which dates from 1872-1882, II, B2; the **Mercat Sant Josep** or **de la Boqueria** on rambla de les Flors (1840-1914), II, B2; the **Mercat de la Llibertat** in Gràcia (1874), off map; the **Mercat de Concepció** (carrer d'Aragó and carrer del Bruc), II, D1; and **Mercat del Ninot** at carrer de Mallorca 133, II, B1.

A good many shops decorated in the Modernist style have fortunately been preserved and always attract visitors. Among them are:

Farmacia Sastre i Marques, carrer de l'Hospital 109, I, B2, by Puig i Cadalfach (1905). This has a large street lamp, relief work on the façade arches and decorative glass inside.

Farmacia J. de Bolòs, carre de Valencia 256, II, C1, is complete with stained glass panels, lamps and a decorated ceiling. It houses a collection of pots.

Farmacia Puig-Oriol, carrer de Mallorca 312, II, C1, dates from 1913 and has a fine series of stained glass panels and furniture.

Farmacia Genové, Rambla 77, I, B1, by Enric Sagnier (1911) has neo-Gothic decoration on the façade.

Antiga Casa Figueras, Rambla 83, decorated by Antoni Ros i Guell (1902), is a popular spot on the Ramblas that was restored in 1986. There are stained-glass panels, intriguing furniture and magnificent decorations on the front of the building, consisting of carved motifs and mosaics.

The **bakery** at carrer de Girona 73 is another noteworthy establishment.

Filatèlia Monje, carrer Boters 2, has a wooden front and furniture worth seeing.

El Indio, carrer del Carme 24, a fabrics shop, has a typical Art Nouveau façade (1922).

Casa Teixidor, ronda de Sant Pere 16, by J.-M. Raspall (1909), sells drawing materials.

Cemeteries

Not many of Barcelona's old cemeteries still exist. The two most important ones are listed here:

South-west cemetery on the slopes of Montjuïc, facing the sea *(open 9am-5pm).* Bus 637 drives through the cemetery on Sundays, 10am-2pm, stopping frequently. You board it at the main gate, near the cinturó des Litoral road. To get there, take bus 38 from either plaça de Catalunya or plaça d'Espanya.

This enormous cemetery is interesting and gives a fine view of the harbour and the sea. Among the most lavish graves is the sepulchral monument of Prat de la Riba, the first president of the Catalan Mancommunitat, on via de Sant Jordi, and that of Francesc Macià, the first president of the Generalitat, on plaça de la Fe.

The building of the cemetery coincided with the spread of Modernism. Wealthy bourgeois families commissioned architects, sculptors and bronze specialists, artists and casters, to make them sumptuous tombstones; a visit to the cemetery is a lesson in the history of modern art. Among the sculptors, mention must be made of Josep Llimona; the following architects also left noteworthy works: Josep Vilaseca (Batlló vault, 1885, with Egyptian-influenced angels at the entrance), Antoni M. Gallissà (La Riva mausoleum, 1891), Puig i Cadafalch (Terrades grave, sepulchral monument of the barons of Quadras, Macià tomb, 1917, Damm vault, 1897), and Jujol (tombstones of Gilbert-Romeu, 1910, Planells, 1916 and San Salvador, 1919).

The **East Cemetery** *(open 9am-5pm)* can be reached by buses 6, 36 and 92. It dates from the Romantic period and has severe neo-Classical-style monuments with charming, sentimental epitaphs and beautiful sculptures.

Public gardens, squares and sculpture: 1982-1986

Barcelona's urban planning has made a complete break with that carried out over 40 years by the first municipality after the Civil War. In an attempt to modernize the city, the present development of open spaces is characterized by strong vitality. Recently constructed parks and squares are well worth a visit. One of the most impressive aspects of the urban planning policy led by Oriol Bohigas and J.-A. Acebillo, is the inclusion of contemporary sculpture in the urban environment. You can either work out a special itinerary around the theme of contemporary art in Barcelona or simply include the odd detour during a walk.

This huge park with its sculptures and lake was laid out on the site of the former Espanya Industrial factory; it is a good example, among others in Barcelona, of the talent of local architects and landscape artists in creating highly pleasant settings out of uninviting urban spaces.

Plaça Àngel Pestanya, off map II, D1, metro Roquetes (L4).
This square by the architect E. Pericas in the Nou Barris district, is laid out on the spot where two main streets cross. There's a lake, a monumental staircase and a sculpture-fountain by Enric Pladevall.

Passeig de Picasso, II, D3, metro Jaume I (L4) and Arc de Triomf (L1).
Bordering the parc de la Ciutadella, opposite the Porxos d'en Fontsère (a neo-Classical portico), stands a fountain-monument enclosed in a glass cube with 13 ft/4 m sides. It is the work of Antoni Tàpies, a homage to Picasso's nonconformity. The architects were R. Amado and L. Domènech.

Parc del Clot, metro Clot (L1).
This is in an essentially industrial zone in the immediate outskirts of Barcelona where you can see two unfinished blocks of the Cerdà plan. They contain skeletons of constructions from different, mainly industrial periods, as well as a sculpture by Bryan Hunt. The architects were D. Freixes and V. Miranda.

Parc de la Creuta del Coll, bus 28 (Gran de Gràcia).
In one of the town's higher regions in the Coll district, a particularly desolate zone has been converted into a park with an almost circular meeting place and a lake-cum-swimming-pool. Eduardo Chillida's sculpture, *Homage to Water,* is reflected in the lake. The entrance to the park is marked by an Ellsworth Kelly work and the summit is crowned with a multi-coloured monument by Roy Lichtenstein. The architects were J. Martorell and D. Mackay.

Parc de l'Escorxador or **Parc Joan Miró,** II, AB1-2, metro Tarragona (L3).
The transfer of the old abattoirs out of town meant that a good piece of land, the equivalent of four blocks of the Cerdà plan, could be transformed into a park. It has since been developed into various built-up or wooded areas where people can walk, play games or gather for large meetings. The central lake is dominated by one of Miró's best-known coloured statues, *Dona i Ocell* ('Woman and Bird'). The architects were A. Solanas, M. Quintana, B. Galé and A. Arriola.

Parc d'Estació del Nort, II, D2.
This now abandoned 'north train station' located near the parc de la Ciutadella will be integrated into the new area around plaça de les Glòries Catalanes. The space occupied by railway lines on the southern side of the station will be replaced by Beverly Popper's 'sculpture-gardens'. These will be surrounded by a wall with ceramic decoration in honour of Gaudí. The architects are A. Arriola, C. Fiol and E. Lesicas.

Fossar de la Pedreda, buses 8 and 48 (passeig de la Zona Franca).
A former quarry *(pedrera)* on Montjuïc mountain with its back to the sea, once used as a communal grave and then abandoned, has been redesigned to commemorate those shot during the Civil War. The tragic aspect of the place combined with the peaceful forces of nature, blend together to form a unit dominated by a mausoleum-sculpture surrounded by water. The sculpture, *Homage to Those Sacrificed for Freedom,* is by F. Ventura. The architect was G. Galí.

Parc de la Pegasso, metro Sagrera (L1 or 5).
The park is located on the former site of a Pegasso truck factory. It was designed to relieve congestion in the densely built-up Sagrera district. The gap created by a difference of level between the park and the street has been filled by a raised passageway. Romantic gardens reflecting an oriental influence have been landscaped on an undulating terrain. There is a sculpture by Ellsworth Kelly. The architects were J. Roig and E. Batlle.

Velodrom d'Horta, metro Montbau (L3).
Barcelona's velodrome (passeig de Vall d'Hebron) was built in 1984. It looks like a large crown and was designed to be covered if necessary by a cupola. Inside is the cycle-racing track and rows of seats that form an oval, while lighting towers have been arranged on a diagonal plane within the stadium. The formal purity of the whole design is quite remarkable. The immediate surroundings have been developed into a natural park dominated by a large sculpture by Joan Brossa *A Visual Poem* — a huge letter 'A' forms the entrance to the park and at the other end there is a second, identical letter 'A', but this time it is broken. This has been interpreted as representing the normal course of life. The architects were E. Bonell and F. Rius.

Plaça de la Palmera, metro La Pau (L4), (carrers de Puigcerdà, de Maresme, d'Andrade and de Trento).
This former wasteland on the edge of Eixample is one of the best examples of the effort made to fill the spaces left by the disorganized urban planning of the 1960s. The sculptor Richard Serra has created an ensemble around a pre-existing palm tree which he has imprisoned between a music kiosk and a tall lighting tower. The whole is a fine example of free interpretation of space. The architects were P. Barragán and B.-D. Sola.

Plaça Països Catalans, II, A1, metro Sants-Estació (L3 or 5).
The desolation of the wasteland that stretched in front of Sants station was matched only by the architects' initial perplexity when faced with the problem. The result, however, is fascinating and the objects that fill the space, including pedestrians, all contribute to the effect. The square features a large pergola with curved roofing reminiscent of smoke from a locomotive, a double row of fountains, podiums without statues and blank billboards — all objects which recall the artistic avant-garde of the first quarter of the century. The result is a completely original topography. The architects were H. Piñon and A. Viaplana.

Plaça de Soller, metro Llucmajor (L4) or Virrei Amat (L5).
This square in the Nou Barris district is an attempt at unifying and condensing a difficult environment. The inner part is comprised of a kind of paved salon with porticoes and a landscaped garden. A group of sculptures by Xavier Corberó serves as a link between the ensemble and a pond. The architects were Julià, Delgado, Arriola and Ribas.

Plaça del Sol, metro Fontana (L3).
The largest and most traditional of Gracià's squares has been remodeled by widening the pedestrian area. A geometric plan was adopted for the space with two groups of trees — magnolias in the north, plane trees in the south. Dominating the whole is a sculpture, *Astrolabi,* by Joaquim Camps. The architects were J. Bach and G. Mora.

Plaça Trilla, metro Fontana (L3).
This was one of the rare existing open spaces in the Gracià district and the only one opening onto carrer Gran de Gracià. It has been developed into a square with a grid pattern of palm trees forming a hypostyle construction where the trees serve as columns. The architects were J. Bach and G. Mora.

Plaça de la Mercè, I, C3, metro Drassanes (L3).
The square was made possible thanks to the demolition of a block of houses. The uniform paving recalls the open spaces in the Gothic quarter and the highlighted church façade dominates the whole. An 18th-century statue of *Neptune* by Adrià Ferran was taken out of the municipal reserves and placed on the square to counterbalance the church. The architects were R.-M. Clotet, R. Sanàbria and P. Casajoana.

Plaça de Sant Agustí Vell, I, D2, and **Plaça de Sant Pere,** I, D1, Metro Urquinaona (L1 and 4) and Arc de Triomf (L1).
Two small elongated squares in the eastern sector of Barcelona's historic centre have been linked by an irregular esplanade. One recalls the terraces of an antique forum and the other a Roman amphitheatre. R. Cáceres was the architect.

Plaça de Tetuan, II, D2, metro Girona (L4).
The bronze and stone monument in the middle of the square by the sculptor Josep Llimona in honour of Bartomeu Robert, mayor of the town, dates from 1910. It originally stood in plaça de la Universitat but was taken down by the pro-Franco régime after the Civil War. The unusual shape of the podium led people to wonder whether Domènech i Montaner or maybe even Gaudí collaborated in the project. In 1985 the monument was rebuilt in the centre of the square where a garden roundabout (traffic circle) conceals the intersection of two wide streets. The architect was A. Arriola.

▬ *BARCELONA'S MUSEUMS*

Almost all Barcelona's museums are in the process of being restructured. This is true of the internationally renowned Museu Nacional d'Art de Catalunya on Montjuïc hill, formerly the Museum of Medieval Art, which is being reorganized and should include the entire contents of the former Museum of Modern Art. The town's Zoology, Archaeology and History museums are also being reworked. A Museum of Contemporary Art begun in 1989 by the American architect, Richard Meyer, on the grounds of the former Casa de Caritat in the El Raval district, should open in 1992. With the Miró and Tàpies foundations and the Museu Picasso it should confirm Barcelona's status as one of the richest European centres of 20th-century art.

Casa Museu Gaudi**
Parc Güell (no number), 08024, ☎ 214 6446.
Open March-Nov, daily 10am-2pm, 4-7pm. Closed Dec-Feb.
Gaudí's house and mementoes.

Fundació Antoni Tàpies*** II, B2
Carrer d'Aragó 255.
The Antoni Tàpies Contemporary Art Foundation is located in the premises of the former Montaner i Simon printing works.

Fundació Joan Miró*** II, A3
Plaça Neptú (Parc de Montjuïc), ☎ 329 1908.
Open Tues-Sat 11am-7pm; Thurs until 9:30pm; Sun and holidays 10:30am-2:30pm. Closed Mon.

Apart from showing paintings and sculptures by the great Catalan artist, the foundation regularly holds exhibitions, retrospectives and other cultural activities. The present Miró collection of over 10,000 works mainly represents the later period in the life of the artist. However, works from earlier stages can be seen as well, thanks to donations made by his wife and family. The foundation also houses the Contemporary Art Study Centre.

Museu Arqueològic de Barcelona*** II, A2
Passeig de Santa Madrona (no number), 08004, Montjuïc, ☎ 423 2149/423 5601.
Open Tues-Sat 9:30am-1:30pm and 4-7pm; Sun and holidays 9:30am-2pm. Closed Mon. Currently being restructured.

The museum gives a general survey of prehistoric life, which includes: the Carthaginian culture of Eivissa (Ibiza) and the famous *Lady of Eivissa;* the ancient Greek colony of Empúries and the sculpture of Asclepius (Aesculapius); and Roman culture through the reconstitution of thermal baths and houses lined with mosaics showing races in the amphitheatres of Barcelona and Girona.

Museu Clarà*
Carrer de Calatrava 27-29, 08017, ☎ 203 4058.
Open Tues-Sun 9am-2pm. Closed Mon.

The studio belonged to Josep Clarà (1878-1958), a famous Catalan sculptor from the turn of the century.

Museu d'Autòmates del Tibidabo*
Parc d'atraccions del Tibidabo, 08022, ☎ 211 7942.
Open Oct-Mar, weekends and holidays, 11am-8pm; April-Sept daily 11am-8pm.

Collections of automatons and models.

Museu de Cera (Wax Museum)*** I, B3
Passatge de la Banca 7, 08002, ☎ 317 2649.
Open Mon-Fri 11am-1:30pm and 4:30-7:30pm; weekends and holidays 11am-1:30pm and 4:30-8pm.

More than 300 wax models of celebrities from all over the world.

Museu de Ceràmica**
Avinguda Diagonal 686, 08034, ☎ 205 1967.
Open Tues-Sun 9am-2pm. Closed Mon.

Medieval and modern ceramic collections (currently being rearranged).

Museu de Geologia (Museu Martorell)* II, D3
Parc de la Ciutadella (no number), 08003, ☎ 319 9312.
Open Tues-Sun 9am-2pm. Closed Mon.

The oldest museum in Barcelona. Palaeontology, natural sciences and library.

Museu de la Ciència**
Carrer Teodor Roviralta 55, 08022, ☎ 212 6050.
Open Tues-Sun 10am-8pm. Closed Mon.

Conceived along the lines of American science museums, visitors take an active part in the exhibits. Among the events organized are scientific films, conferences, courses and temporary exhibitions. The Planetarium has shows in Catalan, Castilian, English and French. There is also an observatory.

Museu de la Música* II, C1

Avinguda Diagonal 373, 08808, ☎ 217 1157.
Open Tues-Sun 9am-2pm. Closed Mon.

The collections are in an elegant setting and cover the period from the 16th to the 20th century. There are displays of instruments, music scores, mementoes of famous musicians and so on.

Museu de les Arts Decoratives**

Palau de Pedralbes, avinguda Diagonal 686, 08034, ☎ 204 6319/203 5285/203 7501.

Large collections from the 16th to the 20th century of furniture, Catalan glassware, precious metalwork, and porcelain (currently being rearranged).

Museu de les Arts de l'Espectacle (Institut del Teatre)** I, B2

Nou de la Rambla 3-5, 08002, ☎ 317 3974 and 317 2078.
Open Mon-Sat 11am-2pm and 5-8pm. Closed Sundays and holidays.

The museum was opened in 1954 on the basis of several legacies, and contains artifacts relevant to the history of Catalan theatre. Among the most noteworthy articles are the mementoes of Frederic Soler 'Pitarra', Àngel Guimerà's personal office (moved from Casa Aldavert in carrer Petritxol), Enric Borràs's costume for his role in *Manelic,* and collections of posters, scripts and programmes. There's also a section devoted to the **Gran Teatre del Liceu** and a specialized library.

Museu del Monestir de Pedralbes*

Baixada Monestir 9, 08034, ☎ 203 9282.
Open Tues-Sun 9:30am-2pm. Closed Mon.

Cloisters and Gothic wall paintings.

Museu del Textil i de la Indumentària* I, D2

Carrer de Montcada 12-14, 08003, ☎ 310 4516.
Open Tues-Sat 9am-2pm and 4:30-7pm, Sun 9am-2pm. Closed Mon.

There are three sections: textiles, clothes and lace.

Museu de Zoologia* II, D3

Passeig Picasso (no number), Parc de la Ciutadella, 08003, ☎ 319 6950/319 6912.
Open Tues-Sun 9am-2pm. Closed Mon. Admission free for under 18s.

This natural history museum is located in the former restaurant of the Universal Exhibition of 1888. There is a specialized library and sound archives.

Museu d'Història de la Ciutat** II, C3

Plaça del Rei (no number), 08002, ☎ 315 111.
Open Tues-Sat 9am-8:30pm; Sun and holidays 9am-1:30pm. Closed Mon.

Museum of the history of Barcelona. Archaeological excavations.

Museu Etnològic** II, A2

Passeig de Santa Madrona (no number), 08004, Montjuïc, ☎ 424 6807/424 6402.
Open Tues-Sat 9am-8:30pm; Mon 3-8:30pm; Sun and holidays 9am-2pm.

Ethnological collections from all five continents.

Museu Frederic Marès*** I, C2

Carrer dels Comtes 10, 08002, ☎ 310 5800.

Open Tues-Sat 9am-2pm and 4-7pm; Sun and holidays 9am-2pm. Closed Mon.

The museum contains a fine collection of sculptures assembled by sculptor Frederic Marès who is the curator. The works are mainly Spanish and cover the Middle Ages for the most part, with some works from the Renaissance and the 17th century. There is also a section of liturgical objects known as the Museu Sentimental, as well as unusual odds and ends including locks and keys, combs, fans, clocks, pipes, photographs and so on.

Museu Marítim** II, C3

Portal de la Pau 1, 08001, ☎ 318 3245/301 6425.
Open Tues-Sat 10am-2pm and 4-7pm; Sun and holidays 10am-2pm. Closed Mon.

The museum traces the history of the Catalan navy and its feats from the Middle Ages to 1859 when the first submarine (invented by Narcis Monturiol) was immersed in Barcelona's waters. Entrance to the museum includes a visit to the harbour nearby where you can see a replica of the *Santa María*, the caravel that took part in the first expedition to the Americas *(open 9am-3pm and 4pm to nightfall)*. There is also a library and photographic archives.

Museu Militar de Montjuïc* II, A3

Castell de Montjuïc, 08004, ☎ 329 8613.
Open Tues-Sat 10am-2pm and 4-7pm; Sun 10am-7pm. Closed Mon.

Collections of ancient and modern weapons, uniforms, models and tin soldiers. Artillery, mostly from the 1936-1939 Civil War.

Museu Nacional d'Art de Catalunya*** II, A2

Mirador del Palau 6, 08004, Montjuïc, ☎ 423 1824.
Open Tues-Sun 9am-2pm. Closed Mon.

The world's most important collection of Catalan Romanesque and Gothic art. There are three sections: Romanesque art with wall paintings from the 11th to the 13th century, Gothic art (including art from neighbouring areas) and works from the 16th and 17th centuries by Tintoretto, El Greco, Zurbarán, Ribera, Viladomat and so on. The museum will soon also house the town's collections of modern art.

Museu Picasso*** II, D3

Carrer de Montcada 15-19, 08003, ☎ 315 4761/319 6310.
Open Tues-Sun 10am-7:30pm. Closed Mon.

The collection consists of the Sabartés legacy, the Plandiura collection bought by the Generalitat de Catalunya in 1932, and donations from the artist in 1968 (series of *Ménines*) and in 1970 (works from his youth).

Youthful masterpieces

Although the Picasso museum covers all the periods of the artist's works, it is especially renowned for its collections of work from his youth. The highlight is the room of *Ménines,* a series of paintings in which Picasso gives his interpretation of the famous picture *(Las Meninas)* by Velasquez. Among his early paintings are: *First Communion* (1896), *Science and Charity* (1897), *Portrait of the Artist's Sister* (1899), *The Teller* (1900) and *La Nana* (1901). Among those of the Cubist period is *Les Manolles* (1917) and from the 'Rose period' the *Portrait of Senyora Canals.* Note also among his early works, *The Sick Child* from the 'Blue period' (1904) and perhaps the most famous painting in the museum, *Harlequin,* dating from 1917.

The architecture of Martorell-Bohigas-Mackay (1974-1988)

The MBM group was formed by the architects Josep Martorell and Oriol Bohigas in 1961 and joined by David Mackay, an Englishman, in 1962. Through its firm intention to integrate architecture into the environment and by its continued attention to the development of architecture, MBM is without doubt the most impressive group of the past thirty years.

A number of buildings from MBM's early period break firmly with the aesthetic formula prevalent in Franco's day by calling upon what Bohigas, an architectural theorist, has defined as realist architecture. Three buildings are representative of their first steps: the Escorial apartments (carrer de l'Escorial 50) built between 1952 and 1962, the Pallars workers' accommodation built from 1958-1959 (carrer de Pallars 299-317) and the group of 121 apartments on avinguda de la Meridiana 312-318 (1960-1965).

The following are representative of one of the main architectural trends in the 1970s and 1980s:

Apartments in the Sarría district (carrer d'Ossio 43-45; carrer Eduard Conde 50). This is a group of 95 apartments in three detached buildings. An effort has been made to adapt to the narrow street system through the use of alleyways that open onto an inner garden, creating at the same time a green space for the quarter (1975-1979).

Can Sumarro, Hospitalet de Llobregat. This is fine example of the rehabilitation of a farmhouse through its conversion into a public library. Still keeping the traditional structure, the courtyard has been transformed into the access area to the library, the children's reading room has been set up in the old barn and the adult's reading room in the house itself.

La Maquinista in Barceloneta district. In 1976 the council bought up the area belonging to the Maquinista factory and 250 apartments were built. Linear blocks of accommodation were arranged around a rectangular area which meant special care had to be taken with the corner buildings (1979-1989).

Nestlé offices, Esplugues de Llobregat (avinguda Països Catalans 33-49). The new Nestlé office building is an extension of an ensemble built in the 1970s that gave rise to constraints in terms of space and use. The façade is a kind of wall-curtain, a wonder of technology and aestheticism. A red column at the entrance testifies to the present preoccupation of the group with colour. This concern has burst forth in the more recent project for the single-family house of Son Vida in Majorca (1982-1987).

ENVIRONS OF BARCELONA

Sant Cugat del Vallès**

7 mi/12 km north west of Barcelona.

This famous Benedictine monastery is the largest in the whole county of Barcelona. The prettiest roads from Barcelona to Sant Cugat either pass through Arrabassada where you have fine panoramic views of the town, or through Vallvidrera. In both cases you can combine your visits to Sant Cugat and Tibidabo. An alternative is to take an FC train (city trains run by the Generalitat) from plaça de Catalunya.

Sant Cugat del Vallès in the past

St Cucufas (Cugat), a Christian of North African origin, was martyred in 303; during persecutions by Diocletian. Excavations in the 1930s uncovered a palaeo-Christian funerary basilica in the cloisters surrounded by numerous tombs. Though the community of Sant Cugat probably dates back to the 6th or 7th century, evidence of its existence dates back only to the 9th.

What to see

Some of the monastery's medieval walls have been preserved. The building of the church itself was undertaken at the end of the Romanesque era and was finished during the Gothic period in the 14th century. The main rose window is a fine example of Catalan Gothic

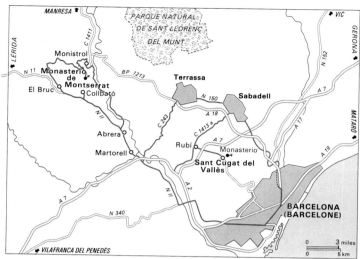

ENVIRONS OF BARCELONA

art with its full, heavy shapes where the decoration is due more to the wide cut of the stone than to the stained glass.

The monastery's reputation as a site of interest is due especially to its carved Romanesque **cloister*****, one of the country's largest and most beautiful. The four galleries which open onto an immense central courtyard are adorned with extremely fine carved capitals. Rich and varied, they testify to the high quality of Romanesque art at the end of the 12th century. The capital decorations include animals, plant motifs and a number of biblical themes — all aimed at enhancing the reflective life of the religious community. On one of the corner columns in the north east you can read the inscription Arnau Cadell, the name of the sculptor or foreman whose portrait can be seen on the adjoining capital.

Inside the **church** several Renaissance and Baroque altarpieces have been preserved.

At the end of the 19th and beginning of the 20th century, the town of Sant Cugat was prized as a holiday resort by the inhabitants of Barcelona and there are still a number of Modernist-style houses.

Terrassa**

11 mi/17 km north of Sant Cugat.

You reach Terrassa after passing through the town of Rubí. Terrassa shares the greater part of Spain's textile production and wool industry with nearby Sabadell. Today the town has a population of 150,000 and has become an integral part of Barcelona's outer suburbs, directly linked to the capital by the A18 highway.

Terrassa in the past

The town of Egara was already known in Roman times but suddenly gained importance when in 450 a bishopric was installed, independent of that in Barcelona, led by Bishop Irenæus. In the 9th century the centre of power moved from the bishopric to the castle of Terrassa around which medieval and, later, modern life revolved. The traditional manufacture of cloth sheets dates back to the Middle Ages.

What to see

Three **churches***** deserve a detailed visit as they are among Catalonia's most important religious buildings from the early Middle Ages. Once inside the town's perimeter walls you will see the church of Sant Pere on the left, Sant Miquel in the middle and Santa Maria behind.

The church of **Santa Maria** dates from the Romanesque period. South of it are the remains of a 12th-century Augustinian cloister. In the apse some faded paintings organized on a concentric basis date from the early Middle Ages and illustrate scenes from the life of Christ. The church has other important paintings dating from the late Middle Ages. In the apse of the southern arm of the transept a series of Romanesque paintings from the second half of the 12th century depict the martyrdom of Thomas à Becket. In the nave, fragments of Gothic wall paintings hide those from the early Middle Ages still faintly visible in the apse. Finally, and most importantly, there are some fine Gothic altarpieces for which the church is renowned: that of St Peter by Lluís Borrassà (1475), another of St Michael by Jaume Sirera and Guillem Talarn (middle 15th-century) and the famous altarpiece of St Abdon and St Senen by Jaume Huguet (1460) that once adorned the altar of the church of Sant Pere.

The church of **Sant Miquel** is the former baptistery of the episcopal buildings. At the back of the apse you can see wall paintings from the early Middle Ages and under the apse there is a small crypt.

The church of **Sant Pere** still has its trefoil apse and its transept from the early Middle Ages. The central apse is closed off by an altarpiece from about the year 1000 and the floor is covered by a mosaic dating from the same period. The nave is 12th-century.

At the exit of the church enclosure near the stream you will see the **castle** and **Charter-house of Vallparadis** which house the Municipal Art Museum *(open 10am-1pm, 4-7pm; Sun and holidays 11am-2pm; in winter Tues-Sat 10am-1pm and 3-6pm. Closed Mon).*

Of the Charter-house founded in 1364, the chapel, the cloister and admirable walls with towers remain. Various other monuments offer historical interest: among them are the **keep** of the former medieval castle and the parish church of the Holy Spirit, built between 1574 and 1616, an example of the persistence of Gothic architecture in religious buildings. Inside there is a fine carved group from the Renaissance, *The Burial* by Martí Diez de Liatzasolo (1539-1540). The church of the former convent of **St Francis,** from the same period, can also be visited along with the cloister embellished with 18th-century ceramics representing scenes from the life of the saint.

Terrassa has a good number of Modernist architectural treasures that testify to the town's industrial and economic boom in the 19th century. In the middle of the public park of Sant Jordi the **Masia Freixa** (1907-1910), a neo-Moorish building by Gaudí with parabolic arches, has been preserved. At that time Lluís Moncunill, a local architect, dominated the construction of new buildings in the town. The Romanesque-style **Industrial School** (1903) is his; so is the neo-Gothic **Town Hall** (1903) and the Aymerich textile factory on the Rambla built between 1907 and 1908. This has since been converted into the **Museu de la Ciència i de la Tècnica*** and exhibits important collections of industrial and archaeological interest. It is destined to play an essential role in the study of industrial art *(open Mon-Sat 4-7pm; Sun and holidays 10am-2pm; presently being reorganized,* ☎ *780 6755/780 6399).*

Terrassa also has an interesting **Museu Tèxtil**, carrer de Salmeron 19-21 *(open 10am-1pm and 5-8pm; Sun and holidays 10am-2pm; closed Mon.)*

Montserrat, the holy mountain**

25 mi/40 km north west of Barcelona.

If you are traveling by car, take the N11 (Barcelona to Lleida), branch off at Abrera and continue via Monistrol. There is also a bus service from Barcelona to the monastery. Finally, you can take the train from Barcelona to Monistrol station and from there the aerial cable car that takes you up the slope in no time at all.

The monastery of Montserrat stands on one of the jagged pinnacles of the Montserrat mountain; venerated as a holy site since the 9th century when Christian hermits lived there, it became the home of the Benedictines in the 11th century.

Montserrat mountains' silhouette of bare jagged rock rises in isolation 4052 ft/1235 m above sea level over an area of about 6 mi/10 km.

Montserrat monastery is Catalonia's national sanctuary. It shelters a Benedictine community of about 100 monks and is a cultural centre of the highest importance with its library and extensive archives. The monastery's thousand-year-old history mirrors that of Catalonia.

Montserrat in the past

The sanctuary at Montserrat, known since the 9th century as a hermitage, became a Benedictine monastery in 1025 when it was founded by Abbot Oliba from Ripoll. It obtained its independence in the 14th century. The basilica you see today was begun in 1560 and consecrated in 1592. It was built in the Gothic tradition and has a single nave with six chapels on each side. The apse is a neo-Romanesque construction dating from the end of the 19th century while the Baroque-style modern façade has marble decoration and sculptures by the Vilamitjana brothers (1900-1901).

What to see

Architectural and decorative remains of former monasteries on the site have been preserved. The doorway of the 12th-century Romanesque church has been re-used in one of the sides of the atrium preceding the basilica. Outside on one side of the square you can see a few arches from the Gothic cloister. Inside the basilica the most highly esteemed work is the Romanesque statue of St Mary of Montserrat, the Black Virgin *(la Moreneta)* which has undergone a number of restorations.

You can climb the stairs to the statue of the Virgin above the high altar, visit the crypt or wander around to admire the church's many works of art — notably modern and contemporary. Or pause to listen to the famous abbey student choirs.

The **Monastery Museum** comprises three main sections — local pre-history, the Holy Land and an art gallery that also displays pieces from the treasury. Thanks to the Sala legacy a **Museum of Modern and Contemporary Catalan Painting★** has been opened. *Rooms of ancient works open in winter 10:30am-1pm; in summer 10:30am-2pm and 3-6pm. Rooms of modern works open in winter 3-6pm; in summer 10:30am-2pm and 3:30-6pm.*

Among the religious services in the basilica open to the public, mention should be made of early mass sung by the boys' choir, the conventual mass, then at midday the *Salve Regina* which is sung and, at nightfall, the rosary, vespers and the *Virolai* (hymn to the Virgin of Montserrat).

Places to visit in the area surrounding the monastery include the **Holy Cave** (Santa Cova) in which, according to legend, the statue of the Virgin was found (access on foot or by the Sant Jeroni funicular railway); the **Hermitage of Sant Joan** (Sant Jeroni funicular railway); various lookout points for magnificent panoramic views; and the church of **Santa Cecilia** — one of the finest examples of 11th-century Romanesque architecture.

AROUND CATALONIA

To give you a glimpse of the rich landscapes and varied life-styles in Catalonia we have designed five itineraries, in addition to the one covering the immediate surroundings of Barcelona. Each itinerary can be regarded as a specific trip, introducing you to Romanesque art, the Pyrenees, the Catalan hinterland, the Vall d'Aran and the coast from Girona to Tarragona, with its natural and artistic resources. The itineraries are designed to form a circular route from Barcelona that takes in the whole of Catalonia beginning with Vic and Ripoll, followed by the Costa Brava and the Pyrenees, and finishing with Lleida (Lérida) and Tarragona.

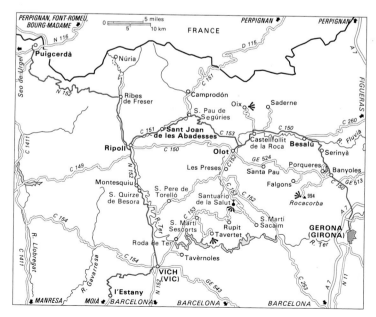

ROMANESQUE ART ITINERARY

The Sant Pere Cathedral in Vic.

VIC, RIPOLL, SANT JOAN DE LES ABADESSES — ROMANESQUE ART

Catalonia is superbly rich in Romanesque art. This medieval style developed throughout the 11th century and reached its culmination in the 12th. For this itinerary we've selected only a few of the most important from several hundred monuments, the Ripoll monastery being the main destination. The sites are easy to reach and, taken as a group, will give you a good idea of the scope of the cultural wealth of Catalonia during the Middle Ages.

BARCELONA TO VIC

Take the A7 highway north to **Granollers** (16 mi/26 km) where you can see the 16th-century **grain market** (Porxada) and the new **Archaeological and Regional Art Museum**, interesting also from a museological point of view as it is particularly well laid out. *Open in summer 6-9pm, Sun 11:30am-1:30pm and 6-9pm; in winter 5:30-8:30pm, Sun 11:30am-1:30pm; closed Mon.* Then take the N152 and after passing the former holiday resorts of La Garriga, El Figaro and Aiguafreda, where Barcelona's middle classes used to meet at the beginning of the century, you reach Vic, capital of the Osona region.

VIC★

Telephone area code: 93.

Access: By car, take the A7 highway north to Granollers, then the N152; by train, on the Barcelona-Puigcerdà line.

Vic stands in the centre of a plain of the same name, 41 mi/66 km north of Barcelona. It is not only of great artistic interest but is also the capital of a large diocese which has produced a good number of Catalan priests. Today it is a commercial, industrial town renowned for its markets on Tuesdays and (especially) Saturdays. Some of them take on the proportions of a fair, particularly those held on All Saints' Day, at Christmas and at the beginning of Lent. The best known is the *del Ram* (Palm Sunday) market, famous for its salt meat and sausages.

Vic in the past

During the early Middle Ages, Vic was one of the country's most important cultural and historical centres. In the 9th century the town was divided into two large zones — the upper part contained the castle and the count's seat of influence, and the lower part dominated by the cathedral was the centre of episcopal power. Vestiges of the Gothic walls have been preserved. Numerous monuments testify to the town's importance through the centuries and a visit to the Episcopal Museum is an absolute must.

What to see

The **Roman temple,** B2, with a cella and atrium gives an idea of what the smaller temples of Antiquity were like.

The town's most important monument is the **Sant Pere Catedral★,** B3, the religious centre of Vic since Carolingian times. Only the crypt remains from the first Romanesque construction built in 1038. During the 11th century a Romanesque belfry was added to the church. This is well-preserved and can be admired on the northern flank of the cathedral. During the second half of the 12th century the cathedral was adorned with a carved façade like that on the abbey church of Ripoll, many fragments of which are kept in the museum. The present cathedral is a neo-Classical edifice built by Josep Moretó between 1781 and 1803. During this reconstruction the Gothic cloister from the first half of the 14th century (which had been built over the previous Romanesque one) was preserved. Inside the cathedral you can see the alabaster altarpiece carved by Pere Oller between 1420 and 1427. The Sant Bernat Calbó chapel is Baroque. Today the cathedral is visited mainly for its murals by Josep Maria Sert, repainted by the artist himself after the Civil War. His illustrations of religious scenes bear a dramatic stamp.

The **Episcopal Palace**, adjoining the cathedral, houses the episcopal library and one of the largest collections of documents in Catalonia, including a fair number of parchments from the 9th and 10th centuries as well as illuminated manuscripts.

The **Episcopal Museum★★★**, plaça Bisbe Oliba 3, B2 *(open in winter 10am-1pm; in summer 10am-1pm and 4-6pm; Sun and holidays 10am-1pm)*, was inaugurated in 1891. This is one of Catalonia's most

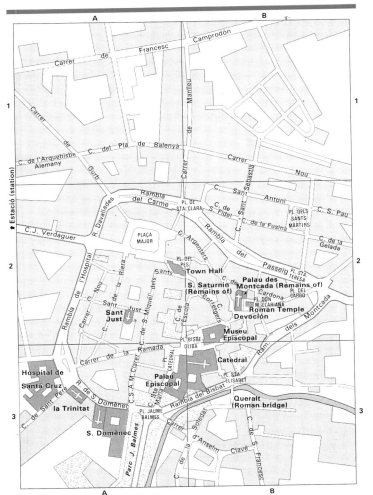

VIC

important museums, especially from the point of view of medieval art (painting and sculpture). There are also sections on prehistory, ceramic collections, Egyptian art, fabrics, glassware, weapons and stones. Among the most important works are Romanesque murals and wood paintings (by Puigbó, Espinelves, Sescorts, Vidrà, Osormort and El Brull among others) and wooden sculptures (like the *Descent from the Cross* by Erill). Of the great Gothic artists represented in the museum, be sure to see Ferrer Bassa, Pere Serra, Lluís Borrassà, Jaume Huguet and Bernat Martorell.

Plaça Major, A2 located near the ancient walls, is the medieval centre of town. Its present architecture gives an idea of the development of different styles since the 16th century.

The **Town Hall,** A2 on the south-west corner of the square has Gothic elements with mitre (Gothic) arches on the ground floor and what is known as the Column Room on the first floor.

Other places of interest in Vic can be seen near the rambla de Sant Domènec which was once an esplanade outside the walls. They include the former **Hospital de la Santa Crey** with its Gothic rooms, and, along the same rambla, the church of **Sant Domènec**, a large Baroque edifice begun in 1708 by Josep Moretó that has a fine cloister with suspended arches. Other buildings in Vic by the same architect include the Carmelite church on rambla de Santa Teresa and the Santa Teresa convent opposite. If you are interested in Modernist architecture, there is Palau Comella, the Casino, on plaça Major, by the architect Gaietà Buïgas (1896), and Casa Colomer on the cathedral square built in 1906 by J.-M. Pericas.

Accommodation
▲▲▲▲ **Parador Nacional**, 9 mi/14 km north east of Vic off the Roda de Ter road, ☎ 888 7211. 31 rooms. A little far from town but ideal for a quiet stay beside the Sau dam. Good food.
▲▲▲ **Can Pamplona**, out of town on the carretera N152 from Vic to Puigcerdà, (no restaurant), ☎ 885 3612. 34 rooms. Comfortable, regional hotel, ideal place to break a trip.
▲▲ **Ausa**, plaça Mayor 2, A2, ☎ 885 5311. 26 rooms. In the town centre. Simple, unpretentious, pleasant and inexpensive.
▲ **Colon**, rambla del Passeig 1, B2, ☎ 886 0220. 38 rooms. Modest hotel frequented by people passing through who know it well. Reliable and economical.

Food and drink
♦♦♦ **Anec-Blau**, carrer de Verdaguer 21-23, A2, ☎ 885 3151. *Closed Mon.* Luxurious; gourmet food. For those who love both modern and regional types of cooking.
♦♦ **Mamma Mia**, Passeig 61, B2, ☎ 886 3998. Italian cuisine.

ENVIRONS OF VIC

To get to the Romanesque **monastery of Estany★★**, a former Augustinian college 12 mi/20 km from Vic, first take the Balsareny road (south-west) and then branch off (south) onto the road to Moià. The monastery was founded in 1080 but all that remains today is the church of Santa Maria *(open daily 10am-1pm and 4-6pm).* This was consecrated in 1133 and is typical of the fully developed Romanesque style, in spite of its later additions. It has a fine late-Romanesque cloister (the building of which continued into the 13th century) with 72 carved capitals. In the oldest wing, close to the church, these represent the life of Christ but it is mainly the eastern gallery that attracts attention because of its capitals, which are illustrated with secular subjects.

RIPOLL★★

Telephone area code: 972.
Access: By car, on the N152; by train, on the Barcelona-Puigcerdà line.
Ripoll, the highly industrial capital of the Ripollès region, stands at the confluence of the Ter and Freser rivers. Thanks to its monastery and Romanesque abbey it is considered the cradle of Catalonia. Allow three hours for a visit.

What to see
The **Monastery of Santa Maria★★★** was founded by Wilfred the Hairy (Guifré el Pelós) in 879 or 880. The church, which was consecrated by Abbot Oliba in 1032 and heavily restored between 1886 and 1893 by the architect Elies Rogent, is the best preserved part of the monastery. It is also one of the most important monuments of the early Catalan Romanesque style and from an architectural point of view is representative of the generation of churches built during the first half of the 11th century. A nave and four aisles end in a markedly projecting

Detail of the lavish sculpted portal of the monastery of Ripoll: inspired by ancient triumphal arches, the imagery celebrates the recovery of Catalan lands from the Muslims.

transept attached to which are an apse and three chapels after the model of the palaeo-Christian basilica of St Peter's in Rome. The 11th-century church façade was flanked by two square towers of which only the southern one remains today. Churches of this time were characterized by architectural decoration in the form of delicate arcading and shallow niches.

At the beginning of the second half of the 12th century a large carved **portal,** a sort of triumphal arch, was added to the church. This façade is one of the major monuments in the history of Western art as much for its structure as for its sculptural wealth. Unfortunately, its bad condition prevents you from deciphering all the scenes (see plan p. 144).

The grandiose aspect of the doorway is enhanced by the design, which draws upon antique triumphal arches. The upper part is decorated with a scene of the triumph of Christ, and below, with figures of historical characters who took part in the establishment of Christ's kingdom on earth. The whole, seeming to be a glorification of imperial leadership, takes on its full meaning when you consider the country's political situation at the time; when the doorway was set into the façade of the church — a pantheon of the Catalan dynasty — Ramon Berenguer III and his son, Ramon Berenguer IV, had just retaken Catalan lands from the Muslims.

During the Middle Ages the Ripoll abbey contained several carved sarcophagi belonging to abbots or high ranking people. That of Ramon Berenguer III, Count of Barcelona, who died in 1311, lies today in a vast funerary monument at the end of the transept.

Work on the **cloister**** *(access to the right of the church porch; open 9am-1:30pm and 4-7:30pm)* began in the Romanesque era and was continued in the Gothic period. The cloister consists of four galleries organized around a large courtyard. The capitals of the 13 arches in the Romanesque gallery are similar in conception to the reliefs of the portal. This section was finished under Abbot Ramon de Berga (1172-1206), according to the inscription above a bas-relief of the abbot on the pillar in the north-east corner. The Gothic galleries were built in the second half of the 14th century under Abbot Galceran de Besora (1380-1383).

Before leaving Ripoll you should visit the Folk Museum, or **Museum of the Pyrenees** *(open 9am-1pm and 3-7pm; Mon 9am-1pm)*, which contains an ethnographic section and rooms on the industrialization of Ripollès during the last century. There is, in particular, a section on old forges and the manufacture of firearms and nails. The museum also displays vestiges of the medieval period found in the monastery.

The Church of Santa Maria. Scenes on the façade:

1. Christ in majesty, angels and symbols of the Evangelists.
2. Old men of the Apocalypse.
3. Saints.
4. Episodes from the story of Solomon (left) and Moses (right).
5. Scenes from the Old Testament.
6. David among his musicians (left) and historical characters presided over by Christ (right).
7. Daniel's visions, animals.
8. Plinth with decorative patterns.
9. Inner sides of the doorway pillars illustrating the monthly agricultural occupations.
10. Decorative patterns and statues of St Peter and St Paul.
11. The story of Cain and Abel.
12. Stories of Jonah and Daniel.
13. Stories of St Peter and St Paul.
14. Decorative relief with animals. The mystic Lamb in the centre with angels.
15. Northern side wall: scenes of Elijah.
16. Southern side wall: the crossing of the Red Sea, Lazarus in the bosom of Abraham.

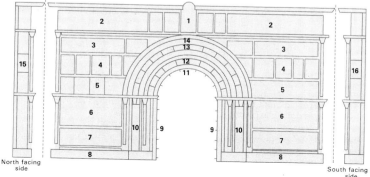

North facing side

South facing side

The Catalan forge

The iron-making process known as the 'Catalan forge' that brought considerable wealth to the Ripollès region in the 19th century is illustrated in the Ripoll museum. It is a process for obtaining iron through the reduction of ore, which, in a single operation, is converted into a malleable substance through the use of charcoal. The metal does not reach a state of fusion but remains a spongy mass known as *'masser'*. Because the iron and steel thus obtained were of a high quality, the process was used in western Europe from the Middle Ages until the end of the 19th century in spite of the development of blast furnaces. Contrary to what its name 'Catalan forge' implies, the technique did not originate in Catalonia but it was perfected there. This type of forge was always located near a river or stream. Note also the display in the museum of Ripoll's portable firearms which in the 16th, 17th and 18th centuries were among the finest in Europe.

Accommodation

▲▲ **Solana del Ter**, carretera Barcelona-Ripoll (no number), ☎ 70 1062. 28 rooms. Slightly out of town. A pleasant hotel with good food.

▲ **Monasterio**, plaça Gran 4, ☎ 70 0150. 40 rooms. In the town centre. Practical, modern facilities.

▲ **Payet**, plaça Nova 2, ☎ 70 0250. 22 rooms. Renowned for its friendly welcome and regional cuisine.

Festivals

The town festival *(Festa Major)* is held on May 11 and the following Sunday is National Wool Day with various traditional rituals including the shearing of a flock, the spinning of wool and the celebration of a country-style wedding.

Useful addresses

Buses: RENFE station. Buses for Camprodon, Girona, Ribes and Sant Quirze de Besora.
Emergencies: ☎ 70 0159.
Tourist Information: plaça de l'Abat Oliva, ☎ 70 2351.

▬ *SANT JOAN DE LES ABADESSES* ★★

Access: About 6 mi/10 km north east of Ripoll on the road to Camprodon and Olot.

The **monastery of Sant Joan de les Abadesses**★★★ was first founded as a convent in 885 by Count Wilfred so that his daughter, Emma, could become the first abbess. After her death in 942 four abbesses succeeded her before the community was dispersed in 1017. Like that of Ripoll, the monastery of Sant Joan was one of Catalonia's major medieval centres of monastic life and throughout its eventful history it had the protection of various counts.

The present church was consecrated in 1150 even though it was not yet completely finished. It has a rather strange plan implying that there was a change in the project as soon as building began. What was originally intended to be a church with a nave, two aisles and a transept, became an edifice with a single nave. Of the monastery's two cloisters, only one remains today, the Gothic one (north) where three arches and three capitals of the older Romanesque cloister have been preserved.

In the church, the magnificent group of the *Descent from the Cross* ★★★ dating, according to documents, from June 16, 1251, is a masterpiece of Romanesque wood sculpture. Legend has it that on the day the church was consecrated a Host appeared in a hollow space on the forehead of the figure of Christ. During the Middle Ages, sculptures representing the Descent from the Cross were common and several examples have been preserved in Catalonia and in Italy. The church contains several altarpieces, among them the alabaster work of Santa Maria la Blanca, dating from 1343.

The **Monastery Museum** inaugurated in 1975 in the former outbuildings houses various sculptures and several works from the former treasury *(open Mar-June and Sept-Oct 11am-2pm and 4-6pm; June-Sept 10am-7pm, Mon 10am-2pm and 4-7pm; Nov-March 11am-2:30pm, weekends and holidays 11am-2pm and 4-7pm).*

Before leaving town you could visit the **abbey palace** with its delightful little 15th-century cloister and the church of St Paul, a Romanesque ruin, once the parish church. It retains vestiges of its chevet, notably a carved tympanum. As you leave town, an elegant Gothic bridge spans the river Ter.

From here you can either return to Barcelona or head straight on to Puigcerdà where you are within easy reach of the Pyrenees (see p. 159). Alternatively, you could go on to Girona (visiting Olot on the way) to continue the itineraries proposed below.

▬ *SANT JOAN DE LES ABADESSES TO GIRONA*

Olot is a medium-sized industrial town in the La Garrotxa region, specializing in textiles, cooked processed meats (delicatessen) and up until the middle of the 20th century, holy pictures.

In a walk around town you will see a number of 18th-and 19th-century buildings (such as the neo-Classical parish **church of St Stephen,** the former **hospice** dating from the end of the 18th century and the **Carmelite convent** with its Renaissance cloister). Another worthwhile visit is the **Museu Comarcal de La Garrotxa,** carrer de Hospici 8 *(open 11am-2pm and 4-7pm; Sun and holidays 9am-2pm; closed Tues).* This is made up of the former Archaeological Museum and the Modern Art Museum with its sizeable collection of Catalan paintings and drawings from the 19th and 20th centuries with an emphasis on the Olot school of landscape painting.

In the **Parish Museum** there is a painting by El Greco of *Christ carrying the Cross.*

Besalú★★

A worthwhile second stop on the way to Girona is the village of Besalú which has not changed much since the Middle Ages. Because cars are not allowed, you park outside the village and enter it on foot across a medieval bridge. Among the monuments to visit are the Romanesque churches of **Sant Pere, Santa Maria** and **Sant Vincent,** all of great interest, and the remains of the synagogue and *Mikvah* (ritual bath) in the former Jewish quarter.

Banyolés

The town of Banyolés makes a pleasant stop. Banyolés has a porticoed square in the centre of the town, the 14th-century Pia Almoina building and the Romanesque monastery of Sant Esteve. The town is mainly known for its position on the shores of a large **lake** — an ideal spot for water sports. For information, ☎ (972) 57 0050. With an area of more than 1 million square metres, the lake has become Spain's largest water sports centre and international competitions are held here on a regular basis.

The **Archaeological Museum** *(open daily in summer 10am-1pm and 5-8pm; in winter 10am-1pm and 4-7pm; closed Mon)* houses a reproduction of the human jaw found in Banyolés (the original is in a private collection) — a rare regional vestige of Neanderthal man.

The Olot school of landscape painting

The Olot school came into being in the second half of the 19th century embracing on the one hand local Olot artists and on the other, all those artists inspired by the environs of Olot. It is often compared to the Barbizon School in France. Its founder, the painter Joaquim Vayreda, was a student of Ramon Martí Alsina. Vayreda's paintings drew a number of artists to Olot including Barrau, Galwey, Urgell, Casas and Rusiñol. The school was later to become institutionalized with the founding of the Olot Artistic and Cultural Centre and the Public School of Drawing. The prestige of the Olot School is such that today a landscape painting may commonly be referred to as an 'Olot'.

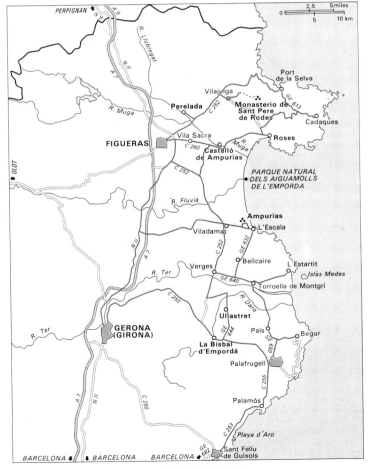

GIRONA AND THE COSTA BRAVA ITINERARY

GIRONA AND THE COSTA BRAVA

Girona (Gerona in Castilian) is the centre for the Costa Brava itinerary. With the town as your base you can tour the Costa Brava's two main regions, the Alt (upper) and Baix (Lower) Empordà, as well as the area around the Pyrenees. For a time after 1908 the name Costa Brava covered the section of the coast between Blanes and Begur but it has since been applied to the entire coastal region of Girona.

The most northerly zone of the Alt Empordà is indistinguishable from the Côte Vermeille just above it in Roussillon, France. The rocky section of the coast immediately south has little creek areas that have become quite residential, such as Llançà, El Port de la Selva and Cadaqués. Then you come to the Golfo de Roses and its two tourist centres, Roses and L'Escala. The southern part of the Costa Brava, the Baix Empordà, has the steepest shore and a dense vegetation of pines and oaks. Because of its many beaches and well-developed infrastructure it is Catalonia's most popular tourist attraction. (See map p. 147).

▰ *GIRONA*★★★

Telephone area code: 972.

Access: By car, on the N11 from Madrid to La Jonquera and the A7 highway from Barcelona to the French border; By plane, the airport is 7 mi/12 km south-west of the town centre.

Girona is a regional capital in the Ter valley located a short distance before the river flows into the Empordà plain, on the route between Barcelona and France. The town has grown rapidly over the last few decades and, with its 65,000 inhabitants, has acquired industrial and cultural importance. From a political and economic point of view Girona has benefited from its central position in relation to the rich *comarques* (counties) of Selva, La Garrotxa, El Gironès and the Alt and Baix Empordà.

Girona in the past

The Roman settlement of Girona was situated in the upper part of the present town. It was surrounded by a roughly rectangular enclosure; some of the walls remain to this day. The main street, corresponding to today's carrer de la Força, and one of the gates to the city were located

---

The Jews in medieval Catalonia

Many towns in Catalonia have preserved important vestiges of their Jewish quarters but the most prestigious is that of Girona. The oldest documents of the Jewish community in Girona date back to the 9th century.

Throughout the Middle Ages, the Jews formed organized urban communities centred in quarters known as *calls*. Their medieval history can be divided into four main periods: the first (876-1213) was one of economic prosperity — evident in the building of houses, synagogues, baths and so on; the second (1213-1283) was marked by increased participation in town life and commercial matters; during the third (1283-1391) fewer Jews held posts as civil servants but there was a renewal of their participation in professional fields (especially medicine and high finance); the last and unhappiest period (1391-1492) was marked by the increasing hostility of Christians, ending with the expulsion of the Jews from the city.

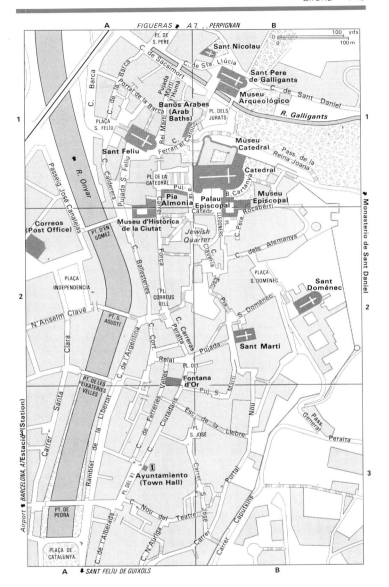

GIRONA

behind the church of Sant Feliu. The Roman road, via Augusta, today's rambla Verdaguer, was built in the lower part of the city parallel to the Onyar river.

Christianity came to Girona in the 3rd century and spread in the 4th — a fact confirmed by the sarcophagi in the church of Sant Feliu. In 785, Charlemagne took the city from the Muslims and from that time on the region fell under the political auspices of the Carolingians, serving as a frontier county. In 878, under the first count, Wilfred the Hairy, Girona became an important centre of New Catalonia. During the Middle Ages the town continued to prosper, growing beyond its walls into new districts such as Santa Maria, Sant Pere, Sant Feliu and Mercadel.

The expansion of the recently restored Jewish quarter dates from the Romanesque period. During the Middle Ages Girona's Jewish community was one of the largest in Catalonia and is one of the best documented.

In the Gothic period the city centre moved gradually towards plaça del Vi and the lower town. Under Pedro the Ceremonious in the last third of the 14th century the town was endowed with new walls. These were severely put to the test in the course of the town's later history by a succession of sieges: 1462-1463 and again in 1467, civil war against Jaume II; 1640 and 1642, the War of the Reapers *(Segadors)*; 1675, 1683-1684 and 1694, wars with France; 1710 and 1712, the War of the Spanish Succession; and 1808-1809, Napoleonic sieges. Because of its geographical position on the major route to France, Girona has had an extremely eventful history, one that has earned it the sobriquet 'Town of Sieges'.

What to see

Barri Vell, B1, the old quarter of Girona, preserves a good many monuments, mainly from the Middle Ages, all grouped together in a small area. By wandering through the narrow streets you will easily be able to conjure up life here in the Middle Ages, with its squires, merchants and clergymen. The old Jewish quarter is atmospheric too, with its alleyways and steep slopes dominated by the Cathedral.

The **Cathedral★★★**, B1, rising above the town, is a Gothic edifice dedicated to the Virgin Mary. It was built in the 14th century to replace the former Romanesque cathedral and its architecture throws light on the way large Catalan Gothic monuments were built at that time. Building began in the first quarter of the 14th century with the apse; the vaults and their painted keystones went up in the 15th and 16th centuries, while the Baroque façade, which was begun in 1680, was not finished until the 20th century. Among the works preserved in the cathedral is the so-called Charlemagne throne. Of the Romanesque cathedral there remains what is known as the Charlemagne Tower, a vestige of the 11th-century edifice, and the cloister which was an added embellishment in the 12th century and which should be visited first if you want to follow the chronological order in which the cathedral was built.

The **cloister★★★**, B1, is renowned for its exceptional decoration on the capitals and the carved friezes that form a vast series of illustrations. Biblical scenes from Genesis (Adam and Eve) and from the life of Christ unfold on the pillars, together with various representations of daily life (craftsmen at work, for example). Because of its great narrative capacity and the quality of its style, the cloister deserves comparison both with its neighbour Sant Pere de Galligants and especially with Sant Cugat del Vallès in the suburbs of Barcelona (see p. 133).

The **Museu Catedral★★**, *(open daily in winter 10am-1pm and 3:30-6pm; in summer 10am-7pm)* houses the richly illuminated **Beatus manuscript★★★** and the immense embroidery known as the **Tapestry of the Creation★★★**, one of the most beautiful wall hangings from the entire Romanesque Middle Ages. In a sense it is Catalonia's equivalent of France's famous Bayeux tapestry. The tapestry portrays a vision of the world dominated in the middle by the Divine Majesty presiding over all the different stages of Creation.

The **Palau Episcopal★★★**, B1, (Episcopal Palace), a recently restored Romanesque-Gothic edifice, is of one of Catalonia's most important museums of medieval art. *(open 10am-1pm and 4:30-7pm; Sun and holidays 10am-1pm; closed Mon.)*

On returning to the front of the Cathedral and standing with your back to it, you will see a Gothic building, the **Pia Almoina**, on the left. This was built in the 14th century to house a charitable institution that helped the poor. Today it is Girona's College of Architects. The Gothic façade with its central 15th-century tower was restored and heightened a little at the

A view of one of the brightly painted residential quarters of Girona, not far from the magnificent cathedral and the narrow streets of the old district, unchanged since the Middle Ages.

beginning of this century. **Casa Pastor** opposite the Cathedral was a diocesan seminary in the 17th and 18th centuries and now houses the Law Courts.

The **Arab Baths*****, A1, in carrer de Ferran el Catòlic, are in an exceptional building, one of the few public baths preserved in Europe. They were built at the end of the 13th century along the lines of Roman baths with hot, warm and cold rooms. The main room consists of a central pool with a fine canopy and carved capitals surmounted by an elegant little cupola that gives the baths a distinctive look from the outside. Because of the horseshoe shape of the arches the baths are thought to have been built by the Muslims — hence the name.

Sant Pere de Galligants**, B1, plaça del Jurats, is a Benedictine abbey known to have existed from the end of the 10th century and which was rebuilt during the 12th. The imposing Romanesque church has three aisles and four apses flanked to the south by a cloister built between 1154 and 1190. Today the buildings house the **Archaeological Museum**** with fascinating artifacts from the town, the surrounding region and, in particular, from the site of Empuries (see p. 156). *Open 10am-1pm and 4:30-7pm; Sun and holidays 10am-1pm; closed Mon, Jan 6, Easter Sunday and Dec 25 and 26.*

The **church of Sant Nicolau***, B1, stands opposite, on the other side of the carrer de Santa Llúcia. Formerly the local parish church, it was built in the 12th century on the site of an older, probably paleo-Christian monument. From here you can reach the **monastery of Sant Daniel** by taking the street of the same name. The monastery is a fine Romanesque building with a cloister and the Gothic tomb of the saint by Master Aloi, dating from 1345.

Alternatively, on leaving the church of Sant Nicolau you could go on the **archaeological walk** set up in 1958 to see the old town walls. After this, return to pujada del Rei Martí to visit the **church of Sant Feliu****, A1, which, after the Cathedral, is the most representative monument of the medieval town. It was built over a paleo-Christian basilica, on the site where the saint was martyred — this is confirmed by the sarcophagi inside. The church is an example of the transitional style of architecture between Romanesque (the layout) and Gothic (the vaults). Its Baroque façade is also worth a look.

The Sardana

The Sardana is by far the most popular Catalan folk dance. It requires astonishing precision and accuracy and is danced by people from all age groups. The dancers hold hands and form a circle. As the circle moves around, each participant 'marks time' and 'sets', ending each part of the dance with feet together. Prior to the dance there is an introductory passage of flute and tambourine music and during the dance itself a *cobla* (orchestra) plays music in which the *tenora* (oboe) dominates.

Attempts have been made to date the Sardana back to Antiquity, to prehistoric dances in the Cogul cave, or to Greek dances illustrated on vases. Similar circles to those formed in the dance adorn some Romanesque capitals. The name itself appears in 16th-century documents. The Sardana was modernized during the mid-19th century thanks to various changes made by Pep Ventura. It then became the national dance of Catalonia, performed in squares throughout the country and was the subject of competitions and studies.

First and foremost among the artists who illustrated the dance in the 20th century is Picasso who, in 1906, drew sketches of the dance in his note books. In later years, the artist returned repeatedly to this theme. He did a series of studies of hands entwined around a dove inspired by the dance, as well as his *Sardana of Peace* and *Long Live Peace.* In Barcelona, the mural decorating the College of Architects opposite the Cathedral is the best evidence of Picasso's interest in the Sardana.

At the end of the 19th century the poet Joan Maragall described the Sardana as 'the complete dance of a people who, with hands clasped, advance with love'.

Max Jacob, a French poet, paid homage to the Sardana with these words :
'To the pleasing sound of the ardent *tenora*
the balconies draped themselves in Catalan colours
the shock of yellow and red going together well.'

By returning to the Cathedral and before taking carrer de la Força, you can visit the **Municipal Historical Museum,** A2, on the right *(open 10am-2pm and 5-7pm; Sun and holidays 10am-2pm; closed Mon)*.It is installed in a former Capuchin convent which became the **Casa Cartellà** in the 18th century. The collection traces the history of the town from Antiquity up to the present day.

Carrer de la Força is the former *cardo* (main street) of the Roman town and also the street which from the early Middle Ages onward ran to the Jewish quarter. The Jewish community in Girona during the Middle Ages was not a large one but nonetheless contributed decisively to the town's economic, scientific and cultural progress.

The house known as **Isaac el Cec** preserves the archaeological remains of a public building. You can continue your walk towards carrer dels Alemanys, a street lined with fine medieval houses, up to the **Sant Doménec convent,** B2, beside the old walls. Its architecture is reminiscent of the Gothic style of the new Franciscan and Dominican religious orders set up in medieval towns from the 14th century onwards. As you go down towards plaça del Vi you will see some intriguing buildings, including the **Palau Agullana,** a fine stately mansion built between the 14th and the 17th centuries, the former **Carmelite convent,** a Baroque building, now the provincial Diputació, and especially the **Fontana d'or,** A2, (Fountain of Gold) beside plaça de l'Oli, a Romanesque-Gothic palatial residence.

In carrer dels Ciutadans, A3, there are more town houses that belonged to noble families from the Middles Ages to the 18th century. These include **Casa Desbac-Cartellà** (n° 16), **Casa Solterra** (n° 18), **Casa Delàs** (n° 14) and **Casa Massaguer** (n° 12). The **Generalitat palace**   on the corner of plaça del Vi has preserved part of the layout of the 16th-17th-century façade. The **Town Hall,** originally Gothic, is for the most part a 19th-century building. The local theatre was set up here in the 19th century.

Plaça del Vi, A3, can be considered the centre of the old town. It serves as a link between the upper town and the lower town on the other side of the Onyar river. As you cross the river don't miss the picturesque view of the houses along the banks; these were built here after the Middle Ages. Once Girona's first industries had been set up in 1840 the city developed rapidly and expanded beyond its walls. In 1897 Eugeni Campllonch put forward a project for the *eixampla* (expansion) of the town, centred around the Gran via de Jaume I. His town planning is still visible today. Among the important 19th-century developments are the stone bridge across the river, built between 1850 and 1856 to link plaça del Vi to carrer Nou, the porches on plaça de Sant Francesc (plaça del Gra), the plaça de la Independència and the parc de la Devesa. This latter is a large park which since last century has become Girona's leisure centre as well as a public garden. If you are interested in Modernist buildings, Girona has a number of works by the architect Masó (1880-1935), a well-known writer and an important culturtal figure in the town. **Casa Teixidor****, also known as Casa de la Punxa (carrer de Santa Eugènia), with its distinctive green ceramic tower, is perhaps the most representative edifice of this new urban development. Farinera Teixidor nearby (a flour mill dating from 1910-1919) consists of a group of offices, apartments and other buildings for industrial use. Note also Casa Batlle (carrer Nou), Casa Ensesa (carretera de Barcelona) and Casa Gispert Saüch (avinguda de Jaume).

Accommodation

▲▲▲ **Costabella,** carretera N 11, avinguda de França 61, ☎ 20 2524. 22 rooms. Out of town. Convenient for motorists.

▲▲▲ **Immortal Gerona,** carretera de Barcelona 31, ☎ 20 7900. 76 rooms. The largest hotel and the nearest to the airport. Comfortable.

▲▲▲ **Ultonia,** avinguda de Jaume I 22, ☎ 20 3850. 45 rooms. Well-located. Within walking distance of the old town and the Cathedral.

▲ **Peninsular,** carrer Nou 3, ☎ 20 3800. 68 rooms. Slightly cheaper, large hotel in the modern part of town.

▲ **Residencia Bellmirall,** carrer de Bellmirall 3, ☎ 20 4009. 7 rooms. In a magnificent medieval setting, tastefully decorated. Few rooms, so reserve well ahead.

Food and drink

Girona's cuisine consists of the most typical Catalan dishes, which make use of products from both land and sea. Specialities include the famous *carn d'olla* (stew), *botifarres dolces* (sweet sausages), a special rice dish, *suquet de peix* and *xuixos*. These are accompanied by white wine, *cava de Perlada*, rosé from Espolla or vintage red from Capinay.

◆◆◆ **Can Roc de les Matinades,** carrer de Santa Llúcia 4, ☎ 20 4519. *Closed Wed*. In the historic centre. Gourmet food.

◆◆◆ **Cal Ros,** carrer de Cort Reial 9, ☎ 20 1011. *Closed Sun evening and Mon in winter, Sat evening and Sun in summer*. The oldest restaurant in town. Meat specialities.

◆◆◆ **Isaac el Cec,** carrer de Força 10, ☎ 21 6761. *Closed Mon*. A historic setting in the Jewish quarter. Inner garden. Elegant, fashionable. Convenient for a quick stop.

◆◆◆ **Rosaleda,** passeig de la Devesa, ☎ 21 3638. *Closed Sun evening and Mon*. Ideal setting for terrific food. Banquets and receptions.

◆◆◆ **Selva Mar,** carrer de Santa Eugenia, ☎ 21 6329. Excellent fresh fish.

♦♦ **Bronsoms,** avinguda Sant Francesc 7, ☎ 21 2493. *Closed Sat evening and Sun evening.* Very typical Catalan fare.

♦♦ **Cipresaia,** carrer de General Fournàs 2, ☎ 21 5662. Seafood and mountain dishes.

♦♦ **El mas de la Creu,** carretera La Creu de Palau, ☎ 20 1006. Outside Girona in a Catalan farmhouse. Great country cooking.

♦ **Els Traguinyol,** ronda Pare Claret 39, ☎ 20 5624. Meat specialities.

♦ **Jim's H,** carrer d'Independència 16, ☎ 21 3661. *Closed Thurs.* Has produced popular dishes since 1918. Simple specialities.

♦ **L'Amfora,** carrer de Força 15, ☎ 20 5010. *Closed Sun evening.* Bistro in the Call district. Traditional cuisine.

♦ **Las Jaras,** carrer de Força 4, ☎ 21 5260. *Closed Sun.* Popular fare in the Call district at very reasonable prices.

♦ **Rhin Bar,** avinguda Jaume I 61, ☎ 20 3031. *Closed Sun.* Popular cuisine as well as take-away dishes.

Useful addresses

Girona/Costa Brava Airport: 7 mi/12 km south west of Girona, ☎ 20 7500.
Tourist Information: plaça Marquès de Camps 17 ter, 17001 Girona, ☎ 20 8401.

▬ THE COSTA BRAVA

Figueres and Alt Empordà

Figueres, capital of Alt Empordà, is 23 mi/37 km north of Girona on both the N11 and the A7 highway. Typical of northern Catalonian towns with a medieval past — as you can see in the fine Gothic **church of Sant Pere,** of which the oldest part dates back to the end of the 14th century — Figueres is renowned for its museums. Its **Toy Museum★,** for instance, is the largest in Catalonia *(open daily in summer 10am-12:30 pm and 4-7:30 pm in winter, Mon and holidays).*The **Empordà Museum** contains regional archaeological collections and also merits special mention *(open 11am-1pm and 3:30-7pm; Sun and holidays 11am-2pm; closed Mon).*

However, the town's greatest attraction is the **Teatre Museu Dalí★★★,** (plaça Salvador Dalí i Gala) *(open Oct 1-June 30 11:30am-5:30pm; Sun and holidays 11:30am-5:30pm; June 1-Sept 30 daily 9am-8:30pm)* in the former local theatre that was built about 1850. Largely destroyed in 1939, it was restored in 1966 and converted into a museum, inaugurated in 1974. The metallic reticulated dome is by Emilio Pérez Piñero. The museum is a kind of temple to Surrealism set in an unorthodox decor.

Castelló d'Empuries (6 mi/10 km east of Figueres on the Roses road) has a large Gothic edifice, the **church of Santa Maria★,** one of the most famous 14th-century Catalan churches. Its French-influenced Gothic façade has earned it the name of the cathedral of Empordà.

Roses (10 mi/16 km east of Figueres), north of the gulf of the same name, is a busy tourist centre with its medieval **church of Santa Maria** and the Roman-Visigoth site of **Puig Rom.**

On the gulf itself, near the mouths of the Fluvia and Muga rivers, a natural reserve, the **Parc Natural dels Aiguamolls de l'Empordà,** covers an area of 11,819 acres/4 783 hectares and shelters a number of bird species. For information, ask in the village of **Cortaler** (near Castelló d'Empúries), carretera de Sant Pere Pescador, ☎ (972) 45 1231.

Cadaqués stands in a bay 12 mi/20 km north east of Roses. It is one of the villages most characteristic of the region, made famous by Salvador

The Teatre Museu Dalí, in the town of Figueres where the artist was born, is a temple to the creator of the «paranoiac critical» process of inducing hallucinations.

Dalí's house in Port Lligat where the painter spent many of his most creative years. The views over Cabo de Creus are splendid. In spite of increasing tourism in the area, the village has kept much of its old charm. It is a good place to stop (if you can find somewhere to park your car!) and wander around the sloping streets, swim, or have a drink on the terrace of one of the many cafés at the harbour.

El Port de la Selva (7 mi/12 km farther north) is typical of villages in the northern section of the Cabo de Creus peninsula. To a great extent the harbour has kept the layout of fishing villages as they were in the 17th and 18th centuries.

From **Llançà** (5 mi/8 km farther on) you can reach Figueres-France road via Portbou (where there's a 1900s-style border train station).

Salvador Dalí (1904-1989)

After exploring his interest in both Cubism and metaphysical painting, Dalí became a leading figure in the Surrealist movement. He developed a distinctive style in which he tried to illustrate irrational dream images using a clean, precise and detailed realism. His compositions, especially those of the 1930s, call upon a repertory of fantastic and often erotic shapes that spring up out of the shore, evoking the seascape that spread beneath the windows of his house in the port town of Cadaqués on the Costa Brava.

The artist's eccentric behaviour made him very popular and he was a lively figure in the media — recognized internationally by his excessively long, waxed handle-bar moustache and his exhibitionism.

Detractors have accused him of being merely gimmicky as an artist while masterful as a manipulator of the media. Decide for yourself; his works can mainly be seen in the Figueres museum. 'It is necessary', said Dalí in his provocative style, 'that all of the people who come out of the museum have false information'.

Cadaqués is a lovely fishing harbour that has miraculously escaped the rampant urbanism of the 1960s; Picasso came here on vacation and Dalí bought a house in nearby Port Lligat that can be visited today.

If you turn back towards Figueres, after 5.5 mi/9 km you will see a branch off to the village of Vilajuïga from which you can reach the Romanesque **monastery of Sant Pere de Rodes***** *(open 9am-2pm and 4-8pm)*. The road leads to the pre-Romanesque church of Sant Creus (Santa Elena), a 10-minute walk from the monastery which is one of the region's most important. Its ruins stand high above the sea and continue to delight lovers of medieval architecture and grandiose landscapes. The abbey church is exceptional as it dates back to the first half of the 11th century. It was built on two levels and its astonishing loftiness makes the three aisles unusually high. In the 12th century a carved marble portal was added (no longer visible) as well as a cloister which can be visited. You can also walk around the various monastic outbuildings.

Return to the junction with the Figueres road and you will find another branch which leads to **Peralada***, which was, in 1080, the family seat of a viscount.The castle still remains, most of it dating from the 16th and 17th centuries. Here in the castle you can indulge in two very different activities: you can either improve your mind in the **Library-Museum** *(open 10am-noon and 2:30-6:30pm; Sun and holidays 10am-noon 4:30-6:30pm)* or gamble in the **Casino** *(open 5pm-4am)*, a popular alternative. There's a restaurant and a bar; formal-dress required; ☎ (972) 53 8125. Other places of interest include the main square, lined with part-Gothic houses. Several buildings here form a harmonious whole: the parish **church of Martí** (which has re-used parts from an earlier medieval construction), the Romanesque **Sant Domenec cloister,** and the **Carmelite convent.**The convent church has a polygonal apse and tombs of the Rocabertí and other great families. The town's wines and *caves* (champagne-wines) are well-known.

After passing through Vilabertran you return to Figueres to begin the Baix Empordà itinerary.

Empuries and Baix Empordà

Sant Martí d'Empuries and the former antique town of **Empuries***** (Ampurias in Castilian) can be reached from the Figueres-La Bisbal road, the C252. The town is north of L'Escala and has been regularly excavated since 1907.

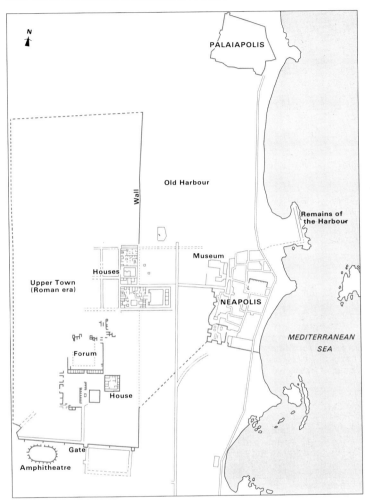

EMPURIES

Empuries in the past

The first Greek settlement here, Palaiapolis, was established at Sant Martí d'Empuries. Then, further south, during the 6th century BC, Neapolis was built — now the lower town that stretches towards the sea. The general layout of the streets and houses gives an idea of the way the early Greek colonists conceived town planning. A short time after their arrival, the Romans set up a military fortress on the top of the hillock. In about 100 BC, a new town was built to a right-angled plan. It grew up around a monumental forum endowed with a group of public buildings. There are some large villas where excavations have revealed mosaic decorations illustrating life in Empuries between the 1st and 3rd centuries AD. During the 5th century AD, a Christian funerary basilica was built in the lower part of Neapolis, the sarcophagi of which are displayed in adjoining rooms.

What to see

The **Museu Monògrafic d'Empuries*** contains archaeological artifacts, mosaics, lamps, vases and so on. Although the most important finds from the site are displayed in the archaeological museums of Barcelona and Girona, this museum is nonetheless worth a visit. *Open summer 10am-2pm and 3-7pm; winter 10am-1pm and 3-5pm; closed Mon. These times are also valid for a tour of the site and the open-air excavations.*

La Bisbal, the capital of Baix Empordà, distinguishes itself by its castle-palace, notable for its Romanesque design.

The town's main street is lined with shops specializing in ceramics, all selling more or less the same things. They're worth a stop though; you'll find inexpensive decorative garden objects and tableware in attractive shades of blue, green or yellow.

Ullastret** (3 mi/5 km farther north) is a fortified *oppidum* (citadel), dating back to the end of the 7th century BC, that was built on a natural mound. Today you can still see some of the walls and their towers, the acropolis in the upper part of town and some houses. The museum displays artifacts from local excavations including numerous ceramic pieces and inscriptions. *Open summer 10:30am-1pm and 4-8pm; winter 10am-2pm and 4-6pm; closed Mon.*

Begur, an ancient fortified town with five remaining towers, is dominated by the remains of its castle. The surrounding area has a lot of inlets and busy tourist centres characteristic of the Costa Brava.

You can get to **Palafrugell** by both coastal and inland roads. The town grew rapidly at the end of last century thanks to its cork industry (bottle stops and other products). The **Catalan Cork Museum**, carrer de Cervantes 10, *(open 5-8pm)* traces the development of the industry.

Palamós to the south is a coastal town built as the Royal Port of Baix Empordà in 1279. Today it is an active fishing centre and seaside resort. The old quarter on the hilltop of the formerly enclosed city retains its medieval feel while 19th-20th-century expansion created nearby reveals a very different kind of town with long straight streets and rectangular housing blocks.

The seafront of **Calella de Palafrugell** combines the joys of the beach with the charm and beauty of its little shady streets.

After crossing **Platja d'Aro**, one of the largest beach resorts in the region, you reach **S'Agaró** and **Sant Feliu de Guíxols**. The latter grew up around the monastery of Sant Feliu which was known to exist in the 10th century. Its Romanesque-Gothic abbatial church remains. The most important vestige however is the monastery porch, known as **Porta Ferrada***, a large façade with two levels of arches that date back to pre-Romanesque times. Among the buildings that testify to the town's wealth secured by the cork industry, during the Modernist era, is the beautiful building by the architect Guitart i Lostaló (1890-1903).

Havaneres: songs of the Costa Brava

Along with the Sardana dance, considered to have originated in Empordà, *havaneres* are sung year round. These initially Creol tunes, with their leisurely rhythms were brought back to Spain by sailors returning from the West Indies during the last century. They were popular with seafarers and over the last few decades singing evenings have become fashionable in most of the coastal towns of Empordà and La Selva. They are especially characteristic of Calella de Palafrugell. As you listen, it is customary to drink a *cremat* (coffee flambéed with rum).

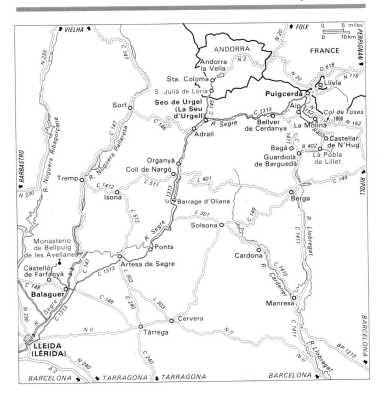

THE PYRENEES ITINERARY

THE PYRENEES, CERDAÑA, LA SEU D'URGELL AND ANDORRA

This itinerary takes you through the grandiose landscapes of the Pyrenees where you can visit numerous little Romanesque churches, fish for trout or indulge yourself in all sorts of winter sports. Gourmets will be able to sample such delicious culinary specialities as Pyrenean river trout *(truita de riu a la pirinenca)*, winter hotpot *(escudella hivernenca)* and wild boar.

▬ *PUIGCERDÁ*

Access: By car from Barcelona (106 mi/170 km) and Ripoll on the N152 via Ribes de Freser where you can take a detour to visit the high mountain valley of Núria, the col de Toses and the La Molina ski resort.

Puigcerdá, the capital of Cerdaña, is on the French border. It stands at an altitude of 3986 ft/1215 m and is known as the snow capital. Thanks to an excellent communications network in the area, it is linked to all the mountain resorts of upper and lower Cerdaña.

Puigcerdá in the past

Puigcerdá has been a capital since the Middle Ages. King Alfonso I granted it a settlement charter in 1178 and various sovereigns of

Catalonia were to later keep a watchful eye on the town and its territory. Its municipal structure dates from the 14th and 15th centuries. However, because of its position on the border it has suffered sieges, and the destruction of innumerable wars, especially that of its walls in 1677.

What to see

There is an artificial lake that dates back to the Middle Ages and a watch-tower that affords a spectacular view over the whole of Cerdaña.

A single tower (tour del Moro) of Puigcerdá's ancient walls has been preserved. On plaça Santa Maria you can see the Gothic bell-tower of the church that was demolished in 1936. However, the most important religious monument in town is the church of the former **Sant Doménec convent** with a single nave, side chapels set between buttresses, and an attractive doorway. Gothic paintings (14th-century) were found inside representing a Tree of Life, which stylistically resembles similar examples in southern France and Italy. The remains of the former cloister can also be visited. Objects of local interest can be seen in the small museum of the Institut d'Estudis Ceretans.

Moving on, the road between Puigcerdá and La Seu d'Urgell (29 mi/47 km) crosses the Baix Cerdanya and Alt Urgell regions.

Bellver de Cerdanya (11 mi/17 km south west of Puigcerdà) marks the transition area where Cerdaña itself ends and the valley of the Segre river (that runs through Alt Urgell) begins. It is the capital of Lesser Cerdaña. Pyrenean Romanesque churches in the area include Santa Maria Talló and Sant Julià de la Pedra.

The area between Puigcerdá, Toses and Bellver de Cerdanya has several well-known ski resorts, among them La Masella and La Molina.

Martinet (5 mi/8 km west of Bellver de Cerdanya) is a trout-fishing centre and the departure point for excursions into the mountains and the lakes region.

Els Banys de Sant Vincenç (6 mi/9 km farther on), dominating the Cadí chain of mountains, is a health resort open only in summer.

▬ *LA SEU D'URGELL*★★

Telephone area code: 973.

Map coordinates refer to the map p. 162.

The capital of the *comarca* is a little town, 8 mi/13 km south west of Puigcerdá, with a rich history and a prestigious past. It has a dynamic market and holds the fair of Sant Ermengol.

La Seu d'Urgell in the past

During the Carolingian era, La Seu d'Urgell was the capital of a county, a busy centre of resettlement and, throughout the Middle Ages, a renowned bishopric. Of its vestiges from the Middle Ages, the town has maintained and restored the old centre around the Cathedral and the Episcopal Palace. Apart from the quarters populated at the end of the Middle Ages (carrer Major, plaça de la Vila) this zone has the town's most picturesque streets, the oldest houses and the Jewish quarter.

What to see

The **Cathedral★**, B1, the cloister and the surrounding edifices form the largest group of buildings in the town and one of the most remarkable examples of Romanesque Catalan architecture. The **Santa Maria basilica★★** dates from the second half of the 12th century. The name of the foreman, Ramon Llombard, suggests he was a native of Italy and thus endowed the building with an Italian character. The church has three aisles, a very wide transept and five apses. The interior indicates the high level of vaulting expertise at the time — the central nave has barrel vaults while the side aisles have groined vaults and there is a tower in the crossing. During the Romanesque era, the episcopal group of buildings of La Seu d'Urgell comprised three churches, known to have

The cathedral of La Seu d'Urgell: the town retains many vestiges from the period between the Carolingian era to the Middle Ages when it was an important centre of the surrounding region.

existed since the 11th century. Only the small chapel remains, backed onto the **Romanesque cloister★★**. This latter preserves three original galleries built before the end of the 12th century.

The **Diocesan Museum★★** adjoining the cloister has been reorganized *(open 9:30am-1:30pm, and 3:30-8pm; Sun and holidays 9:30am-1:30pm)*. The collection of religious art ranks among Catalonia's most important, after that of Vic (see p. 140). It includes Romanesque and Gothic murals and wood paintings, sculptures, and various religious artifacts from the Middle Ages to the 18th century. The display is crowned by three major works: the Beatus manuscript illuminated at the end of the 10th century, the Gothic altarpiece from Abella de la Conca by Pere Serra and the silver sarcophagus of St Ermengol by the silversmith Pere Llopard (1755).

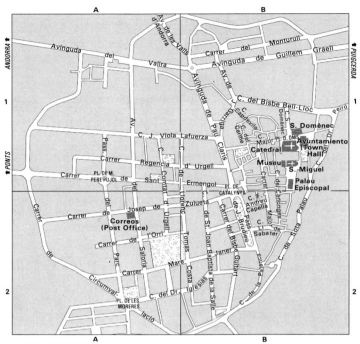

LA SEU D'URGELL

From La Seu d'Urgell, you can go to Andorra (see opposite) or south to Lleida for the next itinerary. Heading toward Lleida and between La Seu d'Urgell and Ponts (39 mi/65 km), you pass through the villages of **Organyà** where the *Homélies d'Organyà*, the oldest text written in Catalan, was discovered, and the **Coll de Nargó** (24 mi/38 km) where you can see the Oliana Dam and especially the Romanesque church which has one of the most unusual pre-Romanesque bell-towers in Catalonia (10th-century).

From Ponts to Lleida you pass through **Balaguer,** capital of Noguera, which retains large stretches of its medieval walls. Also of interest in the town is the Gothic convent of Sant Domènec with its 14th-century cloister, and the former collegiate church of Santa Maria, built between 1351 and 1558.

In the district of **Os de Balaguer,** about 19 mi/30 km north west of Balaguer, the former monastery of Bellpuig de les Avellanes is worth a detour. It contains Gothic graves of the counts of Urgell.

Accommodation

▲▲▲ **El Castell,** ☎ 35 0704. 39 rooms. Luxurious.
▲▲▲ **Parador Nacional,** carrer de Sant Domènec (no number), ☎ 35 2000. 84 rooms. The town's largest hotel. Modern, with luxury service.
▲▲ **Nice,** ☎ 35 2100. 48 rooms.

Family-run boarding houses
The following establishments, all more or less of the same standard, are clean, modest, houses with a restaurant.
▲ **Andria,** passeig Brudieu 24, ☎ 35 0300. 25 rooms.

▲ **Cadi,** carrer de Josep de Zulueta 4, ☎ 35 0150. 42 rooms.
▲ **L'Empordanesa,** carrer de Tomàs i Costa 43, ☎ 35 1028. 18 rooms.
▲ **Mundial,** carrer de Sant Ot 2, ☎ 35 0000. 69 rooms.

ANDORRA

La Seu d'Urgell was the traditional frontier post for Andorra but the customs have been transferred recently to Farga de Moles. Interestingly, the bishop of La Seu d'Urgell is also one of the co-princes of Andorra. The visit to Andorra described here should be considered as an annex to the guide — an extra excursion in the Pyrenees itinerary.

Andorra is a high, mountainous country with altitudes bordering on 9842 ft/3000 m. Abundant snow in winter makes it a popular holiday spot. The area covers 178 sq mi/462 sq km and is divided into seven administrative and ecclesiastical parishes: Canillo, Encamp, Ordino, La Massana, Andorra la Vella, Sant Julià de Loria and Escaldes-Engordany. On the way to Andorra la Vella you first pass through **Sant Julià de Loria** with its Romanesque church of the same name and a wonderful old quarter. In **Santa Coloma,** a short way before Andorra la Vella, you can visit the best-known church in the valley with its pre-Romanesque and Romanesque elements and its original circular bell-tower.

From **Andorra la Vella,** set in a deep valley 6 mi/10 km from the Spanish border and 20 mi/32 km from the French one, you can organize excursions according to your interests. These may include visits to ski resorts, high mountain valleys and lakes, or pre-Romanesque and Romanesque churches.

Tourist Information: Andorra Tourist Office, plaça del Poble, Andorra la Vella, ☎ (974) 202 14.

LLEIDA (LERIDA)
AND THE VALL D'ARAN

Lleida (Lérida in Castilian) is the capital of Catalonia's most western province, the broadest and the least populated of the country. It stretches from the Pyrenees to the Ebro river and has the highest peaks in Catalonia with the Pica d'Estats at 10,312 ft/3143 m.

The Val d'Aran has a wetter, colder climate than other zones in the Pyrenees and temperatures are low nearly all year round. It is a beautiful, wild region, and easy communications, thanks to the Puerto de la Bonaigua and the Viella tunnel, have given a considerable boost to summer and winter tourism.

LLEIDA★★

Telephone area code : **973.**
Map coordinates refer to the map pp. 166-167.
Access. From Barcelona by car, take the Barcelona-Madrid highway, or the N 11; from Tarragona, take the N240 and from La Seu d'Urgell, the C1313.
With 110,000 inhabitants, the town has become the lively capital of western Catalonia and a truly worthwhile place to visit since its prestigious monuments have been restored.

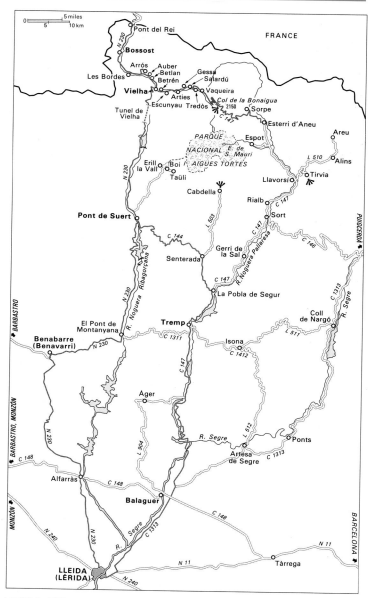

LLEIDA AND THE VALL D'ARAN ITINERARY

Lleida in the past

The town was the ancient capital of the Ilergets, an Iberian tribe. When it came under Roman control, a bridge was built over the river Segre (preserved until the 14th century) and later, in the 5th century, Lleida became the seat of a bishopric. After the Muslim conquest (beginning of the 8th century) it became a stronghold on the northern border of al-Andalus. During the long Arab occupation it grew into a large prestigious centre as the old walls and the Suda fortress testify. It wasn't until 1149 that Counts Ramon Berenguer IV of Barcelona and Ermengol VI of Urgell made their way into the town, bringing with them different religious orders, mainly Templars and Hospitallers. The town was thus repopulated with settlers who spoke Catalan. During the 13th century the city was intensely active from an economic and cultural point of view. A new cathedral was built and in 1300 the first and only university *(Estudi General)* of the Catalan-Aragonese crown was founded. However, the city suffered both from geographical isolation and from various Catalan wars, leading to its impoverishment. The town stagnated until the Napoleonic siege in 1810. During the 19th century it broke free from its walls and was able to spread out. This expansion was accompanied by the arrival of the railway and various town planning projects.

What to see

The old town is concentrated on the southern slope of Puig del Castell where there are some prestigious monuments, namely the Royal Castle or Suda and the Old Cathedral or Seu Villa. In the Middle Ages the heart of the Muslim town was surrounded by walls; this area has become the centre of the modern town. On the top, encircled by a green zone, there are still some vestiges of the Bourbon walls (18th-century). You enter the ancient citadel through the **Lion Gateway**, built in 1826 under Fernando VII.

The **Suda castel**, BC2, (former Arab fortress) north of the Old Cathedral, existed before the Muslim period and may well have been built over the foundations of a Roman fort. After the reconquest from the Arabs, the castle became a residence for the counts of Barcelona. During the 13th century it was embellished by Jaume I who endowed it with stone vaults. Today the only remnants of the monument are stretches of Gothic walls and some towers, marks of its status during the Middle Ages.

The majestic outline of Lleida's Old Cathedral, known as the **Seu Vella****, C2, dominates the town. It rises above the site where the Great Mosque once stood. The Cathedral was consecrated on October 30, 1149, although the imposing edifice you see today was not in fact begun until 1203, under the auspices of the foreman, Pere de Coma (Sacoma). Work progressed rapidly, so much so that at the beginning of the next century the western part, or cloister, was already under way. In the 18th century the town was endowed with a New Cathedral, the Catedral Nova, right in the heart of the modern town, and the Seu Vella was converted into a barracks.

The building of the Gothic Cathedral started with the east side and progressed westwards. The plan includes a nave and two aisles; the nave is double the width of the side aisles. Among the main attractions of the building, mention should be made of the fine doorways. The Sant Berenguer of Palace portal is in the northern arm of the transept. The southern arm of the transept bears the Annunciation doorway, so called because of the two statues, one of the Virgin Mary and the other of the Angel Gabriel, that once adorned either side. The *'dels Fillols'* doorway in the southern part of the nave is typical of 13th-century doorways in the area. Finally, the doorway of the Apostles is on the western façade outside the cloister. The cloister is in front of the church, most unusual for the beginning of the Gothic period. The octagonal bell-tower, which has four storeys, rises above the building, dominating the town and the surrounding area. The major importance of Lleida's Old Cathedral is that it is representative of the transitional style of architecture between Romanesque and Gothic.

Moving down towards the lower town and the river you can take a more or less circular tour, stopping first at **Sant Martí**, B1, a church that dates from the end of the 12th century and first quarter of the 13th. It has a single nave covered with broken barrel and groined vaulting, resting on half-columns adorned with carved capitals. This is the former chapel of

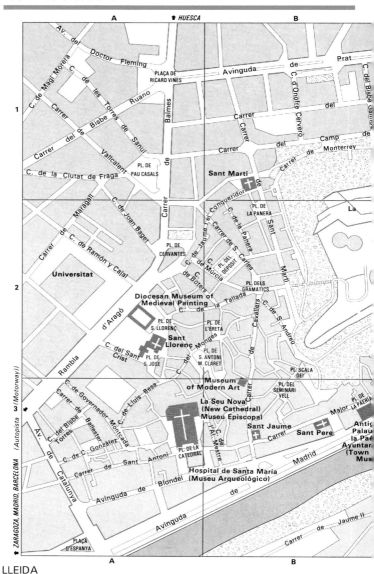

LLEIDA

Lleida's famous university. Recent restoration in the chapel has made possible the installation of the sculpture section of the Diocesan Museum *(open 10am-2pm and 5-8pm)*. You can see statues from the Annunciation doorway of the Seu Vella, Gothic and Romanesque capitals, and 14th- and 15th-century altarpieces.

The **church of Sant Llorenç** stands on plaça de Sant Llorenç beside the **Diocesan Museum of Medieval Painting**, A2. It is one of the remains of a group of buildings constructed by Ramon Berenguer IV after the conquest of the town. The church is mainly known for its sculpture treasures, namely the 14th-century altarpieces by the best artists of the day — Jaume Cascalls and Batomeu Robió. The altarpieces are arranged in the

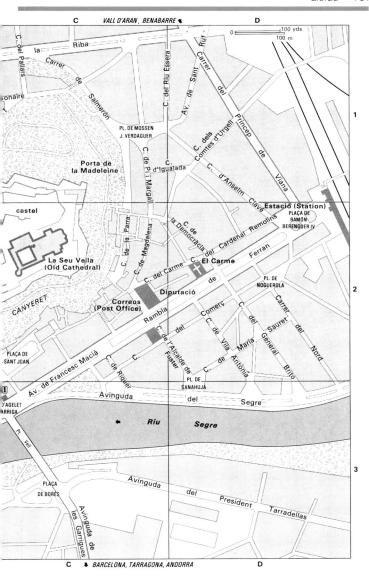

following order: a statue of the saint (to whom the chapel is dedicated) stands in the middle with scenes from the life of the saint on either side.

The **Seu Nova** (New Cathedral), A3, begun in 1761, consecrated in 1781 and finished in 1790, is one of the largest neo-Classical buildings in Catalonia. It has three aisles, all of the same height, as well as vaults, side chapels and an ambulatory. The **Museu Arqueológico** opposite the cathedral, is housed in the former hospital of Santa Maria (presently being restored). Apart from a good many antique and medieval works it also contains palaeo-Christian sculptures from the baptistery of the Bovalar basilica.

The former Rosary convent houses the **Jaume Morera Museum of Modern Art,** B3 *(open 10am-2pm and 7:30-9pm; closed Sun and holidays).* Here you can see 19th- and 20th-century paintings.

A landmark on plaça de la Paeria, the 13th-century **Paeria palace*** (today's Town Hall) is one of the most beautiful civic buildings of the Middle Ages. It was the home of the Sanauja family until 1342 after which it became public property. The façade is distinguished by its elegant windows which light up the reception rooms on the first floor.

If you are interested in Modernist architecture, Lleida has preserved a number of buildings from this period dotted about town together with some very interesting work by Francesc Morera i Gatell, the local architect appointed in 1906. These include the **Escorxador** (abattoirs, 1912-1915), the **Mercat del Pla** (market, 1913), the **Magí Llorenc house** (carrer de Major Cavallers, 1905-1907) and particularly the **Camps Elisis** (Elysian Fields, 1908) or public gardens in which, in 1923-1926, the architect built an aquarium-pavilion. In avinguda de Blondel there is a series of Romantic and Modernist buildings that are very picturesque.

Accommodation

▲▲▲ **Condes de Urgel II**, avinguda de Barcelona 17, ☎ 20 2300. 105 rooms. Ideal for a long stay. Luxurious. Impeccable service.
▲▲▲ **Pirineos**, passeig Ronda 63, ☎ 27 3199. 94 rooms. Has a good reputation for regional cuisine.
▲▲ **Jamaica**, carretera Nal II, located at km 462.5, ☎ 26 5100. 24 rooms. A convenient stop on the road outside town.
▲▲ **Llerda**, carretera Nal II, located at km 467, Ap. 2, ☎ 20 0750. 65 rooms. Out of town.
▲▲ **Principal**, plaça de la Paeria 8, ☎ 24 0900. 53 rooms. In the town centre. Ideal for visiting the sights on foot.
▲ **Ramon Berenguer IV**, Plaça d Ramon Berenguer IV 3, ☎ 23 7345. 60 rooms. Central. Recommended for the price and the service.

Campground
Las Balsas, ☎ 23 3573.

Food and drink

Lleida's culinary traditions and those of the Segrià region are essentially country-influenced, with different varieties of hotpots such as *olla barrejada, escudella* or *carn d'olla* (see p. 25).

Among the most famous typical dishes are those with snails, done *llauna* or *brutesca* style. Their popularity is demonstrated at the Snail Festival *(Aplec del Caragol)* which takes place during Lleida's *Festa Major.* Snails are accompanied by grilled, peeled peppers and aubergines *(escalivada)* or artichokes cooked over coals.

♦♦♦♦ **Sheyton Pub**, avinguda de Prat de la Riba 39, ☎ 23 8197. Luxurious and elegant decor.
♦♦♦ **Cal Molí**, partida dels Buixadors 15, ☎ 24 6640. *Closed Tues.* Catalan cuisine.
♦♦♦ **Forn del Nastasi**, carrer de Salmerón 10, ☎ 23 4510. *Closed Sun evening.* A gourmet restaurant where you can try all Lleida's classic dishes — snails cooked over coals, duck with local fruits, cod cooked in the oven — all accompanied by good regional wines.
♦♦♦ **Molí de la Nora**, ronda de Pingurda (4 mi/6 km from town), ☎ 19 0017. *Closed Sun evening.* Set in an old mill with nautical decor. Good seafood.

Arseguel: one of the typical villages in the region around Lleida.

Useful addresses

Bus station: carrer de Saracibar 2, ☎ 26 8500. Buses for Balaguer, Barcelona, Cervesa, El Cogul, Fraga, L'Espluga, Montagul, La Seu d'Urgell, Solsona and Tarragona.
Emergencies: ☎ 27 1706.
Police: ☎ 23 4340.
Post Office: carrer de l'Alcade Fuster/rambla Ferran 16, ☎ 23 6449.
Train station: RENFE, plaça Ramon Berenguer IV, ☎ 23 7467. Trains for Barcelona, Madrid, Pobla de Segur, Reus, Tarragona and Zaragoza.
Tourist Information: Arc del Pont, ☎ 24 8120; avinguda de Madrid, ☎ 27 2085.

THE VALL D'ARAN

Access: By car from Lleida, take the C147 or the N230 to Viella (104 mi/167 km). There are a lot of tourist services on the way but drivers have to exercise caution on roads and tracks above 3280 ft/1000 m as these are often frozen. The Puerto de la Bonaigua is closed for between six and nine months a year due to snow and if you're planning on going through the Viella tunnel, bear in mind that you often have to use chains. The same is true for the road from Viella to Salardù and Vaqueira.

Crossed by the Garonne river, which rises here, the Vall d'Aran differs greatly from the rest of Catalonia by virtue of its wild landscapes. In addition to Catalan, a local language called Aranés is spoken here. In 1808, while occupied by Napoleon's troops, the valley was annexed to the French *département* of Saint-Gaudens but was evacuated in 1815. In the 19th century it came under the jurisdiction of the bishopric of Urgell.

Viella

Standing at an altitude of 3199 ft/975 m, Viella is the capital of the region. It was an important town during the Middle Ages because of its strategic position between France and Catalonia, a centre not only for the discussion of treaties but also a city vulnerable to sieges and occupations. Today it is an historic town that has maintained its ancient layout and a good number of old houses. The **church of Sant Miquel★** is characteristic of late Romanesque architecture in the region, built during the transitional stage preceding the Gothic period. It contains a Romanesque baptismal font, a 15th-century Gothic altarpiece and, more importantly, the *Christ of Mig Aran* — part of a Romanesque wood carving representing the Descent from the Cross.

If you would like to see more of the region from Viella, here are two possible itineraries:

The first heads north toward France and Saint-Béat. **Betlan-Aubert** (1.2 mi/2 km), at a height of 3415 ft/1042 m, has a Romanesque church; **Les Bordes** (5 mi/8 km) is a typical regional village; **Bossost★** (4 mi/7 km) has a Romanesque church with a carved tympanum that is the largest in the valley; then you will arrive at **Pont del Rei**.

The second itinerary heads toward the **Vaqueria** ski resort (made famous by the annual visit of Spain's royal family) and Puerto (col) de la Bonaigua. **Betrén** (0.6 mi/1 km) has a Romanesque church with a carved façade illustrating the theme of the Virgin and Child; **Arties** (4 mi/7 km) is a thermal centre and an ideal base for excursions into the middle of the valley, while **Gessa** (1.2 mi/2 km), **Salardú** (1.2 mi/2 km) and **Tredòs** (0.62 mi/1 km) are medieval villages. Farther on (6 mi/9 km) you pass through the Puerto de la Bonaigua and continue to the villages of **Sorpe** and **Esterri d'Aneu** (among others) with fine Romanesque churches. Their splendid wall paintings have been moved to the Museu Nacional d'Art de Catalunya in Barcelona.

TARRAGONA AND THE COSTA DAURADA

This itinerary takes you through the southern coast of Catalonia where smooth beaches stretch as far as the eye can see, a surprising contrast to the landscape of the Costa Brava. The sand seems to have turned gold in the sun and the sea is calm and warm. Tarragona, an imperial town, is a centre of art and culture which deserves a lengthy stay. From here you can also visit the famous Cistercian abbeys of Poblet and Santes Creus in the heart of medieval Catalonia. These are oases of spiritual peace set in an area which produces some of the best Catalan wines.

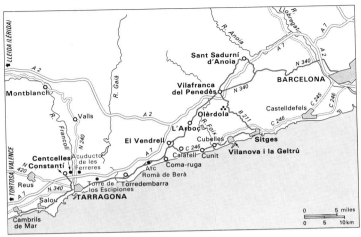

TARRAGONA AND THE COSTA DAURADA ITINERARY

▬ *VILAFRANCA DEL PENEDÈS*

29 mi/47 km south-west of Barcelona.

Access: Travelling from Barcelona to Tarragona you can take the A7 highway which passes through Vilafranca del Penedès or the C246 which goes to Sitges. The B211 links Vilafranca del Penedès to Sitges.

One of the delights of the town is the magnificent **church of Santa Maria**, a 15th-century Gothic edifice with a single nave, a polygonal apse and a fine neo-Gothic façade built in 1903. Opposite the church on plaça Jaume I stands the former **Royal Palace****, in which, according to the chronicler Ramon Muntaner, King Pere the Great died in 1289. It was built at the beginning of the Gothic period (13th century) and today houses a museum with a section on wine *(open winter 10am-2pm and 4-7pm; summer 10am-2pm and 4:30-7:30pm; closed Mon).*

The Gothic **church of Sant Joan and Sant Francesc** has a very large Gothic **altarpiece**** painted by Lluís Borrassà in 1392.

The *comarca,* of which Vilafranca del Penedés is the capital, is known for its historic tradition of winegrowing. The best *cava* (champagne-like wine) is produced in this region.

In **Sant Sadurní d'Anoia** (7 mi/12 km) you can visit the best-known wineries, among them that of Cordoniu, a large Modernist complex by the architect Puig i Cadafalch (1896-1906) *(open Mon-Thur 8-11:30am and 3-5:30pm; Fri 8-11:30am; closed weekends, holidays and in Aug).* This is where the champagne method was first introduced to Spanish wine-makers. It is an exceptionally fine group of buildings where medieval architectural tradition serves the new needs of large-scale modern production. In the centre of Sant Sadurní a number of Modernist buildings testify to the revival the region enjoyed at the end of the 19th century thanks to the wine boom.

Beyond Vilafranca del Penedés on the road to Sitges you can see the ruins of **Olèrdola**** on a hill. The town was inhabited from the Neolithic era to the time of the Roman occupation. It was protected by a wall made of large blocks of stone and endowed with rectangular towers. Right up until the early Middle Ages the town still played a protective role for the area, as it bordered on the Arab zone. A **museum** displays archaeological material from the ancient city and gives complementary information for a tour of the site *(open 9am-1:30pm and 3-5pm, 3-7pm in summer; Sundays and holidays 9am-1:30pm; closed Mon)*. On the top of the site there is an attractive pre-Romanesque church.

▬ SITGES★

26 mi/42 km south west of Barcelona.

Sitges is a typical Catalan town and an intensely busy holiday resort that gets overcrowded in summer. It dates back to the Middle Ages and has a fine 17th-century parish church.

The town is especially known for its artistic life which at the end of the 19th century and during the first quarter of the 20th century made the place a cultural centre. It was largely frequented by artists, especially in the summer months. In 1892 the famous painter Santiago Rusiñol became the leader of the local art scene and between 1892 and 1899 organized Modernist festivals in a house known as **Cau Ferrat★★**. Today this is a museum (Museu Cau Ferrat), which opened in 1930 *(open summer 10am-1pm and 5-7pm; winter 10am-1pm and 4-6pm; Sun and holidays 10am-2pm; closed Mon)*. The museum was made possible thanks to a legacy left by the painter. It includes collections of medieval and modern art, with two paintings by El Greco and various works by Catalan artists from the end of the 19th century.

The Modernist building beside it, **Maricel de Mar**, built under the supervision of Miquel Utrillo, has, since 1910, housed the medieval and modern collections of the American, Charles Deering. Among the works displayed are some wall decorations by Josep Maria Sert.

The artistic tradition in Sitges has nurtured other museums, such as the **Romantic Museum,** carrer de Sant Gaudenci 1 *(open winter 10am-1pm and 4-6pm; summer 10am-1pm and 5-7pm; Sun and holidays 10am-2pm; closed Mon)*, which reflects life in the 19th century, and the **Costume Museum** (currently being set up).

At Sitges the del Garraf coast ends and the Costa Daurada (Golden Coast) begins. Unlike the Costa Brava you can travel alongside it without ever leaving the sand and the beach. Throughout this itinerary you will be able to find all the necessary tourist facilities. The total length of the Costa Daurada between Sitges and Cambrils is 43 mi/70 km.

Vilanova i La Geltrú (5 mi/8 km west of Sitges) was a luxury holiday resort at the turn of the century. You will get an impression of this when you see the porticoed square in the centre of town and visit the **Balaguer Library-Museum** where you can see some interesting paintings including an *Annunciation* by El Greco *(open 10am-2pm and 4-7pm; Sun and holidays 10am-2pm; closed Mon)*. This same period of splendour is evoked in the **Can Papiol Romantic Museum,** carrer Major 32 *(open winter 10am-1pm and 4-6pm; summer 10am-1pm and 5-7pm; Sun and holidays 10am-2pm; closed Mon)*. The **Castle of La Geltrú** is the main vestige of the medieval town. It was restored at the beginning of the century and retains parts of its 12th- and 15th-century design *(open 10am-2pm and 4-7pm; Sun and holidays 10am-2pm; closed Mon)*.

Continuing along the road through **Cubelles, Cunit** and **Calafell** with its castle and Romanesque church, you reach **El Vendrell,** home of the playwright Angel Guimerà and the cellist Pau Casals. You can visit their respective **Casa-Museu** in carrer de Santa Anna 14 and avinguda de Palfuriana 59-61 *(open winter 11am-2pm and 5-7pm; summer 11am-2pm and 5-8pm; closed Mon)*.

Art lovers may be interested in taking a short detour at this stage, back in the direction of Vilafranca del Penedès to a town called **L'Arboç** distinguished by its neo-Gothic **Giralda** building and its folk-dancing known as 'Dances of the Devils'. Its church possesses the only large group of 14th-century Gothic paintings in the area, they represent *St Bonaventure's Tree of Life★*.

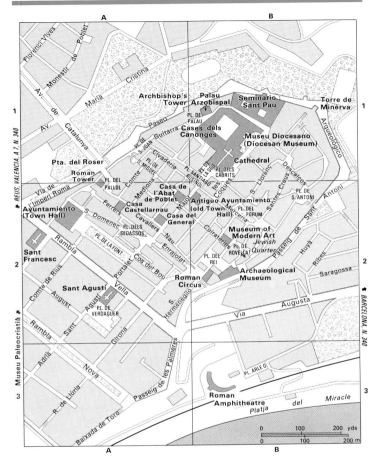

TARRAGONA

Returning to the coast you pass **Sant Salvador, Coma-Ruga** (0.62 mi/1 km) and then, by taking the main road to Tarragona, you reach the **Arco de Berà**** (triumphal arch) which gives you your first taste of Roman Tarragona. The arch straddles the ancient Via Augusta, 12 mi/20 km north west of Tarragona. You then pass **Creixell** and **Torredembarra** with its magnificent Renaissance castle. A little farther on you will notice the **castle of Tamarit** on a slight rise to the left. It is a private residence, halfway between a medieval castle and a Romantic Wagnerian creation. After this, on your right, you will see the **Torre de Scipio*** (Scipio Tower), the real gateway into Roman Tarragona.

▬▬ *TARRAGONA****

Telephone area code: 977.

Tarragona is the regional capital and, with its 112,000 inhabitants, Catalonia's second city. It stands at the mouth of the Francolí river and has over 9 mi/14 km of seafront. It is in the middle of an important communications network, on the road from Barcelona to Valencia (N340) and the road to Lleida (N240).

The town's prestige dates back to Antiquity when it was capital of a province. It has retained a number of monuments from that period, most of them Roman. There are also several medieval buildings, mainly around the cathedral. The archbishop of Tarragona is still the 'metropolitan' (one who presides over other bishops) of all other Catalonian dioceses.

Tarragona deserves a lengthy stay although tourists too often grant it only a quick visit on their way to the beach. Over the last few years its monuments have been increasingly restored and Tarragona has regained its position among universal cities of art.

Tarragona in the past

After being inhabited by the Iberians, the town was occupied by Publius Scipio who set up a military base here in 218 BC as a centre of operations against Iberian tribes. It became capital of *Hispania Citerior*, acquiring the status of Roman colony under Caesar in 45 BC with the title *Colonia Iulia Urbs Triumphalis*. After the reorganization of the Iberian Peninsula by Augustus, Tarragona was the capital of a province that covered a wide eastern stretch of the peninsula between Andalusia and the Duero valley. At that time the town had a population of over 30,000 inhabitants spread over an area of more than 148 acres/60 hectares. Its topography consisted of a series of terraces. The forum and temples stood on the upper terrace, the circus occupied the middle one while the amphitheatre and residential zones were on the lower terrace. Christianity came early to Tarragona. The town's three patron saints, Fructuosus, Augurius and Eulogius, were martyred in the amphitheatre's arena shortly after the middle of the 3rd century.

The town later fell to the Visigoths (see p. 36). Tarragona remained under Islamic control for four centuries following the Muslim invasion of 716. Reconquered by the Count of Barcelona, Ramon Berenguer IV (1131-1162), it took on the status of ecclesiastic metropolis and began its new role under the Catalan-Aragonese crown. From then on, however, it was a distant second to Barcelona of its status as capital.

What to see

The **Cathedral*****, B1, in the upper part of town, is an important example of the transition in religious architecture from Romanesque to Gothic. It was built on a raised site over the ancient Roman public square. Work on the cathedral began in 1171, thanks to a legacy left by Archbishop Hug de Cervelló, and it was consecrated in 1331. It is a large church with a basilica plan in the shape of a Latin Cross. Its two architectural styles are juxtaposed on the façade — the side doorways are Romanesque while the central portal with fine sculptures by Master Bartomeu is Gothic, making an admirable contrast. The western façade was built between 1277 and 1282. Decoration on the façade is thought to have continued into the 14th century because some of the statues belong to the workshop of the prestigious 14th-century sculptor, Jaume Cascalls.

The Cathedral has a good many works of art inside, beginning with the choir. Chronologically speaking, the fore-altar is the oldest work. Made in the 13th century, of white marble, it demonstrates the last flights of Romanesque art, particularly in the scenes of the martydom of St Thecla which surround the central part illustrating Christ in Majesty. Against the wall on the right, the magnificent funerary monument of Archbishop Juan of Aragon, who died in 1354, consists of a sarcophagus with a recumbent statue, several other statues of saints and a relief scene of the ascent of his soul. The main **altarpiece*** is a grand creation by the sculptor Pere Joan dating from the first third of the 15th century. On it are alabaster scenes of the life and martyrdom of St Thecla as well as stories from the life of the Virgin Mary. The three statues sculpted in the round represent the Virgin and Child flanked by St Thecla on the left and St Paul on the right. The whole is a major work of western art, an example of the ornamental trends prevalent at the end of the Middle Ages and a tribute to a great master of alabaster carving.

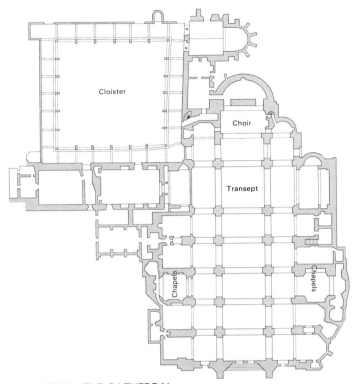

TARRAGONA: THE CATHEDRAL

Before visiting the various chapels, look in on the sacristy to see the Treasury and, in particular, the fine Gothic ceiling. The chapel of Santa Maria or dels Sastres ('of the Tailors') on the left-hand side was decorated under the direction of Bishop Pere de Clasquerí (1358-1380) and is the Cathedral's most ornate. This is mainly due to its decorative architecture consisting of Gothic vaulting above freestanding statues, and an openwork gallery. The 1368 altarpiece by Master Aloi is adorned with a fine illustration of the Virgin and Child in the centre as well as episodes from the lives of Jesus and Mary.

The chapel of St Barb also dates from the middle of the 14th century. The chapel of the Holy Sacrament, the Cathedral's best example of a Renaissance chapel (1583-1592), contains the tomb of Archbishop Antoni Augustin who died in 1586. The next one along is the chapel of Sts Cosmas and Damian, a 16th-century work by the architect Pere Blai that was endowed with a Baroque altarpiece in the 18th century. The chapel of the Holy Sepulchre, founded in 1494, contains a Roman sarcophagus surrounded by a group of sculptures. The chapels of St John the Evangelist and St-Fructuosus were constructed following plans by Pere Blai; building began in 1592.

The chapel of the Immaculate Conception contains the Cathedral's most sumptuous Baroque altarpiece, while that of the Virgin of Montserrat, built in a Plateresque style between 1520 and 1525, contains a highly important work, the altarpiece of the life of the Virgin, begun by Pere Serra and finished (1411) by the painter Lluís Borassà. You can see another large altarpiece from the beginning of the 15th century in the chapel of St Thomas. Facing this on the right-hand side of the Cathedral, you first come to the Baptistery chapel dating from the middle of the 14th century. Its neighbour, the chapel of St Michael, a practically contemporary construction, contains a 15th-century altarpiece of the Archangel and the life of Christ, an important creation by the painter Bernat Martorell. The chapel of St Thecla is a fine example of 18th-century Tarragona marble work. At this point you can leave the chapels to enter the cloister by the door near the choir.

The **cloister,** north east of the church, is based around four vast galleries. Work on these galleries began in the late 12th century and lasted over 50 years. The very rich decoration on the capitals has been compared to that of Sant Cugat del Vallès or that of Girona, and is a beautiful example of late Romanesque art. The entrance to the chapter-house is remarkable with its triple arcading. What especially draws attention, however, is the door into the Cathedral (built at the very end of the 12th century) with its group of capitals and sculptures of great artistic quality. The tympanum surmounts the capital of the pier illustrating the Virgin and Child and is dominated by a Christ in Majesty surrounded by symbols of the Evangelists. The whole is completed by carvings on the capitals. The chapels all around the cloister are well worth a detailed visit as they contain important sculptures and paintings from the Middle Ages. Note the 14th-century works in the chapel of St Thecla, the altarpiece by Master Joan of Tarragona, another by Joan Mates, and the *Annunciation* by Jaume Huguet in the Corpus Christi chapel.

The **Diocesan Museum*,** B1, next to the cloister is currently being rearranged and houses collections of medieval and liturgical works as well as tapestries from the 15th, 16th and 17th centuries *(open 10am-1pm and 3-7pm; closed Sun).*

There are some interesting buildings concentrated around the Cathedral. An example is the former **Cambreria** building on the plaça de la Seu with its attractive porticoed façade. Another is the **Casa del Degà** in carrer Escrivanies Velles. You can see some fine Gothic porches (the only preserved ones in town) as you go down to carrer Merceria, B2. A circular itinerary around the Cathedral begins with a walk up carrer Pare Iglesias alongside the Cathedral flank to the St Thecla portal and the old hospital. The lower part of this dilapidated building dates back to the Romanesque period while the upper sections are 15th-century. In the same street you can see the late 16th-century **Casa dels Concilis** and vestiges of the forum which, during Roman times, occupied the terrace on which the Cathedral was built.

On the corner of carrer de Sant Pau is the former chapel of **Santa Tecla la Vella** which once stood in the Cathedral cemetery. The oldest parts of the building are from the 12th century. You walk past the seminary, a fine 19th-century neo-Gothic edifice where you can see the chapel of Sant Pau in one of its courtyards. This latter is a transitional-style building like the Cathedral, built between 1215 and 1225. The **Cases dels Canonges** (the Canons' houses), B1, on the northern side of the Cathedral date from the 19th century.

Continue across plaça de Palau from where you can see a tower in the ancient wall known as the **Archbishop's Tower,** A1, and take carrer de Gitarra to plaça Sant Joan. From here continue down to the Portal del Roser where the archaeological walk begins. It takes you between the old Roman enclosure and the 18th-century perimeter. You will see the mighty wall with its enormous lower blocks of stone, its imposing gateways and protective towers. Some constructions, like the Archbishop's Tower, date from the Middle Ages and were built over Roman foundations. Return to Portal del Roser and continue from there to plaça del Pallol where the mixture of periods and styles gives the square its particular character — a Roman gateway, Gothic windows and the former Audiença, a porticoed edifice built partly over a Roman tower.

This attractive architectural ensemble continues into carrer dels Cavallers with **Casa Castellarnau,** A2 *(open Tues-Sat 9am-1pm and 4-7pm; Sun 9am-1pm; closed Mon)* and on into carrer Major with its Casa del

Among the many historic monuments of Tarragona is the Roman amphitheatre that was built in the 1st or 2nd century AD.

General, the former Generalitat, the magnificent Casa de l'Abat de Poblet and the old Casa de la Ciutat. You come to plaça Santiago Rusinol and can then take carrer de la Merceria leading off to the right, a street lined with Gothic porches. You end up at plaça del Forum and some Roman remains. Not far from here you can visit the **Museum of Modern Art**, B2, carrer de Santa Anna 8, which houses works by regional artists from the late 19th century and the 20th century *(open summer 10am-1pm and 5-8pm; closed Sun, Mon and holidays — winter 10am-1pm and 4:30-7:30pm; Sun and holidays 11am-2pm; closed Mon).*

Continuing towards plaça del Rei you will find yourself beside the **Town History Museum**, B2, installed in a building that has successively been called the Praetorium, Augustus' Palace, Pilate's Castle and the King's Castle *(open summer 10am-1pm and 4:30-8pm; winter 10am-1:30pm and 4-7pm; Sun and holidays 10am-2pm; closed Mon).* It was in fact a Roman tower which was converted in the Middle Ages by the addition of a Gothic room in the upper part into a place where the Kings of the Catalan-Aragonese crown could stay.

The **National Archaeological Museum★★★**, B2, plaça del Rei (no number), in a modern building fitted out in 1960, contains a significant collection of Roman art that includes important pieces of sculpture, mosaics, vases and so on *(open summer 10am-1pm and 4:30-8pm; winter 10am-1pm and 4-7pm; Sun and holidays 10am-2pm; closed Mon).*

By taking baixada de Sant Hermenegild from here you reach the **Roman circus**, B2. If you would like to visit it, ask at the Town History Museum. This particular zone has been the subject of considerable research since 1984 with the aim of studying and rehabilitating one of the major monuments of the Roman part of town. During Roman times circuses were large constructions built for races (especially chariot races) and that of Tarragona was particularly renowned. It was built a little before AD 100 and measured more than 1066 ft/325 m long and 377 ft/115 m wide. By the beginning of the 6th century it had already been abandoned and during the Middle Ages the area was gradually taken over by a residential zone.

The **Roman amphitheatre**, B3, slightly below this area, was built for public games, including gladiator fights and combat with wild animals. It has an elliptical shape with an arena in the middle surrounded by terraced rows. In a spectacular position facing the sea it is a very popular monument with Tarragona's citizens. It was built towards the end of the 1st century or during the first half of the 2nd century outside the Roman town, turning the natural slope of the ground to good account. It was here that Bishop Fructuosus and his deacons, Augurius and Eulogius, were martyred in 259. During the 6th century a little church with three aisles and an apse was built over the place where they were tortured and the spot became a popular place of pilgrimage. During the 12th century it was replaced by a Romanesque church with a single nave, a transept and a rectangular apse.

This is where the visit of the old town ends. The modern town, however, is also worth visiting thanks to the artistic development in Tarragona during the 19th and 20th centuries. Rambla Nova, parallel to Rambla Vella, A2-3 (where you can see the **church of Sant Agustí**, 1580) is the main street. It has played a determining role in the planning of the new part of town as well as in the Eixample ('expansion') of the old, and it is here that you will see the best Modernist buildings in town. **Casa Salas** (1907) and the **Col.legi de les Teresianes** (1922) by the architect Bernardí Martorell, who uses exposed brick, are the most noteworthy. More of this type of architecture can be seen in the works of Josep Maria Pujol Barberà (1897-1939), a local architect who drew the plans for the Eixample in 1922 and built the Escorxador (abattoir) in 1902, the Mercat Central (1915), a magnificent metallic edifice on plaça Corsini, and Casa Ripoll (1913) on passeig de Sant Antoni.

You could continue towards the Port Serrallo district to end up on the banks of the Francolí river at the Tabacalera (tobacco factory) on passeig de la Independència (no number). While the factory was being built between 1923 and 1926 a large palaeo-Christian necropolis was discovered. A visit will inform you about the funerary customs of Tarragona's early Christians.

The **museum** *(open winter 10am-1:30pm and 4-7pm; Sun and holidays 10am-2pm; summer 10am-1pm and 4:30-8pm; Sun and holidays 10am-2pm; closed Mon)*, built between 1928 and 1930, houses mosaics, sculptures and other items found during excavations. The necropolis was once dominated by a large funerary basilica and today preserves a number of graves, underground mausoleums and tables for funerary meals. Cemeteries like this one often spread well beyond the gates of large Roman towns during the 4th and 5th centuries.

Environs of Tarragona

The village of **Constantí** (3.1 mi/5 km north-west of Tarragona) on the right bank of the Francolí river has one of Spain's largest mausoleums dating from the paleo-Christian era. The **Centcelles Mausoleum★★★** *(open 10am-1:30pm and 4-7pm)* was built at the beginning of the 4th century and is perfectly preserved. The main building compares with the large mausoleums of ancient Rome. It was built to house the tomb of a wealthy owner from the town. Covering it is a cupola adorned with mosaics arranged in concentric circles. They illustrate hunting scenes, episodes from the Bible and personifications of the four seasons in the form of small nude figures. The funerary images as a whole suggest that the villa belonged to someone of high rank, maybe even to a member of Emperor Constantine's family. The deceased is portrayed in the scene opposite the entrance amongst the figures attending the hunt.

A journey through the Costa Daurada could continue south of Tarragona towards **Salou** and **Cambrils**. You'll see more of the life of local fishermen and be able to savour the long stretches of sun and sand which make up Catalonia's southernmost beaches.

Accommodation

▲▲▲▲ **Imperial Tarraco,** rambla Vella 2, A2, ☎ 23 3040. 170 rooms. The hotel stands on a rise dominating the platja del Miracle and the Mediterranean. Magnificent view.

▲▲▲ **Astari,** via Augusta 95, B2, ☎ 23 6911. 83 rooms. Not far from the beach. Tennis courts, swimming pool. Renowned restaurant.

▲▲▲ **Lauria,** rambla Nova 20, A2, ☎ 23 6712. 72 rooms. Centrally located.

▲▲ **Sant Jordi,** via Augusta (no number), B2, ☎ 23 7212. 40 rooms.

▲ **Espana,** rambla Nova 49, A3, ☎ 23 2712. 40 rooms.

▲ **Marina,** via Augusta 151, B2, ☎ 23 3027. 26 rooms.

▲ **Nuria,** via Augusta 217, B2, ☎ 23 5011. 61 rooms.

▲ **Paris,** carrer de Joan Maragall 4, ☎ 23 6012. 45 rooms.

▲ **Urbis,** carrer de Reding 20, ☎ 21 0116. 44 rooms.

Food and drink

Tarragona's best-known culinary speciality is *romesco,* a sauce for fish made with a light oil base, peppers, hazelnuts and Priorat wine, thickened with plain or toasted breadcrumbs. There is an infinite variety of fish dishes based on the local sea catch with devil-fish, hake and tunny included in an abundant choice. Some typical dishes include *zarzuela* (platter of fish in a sauce), *graellada* or *parrillada* (grilled fish), tunny with snails, cod with *samfaina* (a sort of ratatouille), grilled cuttlefish and so on. Don't forget that Tarragona is also in the heart of an area that produces fine wine; the Penedès region has a great winegrowing tradition.

◆◆◆ **Sol Ric,** via Augusta 227, ☎ 23 2030. *Closed Mon and on Wed evening.* One of the most distinguished restaurants in town; fish specialities.

◆◆ **Cal Brut,** carrer de Sant Pere 14, ☎ 21 0405. *Closed Sun evening.* Seafood.

◆◆ **La Galeria,** rambla Nova 16, ☎ 23 6143. Right in the centre.

◆◆ **Meson del Mar,** platja Larga, ☎ 23 9401. Fish specialities; near the beach.

◆ **El Tiberi,** carrer de Martí d'Ardenya 5, ☎ 23 5403. *Closed Sun and on Mon evening.* Buffet where you may eat as much as you like. Catalan specialities. Good value for your money.

Entertainment and leisure

The area around Tarragona has a wide choice of leisure activities. There are beaches, sports centres, summer festivals and, as is the case all along the coast, a lively nightlife in summer.

The Ebro delta

The Ebro delta, an area of 124 sq mi/320 sq km in the south of Tarragona province, is one of the wettest parts of the entire peninsula and one of the largest natural reserves in Europe. Its geological formation is due to gradual sedimentation over the years which has built up the mouth of the river, and its present shape has been sculpted by erosion and ocean currents. Approximately 75% of the area is given over to cultivation, mostly rice and horticulture. Twenty percent of all Catalan fishing is carried out in these waters. The major attraction for tourists, however, is the birdlife outside the settled areas. There are over 300 species of birds making this one of the Mediterranean's richest areas for migratory bird watching.

Castells: Castellers (human castles)

This folk event, known to have existed since at least the 18th century, is often called *Xiquets* (boys) de Valls because of its hometown, Valls. It consists of building human towers called *Castells* (castles) to the sound of the *gralla* (the flageolet or small fipple-flute). There are three types of towers: 'castles', 'towers' or 'pillars', depending on the number of men at the base (whether five, two or only one). As far as height is concerned, the towers can reach eight storeys. The most difficult castles are the seven of three (seven levels of three men), the eight of four and the pillar of six. Tower competitions are very popular in the villages of south-eastern Catalonia and take place during *Festes Majors* (major festivals). They are one of the highlights of summer.

Getting around Tarragona

Except in the upper part of town it is possible to drive around Tarragona in spite of occasional traffic congestion.

Shopping

Tarragona is a commercial town. The Unió and Apocada streets joining the two ends of town are lined with shops and department stores as is the Rambla, the main street of the modern part.

Useful addresses

Car rental: Atesa, avinguda de Catalunya 36, ☎ 21 7493; **Avis,** rambla Nova 125, ☎ 21 9156; **Europcar,** avinguda d'Andorra 10, ☎ 22 2770.
Emergencies: ambulance (Red Cross), ☎ 23 3535.
Police: ☎ 091.
Post Office: Plaça Corsini, ☎ 21 0149 and 21 1165.

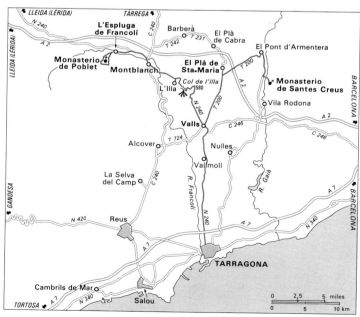

MONTBLANC AND CISTERCIAN ABBEYS ITINERARY

Founded in the 12th century by Cistercian monks, the monastery of Poblet — one of the most important of the Middle Ages — underwent construction work until the 14th century, but has since remained basically unaltered. In 1940, after being abandoned in the 19th century, Cistercian monks once again took up residence in the monastery.

Taxis: Radio Taxi-Tarragona, ☎ 23 6064; Radio Taxi-Cooperativa, ☎ 22 1414; Radio Taxi-Sicart, ☎ 21 5656; Tele Taxi Tarraco, ☎ 22 2000.

Tourist Information: carrer Major 39, ☎ 23 8922; plaça de la Font 1, ☎ 23 4812; **Generalitat Tourist Office**, carrer de Fortuny 4, ☎ 23 3415.

Train station: RENFE Information: ☎ 23 3643/23 2534. Ticket sales: rambla Nova 40, ☎ 23 3034.

Yacht Club: ☎ 21 0360.

▬ *MONTBLANC AND THE CISTERCIAN ABBEYS OF POBLET AND SANTES CREUS*

Leaving Tarragona to the north on the N240 you come to the town of **Valls**. Here you can see the church of Sant Joan with its Renaissance façade, the neo-Classical house of Santes Creus in carrer de la Cort, and the del Roser chapel decorated with exceptionally fine earthenware tiles dating from 1605. Valls is also the home of *Castells* (see p. 180).

Montblanc★★

23 mi/37 km north of Tarragona.

Standing on a rise above the right bank of the Francolí river, this veritable open-air museum was one of the country's most important towns in the Middle Ages and has managed to keep its medieval atmosphere intact. This is especially thanks to the largely preserved walls which spread over about 1 mi/1.5 km. The curtain walls and towers were built rapidly between 1366 and 1377. Several gateways flanked by towers remain, like those of Sant Jordi and Bover. Among the important monuments within the walls are the churches of **Santa Maria★** (1352-1528), **Sant Miquel★** (with a Romanesque façade and Gothic nave) and Sant Marcial (mid 14th-century).

An intriguing street to follow for a wander around town is carrer Major; it runs the length of the town and crosses plaça Major, the main square. Montblanc still has several medieval palaces such as Palau Reial, a royal residence, Casa Alenyà or Aguiló near the Jewish quarter, Palau del Castlà near the church of Sant Miquel, and Casa Josa, now the **Museu Comarcal**, carrer Josa 6, ☎ 86 0349.

Outside town, beyond the walls, you can visit the Gothic church of Sant Francesç, evidence of Franciscan presence here in the middle of the 13th century. Of interest also are the old hospital, the church of Santa Magdalena and the Gothic bridge over the Francolí.

Monastery of Poblet***

3 mi/5 km west of Montblanc.

Arriving from Montblanc you reach Poblet after first going through the town of l'Esplua de Francolí.

This important abbey was founded in the middle of the 12th century by Cistercian monks from the Fontfroide Abbey in France who were granted land by Count Ramon Berenguer IV. By 1185 it already had a hospital, a library, a church (then still under construction) and various outbuildings. In 1343, under Abbot Copons, the manuscript of the *Catalan Chronicle* by Jaume I was copied here and the same year the church was completed from an architectural point of view. The wall around the monastery was built under Pedro the Ceremonious. Finally, at the very end of the 14th century, King Martin the Humane built his palace here.

What you see today is essentially a model of the Cistercian monastery as it must have been at the end of the Middle Ages, with a church and cloister, a chapter-house, dormitory, refectory, royal palace, an abbatial palace, library, store room, secondary cloisters and annexes. Because of its massive size, the architectural quality of its edifices, its wealth and the religious and political power of its abbot, Poblet was one of the most important monasteries of the Middle Ages. It was also the royal pantheon for the kings of the Catalan-Aragonese crown. During the Middle Ages it housed an average of 100 monks. It began to decline at the end of the 16th century and was then abandoned when Church possessions were sold in 1835. Modern restoration began in 1930 and since 1940 a community of Cistercian monks has once again taken up residence in the monastery. Recently, the first president of the Generalitat of Catalonia since its restoration, Josep Tarradellas (1954-1980), bequeathed his personal archives to the monastery.

On entering the monastery through the Porta Daurada (or Golden Door, dating from the 15th century) you will see the small chapel of Sant Jordi (St George) on the left, built by Alfonso V the Magnanimous as a gesture of thanksgiving for the conquest of Naples. There is some fine relief work on the façade, together with the royal coat of arms.

Moving on to the basilica, you will probably be struck as you enter by the sobriety and lack of ornamentation characteristic of Cistercian churches. The immense basilica (nearly 328 ft/100 m long) has three aisles with seven bays, an apse and transept both with an ambulatory, and five radiating chapels (dating from the end of the 12th century and the first half of the 13th). Note the **altarpiece★★** in the main apse which replaced the 14th-century one. It is a large alabaster work by the sculptor Damià Forment, commissioned in 1527; one of the major works of the Catalan Renaissance. Poblet's basilica was renowned in the Middle Ages for its **royal tombs★★**. They were raised, restored and completed in the first half of the 20th century by the sculptor Frederic Marès. They are the work of the best artists in medieval Catalonia: Master Aloi, Pere de Guines, Jaume Cascalls (1349), Jordi de Déu and Jordi Joan, father of Pere Joan. The sarcophagi are made of alabaster with recumbent statues on their lids and funerary scenes on the sides. Starting with the choir, the tombs follow this order: on the right, Alfonso II (d. 1196), Juan I (d. 1396) buried with his two wives, Mata (d. 1380) and Violant

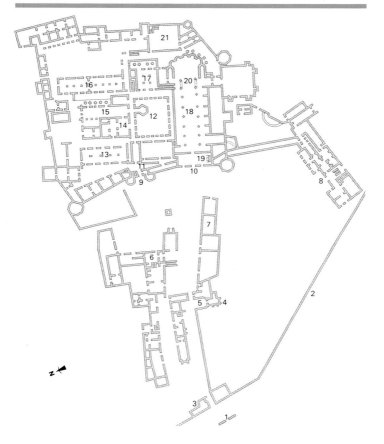

MONASTERIO DE POBLET   (POBLET MONASTERY)

1. *Prades Gateway. Beginning 16th-century.*
2. *Outer walls.*
3. *Gate-keeper's lodge.*
4. *Chapel of Our Lady of the Rosary and of Sant Jordi (St George).*
5. *Porta Daurada (Golden Door) (1470-1492).*
6. *Hostelry for pilgrims and the poor.*
7. *Hostelry.*
8. *Abbot's palace (1583-1598, 1684-1688).*
9. *Royal towers, Porta Reial and walls.*
10. *Former Romanesque portal and Baroque façade (1716-1722).*
11. *Courtyard of the Palace of King Martin the Humane (14th-15th century).*
12. *Main cloister.*
13. *Ground floor: lay brothers' refectory; first floor: older brothers' dormitory.*
14. *Former kitchen (12th-century).*
15. *12th-century refectory.*
16. *First room: scriptorium; second room: noviciate until 15th century, library since 1677.*
17. *Chapter-house from the end of the 13th century.*
18. *Basilica.*
19. *Renaissance Chapel of the Holy Sepulchre.*
20. *Royal Chapel and Pantheon.*
21. *Cloister of St Stephen (1197).*

(d. 1430), Juan II (d. 1479) and his wife Juana (d. 1468). On the left: Jaume I the Conqueror, (d. 1276), Pedro IV of Aragon (d. 1387) and his wives Marie de Navarre (d. 1347), Eleanor of Portugal (d. 1348) and Eleanor of Sicily (d. 1375). The last tomb, which was supposed to be for the remains of King Martin, in fact contains Fernando I who died in 1416. The sacristy is at the end of the left arm of the transept and was built in the middle of the 13th century. The stairs beside it lead to the dormitory.

If you come out of the basilica onto the main square and follow the wall northwards you reach the Porta Reial (Royal Door), one of the largest Gothic constructions of the end of the 14th century. You go through this into a little hallway. This leads to the palace of King Martin on the right, to the convent on the left, and opposite, beyond a Romanesque doorway, to the **cloister****. This is surprisingly large and of great interest with its pointed vaulting in the galleries and austere yet beautiful architectural decor. The oldest wing is the southern one, adjoining the church. It was built under Pedro the Catholic (1174-1213); construction of the rest of the building was carried out during the 13th century.

Monastery of Santes Creus***

To get to Santes Creus from Poblet return first to **Valls,** then take a secondary road to **Pla de Santa Maria** (6 mi/9 km; there's a Romanesque church) and on to **El Pont d'Armentera** (4 mi/7 km). From here take the Aiguamúrcia road to Santes Creus.

Together with the monasteries of Poblet and Vallbona de les Monges, Santes Creus makes up the triad of Cistercian monasteries in Catalonia. It was founded in 1168 by a community from La Grand-Selve in the Languedoc region of France. The main buildings were constructed at the end of the 12th century and the first part of the 13th. Because of the protection Santes Creus received from kings and nobles it became an important centre in the Middle Ages. Although it no longer has a monastic community, it is well worth the visit and there are good tourist facilities in the vicinity.

From the square, before going into the monastery, observe the sober façade of the church and the abbatial palace, which dates to the end of the 16th century.

The church itself was probably finished in 1225. It has the shape of a Latin Cross with three aisles separated by pillars, a wide transept and a typically Cistercian apse with five rectangular chapels, the middle one being the largest. In the transept crossing you can see the tombs of Pedro III the Great, Jaume II and his wife, Blanche d'Anjou. The design of the tombs, the shape of the canopies above them and the quality of the sculptures by Pere de Bonhuyl (dating from the beginning of the 14th century), all contribute to make these resting places unique works of art. The Gothic altarpiece, partly by Lluís Borrassà, is now preserved in the Cathedral in Tarragona; the present one is by Josep Tramulles, commissioned in 1647.

The **cloister**** flanking the church, built between 1313 and 1341, is an important part of the visit. The eastern gallery adjoining the chapter-house is the oldest, followed by the one adjacent to the church. The artist responsible for the other two, begun in 1332, has been identified as Raynard des Fonoll.

USEFUL VOCABULARY

Common words and phrases

English	*Catalan*	*Castilian*
Yes/No	Si/No	Sí/No
Thank you (very much)	(moltes) gràcies	(muchas) gracias
Please	Si us plau	Por favor
Good morning	Bon dia	Buenos días
Good evening	Bona tarda	Buenas tardes
Good night	Bona nit	Buenas noches
Goodbye	Adéu-siau	Adiós/Hasta la vista
See you tomorrow ...	Fins demà	Hasta mañana
What's your name? (formal)	Com us dieu?	¿Cómo se llama usted?
What's your name? (informal)	Com te dius?	¿Cómo te llamas?
My name is	Em dic	Me llamo
Do you speak Spanish/............. English/French/ German?.............	Parleu castèlla/ anglès/francès /alemany?	¿Habla castellano/ inglés/francés/alemán?
How do you say this in Catalan?	Com es diu això en català?	¿Como se llama esto en catalàn?
Please speak more slowly	Parleu una mica més a poc a poc, si us plau	Hable más lento, por favor
Where is...?	On és...?	¿Dónde está...?
I'm looking for	Busco	Cerco ....
I would like	Voldria	Quisiera ....
I need	Necessito	Necessito ....
What time is it?	Quina hora és?	¿Qué hora es?

Numbers

English	*Catalan*	*Castilian*
One	U, Un/Una	Un, Uno/Una
Two	Dos, Dues	Dos
Three	Tres	Tres
Four	Quatre	Cuatro
Five	Cinc	Cinco
Six	Sis	Seis
Seven	Set	Siete
Eight	Vuit	Ocho
Nine	Nou	Nueve
Ten	Deu	Diez

Time

English	*Catalan*	*Castilian*
Yesterday	Ahir	Ayer
Today	Avui	Hoy
Tomorrow	Demà	Mañana
The day before yesterday	Abans d'ahir	Antes de ayer
The day after tomorrow	Demà passat	Pasado mañana
Last week	La setmana passada	La semana pasada
Next week	La setmana que vé	La semana próxima
Morning	Matí	Mañana

Midday	Migdia	Mediodía
Afternoon	Tarda	Tarde
Evening	Vespre	Atardecer
Night	Nit	Noche
Monday	Dilluns	Lunes
Tuesday	Dimarts	Martes
Wednesday	Dimecres	Miércoles
Thursday	Dijous	Jueves
Friday	Divendres	Viernes
Saturday	Dissabte	Sábado
Sunday	Diumenge	Domingo
Spring	Primavera	Primavera
Summer	Estiu	Verano
Autumn	Tardor	Otoño
Winter	Hivern	Invierno

At the station or airport

A ticket for . . .	Un bitllet per . . .	Un billete para . . .
No smoking	No fumeu	Prohibido fumar
Platform	Andana	Andén
Station	Estació	Estación
Stop	Parada	Parada
What time does . . . arrive?	A quina hora arriba . . . ?	¿A que hora llega . . . ?
What time does . . . leave?	A quina hora surt . . . ?	¿A que hora sale . . . ?
(Winter/Summer) Time	Horari (d'estiu/d'hivern)	Horario (de verano/de invierno)

By car

Where is the nearest gas station (filling station)/the nearest garage?	On és la pròxima gasolinera/el pròxim taller de reparació?	¿Donde se encuenta la próxima gasolinera/el próximo taller de reparación?
Full tank, please	Ompliu el dipòsit, si us plau	Llene el depósito, por favor
Car park/parking place	Aparcament/pàrquing	Aparcamiento/parking

In town

To go to . . . ?	Per anar a . . . ?	¿Para ir a . . . ?
Is it near/far?	Es a prop/lluny?	¿Está cerca/lejos?
To the right	A la dreta	A la derecha
To the left	A l'esquerra	A la izquierda
Avenue	Avinguda	Avenida
Cemetery	Cementiri	Cementerio
Church	Esglesia	Iglesia
Garden	Jardí	Jardín
Market	Mercat	Mercado
Museum	Museu	Museo
Palace	Palau	Palacio
Square	Plaça	Plaza
Street	Carrer	Calle
Walk, Promenade	Passejada	Paseo
Open/Closed	Obert/Tancat	Abierto/Cerrado

Credit cards	Targetes de crèdit	Tarjetas de crédito
How much?	Quant val?	¿Cuanto cuesta?
It's expensive	Es car	Es caro
Is there something cheaper/bigger/smaller/in another colour?	En té de mes bon preu/més gran/més petit/d'un altre color?	¿Tiene algo mas barato/más grande/más pequeño/de otro color?
Price according to the weight	Preu segons el pes	Precio según el peso
Price according to what is available in the market	Preu segons el mercat	Precio según el mercado
Lavatories-Men/Women	Lavabos-Homes/Dones	Lavabos/Servicios-Caballeros/Señoras

At the hotel

Do you have a room free?	Té alguna habitació lliure?	¿Tiene alguna habitación libre?
For one night/for two people/with bathroom	Per una nit/per a dues persones/amb bany	Para una noche/Para dos personas/con baño
What time can we have breakfast/lunch/dinner?	A quina hora es pot esmorzar/dinar/sopar?	¿A qué hora se puede desayunar/comer/cenar?
Could you wake me at . . .?	Em poden despertar a . . . ?	¿Me puede despertar a . . . ?
The bill, please	El compte, si us plau	La cuenta, por favor

At a restaurant

Table reserved	Taula reservada	Mesa reservada
Fork	Forquilla	Tenedor
Glass	Vas	Vaso
Knife	Ganivet	Cuchillo
Menu	Carta/Llista de preus	Carta/Lista de precios
Set menu	Menu	Menu
Plate	Plat	Plato
Spoon	Cullera	Cuchara
Teaspoon	Cullereta	Cucharilla
Apple	Poma	Manzana
Beef	Bou	Buey
Bread	Pa	Pan
Butter	Mantega	Mantequilla
Chicken	Pollastre	Pollo
Duck	Ànec	Pato
Egg	Ou	Huevo
Fish	Peix	Pescado
Fruit	Fruita	Fruta
Grape	Raïm	Uva
Ham/	Pernil/	Jamón/
Cooked ham	Pernil dolc	Jamón dulce
Ice cream	Gelat	Helado
Lamb	Anyell	Cordero-lechal
Mustard	Mostassa	Mostaza
Mutton	Be/Xai/Corder	Cordero
Omelette	Truita/	Tortilla
Orange	Taronja	Naranja
Pastry (dessert)	Pastís (Postre)	Pastel (Postre)
Peach	Préssec	Melocotón

Pork	Llom	Lomo
Potatoes (baked, fried)	Patates (Al forn, fregides)	Patatas (asadas, fritas)
Rabbit	Conill	Conejo
Rice	Arròs	Arroz
Salad	Amanida/Ensalada	Ensalada
Salt	Sal	Sal
Sausage	Llonganissa	Salchichón
Sugar	Sucre	Azucar
Tomato	Tomàquet	Tomate
Veal	Vedella	Ternera
The bill, please	El compte, si us plau	La cuenta, por favor
Service included	Servei inclòs	Servicio incluido

GLOSSARY OF ARCHITECTURAL TERMS

Abacus: A level tablet on the capital of a column, supporting the entablature.

Agora: Public square or market-place in an ancient Greek city.

Ambulatory: A covered walk, as an aisle.

Apse: Rounded or rectangular extremity of a church, behind the choir.

Apsidiole: A subsidiary apse.

Archivolt: The under-curve of an arch.

Atrium: The entrance hall or chief apartment, usually of a Roman house.

Barrel vault: A vault with a simple hemicylindrical roof, like a continuous arch.

Bay: The space between two columns.

Cella: The inner chamber of a temple.

Chevet: The apsidal end of a church consisting of a main apse and possibly several apsidioles and chapels radiating from it.

Crenel: A notch in a parapet.

Crossing, transept crossing: The area in a church where the transept intersects the nave.

Curtain walls: The part of a rampart between two bastions.

Entablature: The part of a classical building above the capital comprising the architrave, frieze and cornice.

Escutcheon: A shield on which a coat of arms is represented.

Forum: A level rectangle of ground in the centre of every large Roman town surrounded by the chief civic buildings — in ancient times the focus of the town's political, social and commercial life.

Greek Cross (floorplan): A church built in the shape of a cross with arms of equal length.

Groin, groined vault: The line of intersection of two vaults, also a rib along the intersection.

Hypostyle: Having the roof supported by pillars.

Latin Cross (floorplan): A church in which the nave is longer than the transept.

Mirador: A belvedere or watch-tower.

Mozarabic architecture: A style developed by Christians living in Muslim territory (9th-11th century).

Mudejar architecture: A style developed by Arabs living in Christian territory (11th-15th century).

Ogival arch: A pointed arch.

Pergola: A structure with climbing plants along a walk.

Pier: The support of an arch.

Plateresque style: An ornate style (popular in Spanish Renaissance) resembling silversmiths' work.

Praetorium: A Roman governor's residence.

Ribbed vault: A vault strengthened by a projecting band of stone.

Roman arch: A wide, semicircular, generous arch.

Splay: A slant or bevel as of the side of a doorway, window and so on.

Squinch: An arch or other support across a re-entrant or interior angle.

Stalactite ceiling: Decoration on ceiling similar in shape to icicle-like pendants on a cave roof.

Transept: Part of a church at right angles to the nave.

Trefoil: A three-lobed form.

Triforium: A gallery, storey or arcade over an aisle.

Tympanum: A space between a lintel and an arch over it. A semicircular or triangular surface, usually carved above the door of a church.

▬ SUGGESTED READING

Bettonica, Luis. *Cuisine of Spain* (W. H. Allen, 1983).

Blackstone Franks Guide to Living in Spain (Kogan Page, 1988).

Busselle, Michael. *Castles in Spain: A Traveller's Guide Featuring the National Parador Inns* (Pavilion Books, 1989).

Carr, Raymond. *Modern Spain, 1875-1980* (Oxford University Press, 1980).

——. *Images of the Spanish Civil War* (Allen & Unwin, 1986).

Casas, Penelope. *The Food and Wines of Spain* (Knopf, 1982).

——. *Tapas: The Little Dishes of Spain* (Knopf, 1985).

Diehl, Gaston. *Miró* (Crown Publishers, 1974).

Fusi, J.P. *Franco: A Biography* (Unwin Hyman, 1987).

Grodecki, Louis. *Gothic Architecture* (Faber and Faber, 1986).

Hemingway, Ernest. *The Dangerous Summer* (Hamish Hamilton, 1985).

Hilton, Timothy. *Picasso* (Thames & Hudson, 1987).

Hooper, John. *The Spaniards* (Penguin, 1986).

Jencks, Charles. *The Language of Post-Modern Architecture* (Academy Editions, 1978).

Lewis, Norman. *The Voices of the Old Sea* (Penguin, 1986).

MacMiadhachain, Anna. *Spanish Regional Cookery* (Penguin, 1976).

Martinell, Cesar. *Gaudí Designer: His life, His Theories, His Work* (International Specialist Books, 1982).

McGirk, Tim. *Wicked Lady: Salvador Dali's Muse* (Hutchinson, 1989).

Michener, James. *Iberia: Spanish Travels and Reflections* (Random House, 1968).

Morris, Jan. *Spain* (Oxford University Press, 1979).

Orwell, George. *Homage to Catalonia* (Harcourt Brace, 1969).

Penrose, Roland. *Miró* (Thames Hudson, 1985).

Russel, P.E., ed. *Spain: A Companion to Spanish Studies* (Methuen, 1985).

Walker, Ted. *In Spain* (Secker & Warburg, 1987).

INDEX